THE ONE CREATOR GOD
IN THOMAS AQUINAS
& CONTEMPORARY THEOLOGY

SACRA DOCTRINA SERIES

Series Editors

Chad C. Pecknold, *The Catholic University of America*

Thomas Joseph White, OP, *Pontifical University of St. Thomas Aquinas*

THE ONE
CREATOR GOD
IN THOMAS AQUINAS
& CONTEMPORARY
THEOLOGY

Michael J. Dodds, OP

The Catholic University of America Press
Washington, D.C.

Library of Congress Cataloging-in-Publication Data

Names: Dodds, Michael J., author.

Title: The one creator God in Thomas Aquinas and contemporary
theology / Michael J Dodds, OP.

Description: Washington, D.C. : The Catholic University of America
Press, 2020. | Series: Sacra doctrina | Includes bibliographical references
and index.

Identifiers: LCCN 2020014179 | ISBN 9780813232874 (paperback) |

Subjects: LCSH: God (Christianity)—History of doctrines. | Thomas,
Aquinas, Saint, 1225?–1274. | Catholic Church—Doctrines—History.

Classification: LCC BT98 .D5635 2020 | DDC 231.7/65—dc23

LC record available at https://lccn.loc.gov/2020014179

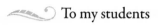 To my students

CONTENTS

FIGURES

ABBREVIATIONS

Works of Thomas Aquinas

Cat. aur. in joann.	*Catena aurea in Joannem*
De aeternitate	*De aeternitate mundi*
De articulis	*De articulis fidei et ecclesiae sacramentis*
De ente	*De ente et essentia*
De malo	*Quaestiones disputatae de malo*
De pot.	*Quaestiones disputatae de potentia*
De ver.	*Quaestiones disputatae de veritate*
In de an.	*In Aristotelis librum De anima commentarium*
In de caelo.	*Commentarium in libros Aristotelis De caelo et mundo*
In de div. nom.	*In librum beati Dionysii De divinis nominibus expositio*
In meta.	*In Metaphysicam Aristotelis commentaria*
In peri herm.	*Commentarium in Aristotelis libros Peri hermeneias*
In phys.	*In octo libros Physicorum Aristotelis expositio*
SCG	*Summa contra Gentiles*
Sent.	*Scriptum super libros Sententiarum*
ST	*Summa Theologiae*
Super ad col.	*Super epistolam ad Colossenses lectura*
Super ad eph.	*Super epistolam ad Ephesios lectura*
Super de causis	*Super librum De causis expositio*

THE ONE CREATOR GOD
IN THOMAS AQUINAS
& CONTEMPORARY THEOLOGY

INTRODUCTION

Hear, O Israel: The Lord our God is one Lord!

These first words of the *Shema*, the basic prayer of Judaism, are an eloquent testimony to divine unity.[1] St. Thomas Aquinas uses them in explaining that the oneness of God is also an essential article of Christian faith: "The first article is therefore that we believe in the unity of the divine essence according to Deuteronomy, 'Hear, Israel, the Lord your God is one God.'"[2] Any Christian confession of divine oneness, however, must also entail a trinitarian profession of the unity of the three divine persons as revealed through Christ and the Holy Spirit.[3] This book is fundamentally a reflection on the oneness of the triune God—on the one divine essence of the God who is Father, Son, and Holy Spirit. Aquinas begins his *Summa Theologica* with just such a reflection: "In treating of God there

---

1. Dt 6:4. This translation is from *The Holy Bible: Revised Standard Version* (New York: Collins, 1973). Otherwise, except for scriptural passages in the works of Aquinas, all scriptural translations are from *The New American Bible,* Revised Edition (Charlotte, N.C.: Saint Benedict Press, 2011). Translations of all other works are those of the author except where a published translation is given in the bibliography. For an overview of scholarship on the emergence of monotheism in Israel, see appendix 2.

2. "Audi Israel: Dominus Deus tuus, Deus unus est" (*De articulis,* Part 1). See also *ST* I, 11, 3, sed contra.

3. "Just as the effect of the mission of the Son was to lead us to the Father, so the effect of the mission of the Holy Spirit is to lead the faithful to the Son. Now the Son, since he is begotten Wisdom, is Truth itself: 'I am the way, and the truth, and the life' (14:6). And so the effect of this kind of mission [of the Spirit] is to make us sharers in the divine wisdom and knowers of the truth. The Son, since he is the Word, gives teaching to us; but the Holy Spirit enables us to grasp it" (*Super ev. ioann.,* chap. 14, lect. 6, no. 1958).

will be a threefold division. For we shall consider (1) Whatever concerns the divine essence; (2) Whatever concerns the distinctions of persons; (3) Whatever concerns the procession of creatures from him."[4] Aquinas will be our guide in what follows, acting not simply as a historical figure but as an enduring source of wisdom with much to contribute to contemporary theological issues.

Aquinas clearly states that his *Summa Theologica* is intended for "the instruction of beginners," but the academic level of those "beginners" is disputed.[5] He starts with a discussion of the nature of theology, whose "chief aim is to teach the knowledge of God, not only as he is in himself, but also as he is the beginning of things and their last end, and especially of rational creatures."[6] In contemporary jargon, this means that theology is concerned with both "God in himself" (God's existence and attributes)

4. *ST* I, 2, prologue. "There are three things to be considered concerning the nature of God, namely the unity of the divine essence, the Trinity of persons, and the effects of divine power" (*De articulis, Part I*).

5. *ST* prologue. According to James Weisheipl, "Thomas wanted to present a comprehensive vision of 'sacred doctrine' for beginners, a handbook suitable for novices" (James A. Weisheipl, OP, *Friar Thomas D'Aquino: His Life, Thought and Works* [Washington, D.C.: The Catholic University of America Press, 1983], 222). Leonard Boyle agrees: "Thomas in particular probably had young and run-of-the-mill Dominicans primarily in mind and not a more sophisticated, university audience when in chiseled prose and in easy, logical steps he put his *Summa Theologiae* together" (Leonard E. Boyle, OP, "The Setting of the *Summa Theologiae*," in *Aquinas's "Summa Theologiae": Critical Essays*, ed. Brian Davies, OP [Lanham, Md.: Rowman and Littlefield, 2006], 12). See also Brian Davies, OP, *Thomas Aquinas's "Summa Theologiae": A Guide and Commentary* (Oxford: Oxford University Press, 2014), 7–13. John Jenkins argues, however, that the work "was meant to serve as a final, comprehensive course for theology students" (John Jenkins, *Knowledge and Faith in Thomas Aquinas* [Cambridge: Cambridge University Press, 1997], 89). Bernard McGinn also pictures more advanced students, perhaps "something like modern graduate students in theology" (Bernard McGinn, *Thomas Aquinas's "Summa theologiae": A Biography* [Princeton, N.J.: Princeton University Press, 2014], 49). Mark Johnson suggests that "the *Summa theologiae* is not a text for beginners in Christian doctrine but a text for the teachers of beginners in Christian doctrine: the precise job description of a *lector conventus* in the Dominican educational system that defined Thomas, the Dominican master of theology" (Mark F. Johnson, "Aquinas's *Summa theologiae* as Pedagogy," in *Medieval Education,* ed. Ronald B. Begley and Joseph W. Koterski, SJ [New York: Fordham University Press, 2005], 140). Denys Turner agrees: "But if this [to be a beginner's manual] is its general purpose it is perhaps better to see it as a manual for the *teachers* of beginners than as a textbook for the use of beginners themselves, for that general Prologue makes clear that the revisionary purpose his work is meant to serve is principally curricular in character, that of setting out the ordering of the questions in a manner which is more coherently teachable than is done in the standard teaching texts available at the time " (Denys Turner, *Faith, Reason and the Existence of God* [Cambridge: Cambridge University Press, 2004], 239–40).

6. *ST* I, 2, prologue.

and "God for us" (God as our Creator and final happiness). With "us" in the picture, theology also needs to consider our moral life, in which we are led to God through grace, and Christ who is "the way."[7]

Writing for "beginners," Aquinas presents these topics in a way that is pedagogically helpful. Over the centuries, his approach has proved useful to beginners while still challenging to proficients.[8] His scholastic method of presentation, through questions and responses, leaves his theology open to new questions and invites innovative responses as different theological issues arise from contemporary philosophy and science.[9] Although in what follows we'll forego the technical apparatus of question and response, we do hope to embrace the broad spirit of Aquinas's enterprise in considering the question of God, both as Aquinas presents it and as it has been shaped by contemporary concerns.

In this introductory chapter, we start with a brief overview of Aquinas's life and then look at his doctrine of God, his understanding of the methods of philosophy and theology, the nature of his *Summa Theologica*, and finally the "Thomism" of his followers. In subsequent chapters, we will consider the One God following the pedagogical order of the *Summa Theologica*: the existence of God (chapter 1); the divine attributes (chapter 2); our ability to know and name God (chapter 3); God's knowledge (chapter 4); will (chapter 5); love, justice, and compassion (chapter 6);

7. Jn 14:6. "In our endeavor to expound this science, we shall treat: (1) of God; (2) of the rational creature's advance towards God; (3) of Christ, who as man, is our way to God" (*ST* I, 2, prologue).

8. Brian Davies offers some encouragement to today's beginners: "The *Summa Theologiae* is very much a 'reader-friendly' text.... This is definitely one of Aquinas's most accessible writings" (Brian Davies, OP, "Introduction," in *Aquinas's "Summa Theologiae": Critical Essays,* ed. Brian Davies, OP [Lanham, Md.: Rowman and Littlefield, 2006], xiv).

9. In Aquinas's method, Josef Pieper finds "an intrepid frankness of affirmation, and enthusiasm for ever new explorations into the wonders of reality. Along with that, of course, there come ever new difficulties in incorporating the new data into our total view of the universe, and hence ever new conflicts, compelling us constantly to rethink our previous positions, to revise all our set ideas, even in theology. This attitude, which neither permits us to cast away an insight already won nor allows us to rest on our laurels with a false sense of finality, is not easy to achieve. It is a highly demanding affair. But it is perhaps the best lesson among the many that can be learned in the school of the 'universal teacher' of Christendom" (Josef Pieper, *Guide to Thomas Aquinas,* trans. Richard and Clara Winston [New York: New American Library, 1964], 141). "This inquiry, however, which seemingly stops at nothing, is characteristic of Scholastic theology as a rational, scientific theology" (Ulrich G. Leinsle, *Introduction to Scholastic Theology,* trans. Michael J. Miller [Washington, D.C.: The Catholic University of America Press, 2010], 12).

providence (chapter 7); power (chapter 8); beatitude (chapter 9); and action, including both God's initial act of creation and his continuous care for all things (chapter 10).

The Life of Thomas Aquinas

In 1224 or 1225, Thomas d'Aquino was born into the noble family of Count Landolf, lord of Aquino, at the family castle at Roccasecca in southern Italy. At age five or six, he began his education as an oblate in the Benedictine Monastery of Monte Cassino.[10] He spent nine years there, fostering his education and apparently plaguing the good monks with his constant question: "What is God?"[11] Political complications led his parents to move him to the newly founded *studium generale* in Naples, but they still hoped he would one day return to Monte Cassino and eventually become abbot. He foiled their plans in 1244 by joining the Dominicans, the Order of Preachers recently founded by St. Dominic.[12] It was an order of mendicants or "beggar monks" who practiced a new brand of religious life marked by preaching, itinerancy, evangelical poverty, prayer, study, and common life. When Aquinas met them, the Dominicans were already spreading throughout Europe—"in full blossom, especially in university towns."[13]

For all their energy, though, the Dominicans lacked the long tradition (and extensive properties) of the Benedictines. Small wonder that his family was horrified at his choice: "By any standard, Thomas's action was dramatic and radical. His decision to throw in his lot with the Dominicans would have verged on the incomprehensible to any parents who, like his, were of aristocratic (if only of a relatively minor) standing, and

---

10. Throughout this section, I have relied on two excellent biographies: Jean-Pierre Torrell, OP, *Saint Thomas Aquinas*, vol. 1, *The Person and His Work*; vol. 2, *Spiritual Master,* trans. Robert Royal (Washington, D.C.: The Catholic University of America Press, 1996–2003); and Weisheipl, *Friar.*

11. Simon Tugwell, OP, ed., *Albert and Thomas: Selected Writings* (New York: Paulist Press, 1988), 203; G. K. Chesterton, *Saint Thomas Aquinas: The Dumb Ox* (Garden City, N.Y.: Doubleday, 1960), 59; Gerald Vann, OP, *Saint Thomas Aquinas* (New York: Benziger Brothers, 1947), 39.

12. Torrell, *Saint Thomas,* 1:6–9.

13. Marie-Dominique Chenu, OP, *Aquinas and His Role in Theology,* trans. Paul Philibert, OP (Collegeville, Minn.: Liturgical Press, 2002), 1.

were correspondingly ambitious for the future career of their child."[14] The family kidnapped and confined him under a kind of house arrest in Roccasecca. There Aquinas busied himself by reading the Bible and studying the *Sentences* of Peter Lombard.[15] After about a year, his parents gave up. Seeing that their stubborn son would not abandon his chosen vocation, they delivered him to the Dominican priory in Naples.

The Order sent him to study first in Paris and then in Cologne, where he served as assistant to Albert the Great, a remarkable friar who had early embraced not only the recently retrieved philosophy of Aristotle but also the full range of scientific inquiry of his day. Hearing that Aquinas's classmates had nicknamed him "the dumb ox" (in virtue of his quiet ways and rather plodding appearance), Albert famously prophesied: "We call him the dumb ox, but he will make resound in his doctrine such a bellowing that it will echo throughout the world."[16]

In obedience to his superiors, Aquinas taught first at Paris (1256–1259), then in Italy at Orvieto and Rome (1259–1268), again at Paris (1269–1272), and finally at Naples (1272–1274). While teaching his Dominican brothers at Orvieto, Aquinas conceived a new approach to theology that would break from the traditional study of the *Sentences* of Peter Lombard. In Rome, this plan took shape as he began his *Summa Theologica,* a textbook for "beginners" designed to avoid bringing "weariness and confusion to the minds of readers."[17]

No ivory tower scholar, Aquinas did not shrink from inserting himself into the hot button issues of his day. As one of the questions at his

14. Denys Turner, *Thomas Aquinas: A Portrait* (New Haven, Conn.: Yale University Press, 2013), 9.

15. Weisheipl, *Friar,* 34.

16. Torrell, *Saint Thomas,* 1:26.

17. *ST* prologue. Torrell, *Saint Thomas,* 1:144–45. "He was, in a word, free to devise a curriculum of his own—one that would have the student body as its focus. More importantly, he was now in a position to expand the students' theological education and to break out of the narrow tradition of practical theology that had hitherto marked the Dominican educational system" (Boyle, "Setting," 8). "Relatively fresh from Paris, friar Thomas launched his course at Santa Sabina in Parisian fashion. But the strictures of an older syllabus and an older textbook soon led him to modify his presentation. In his second year in Rome Thomas Aquinas set to work on what would become not only his greatest legacy but perhaps the single greatest summary of medieval theology, the *Summa theologiae*" (Michèle M. Mulchahey, *"First the Bow Is Bent in Study...": Dominican Education before 1350* [Toronto: Pontifical Institute of Mediaeval Studies, 1998], 280).

inception as a master in sacred theology in Paris in 1256, for instance, he chose the "in-your-face" topic of the legitimacy of the mendicant vocation—a major point of contention between the religious and secular masters.[18] Paris itself was no peaceful college town but more of a minefield. Humbert of Romans describes the plight of the Dominicans in 1256: "No sooner was a friar caught sight of . . . than he was surrounded by the human swarms. . . . Filthy rushes . . . were poured upon the cowled head from above; mud, stones and sometimes blows greeted him from below. Arrows had been shot against the priory, which had henceforth to be guarded day and night by royal troops."[19]

Aquinas was always ready to put his learning to practical use in preaching and answering the needs of the faithful. He wrote a brief tract on study in response to a certain Brother John[20] and composed the massive *Summa contra Gentiles* to support the missionary work of the Church.[21] At the bidding of Pope Urban IV in 1267, he wrote a tract, *Contra errores Graecorum* (Against the errors of the Greeks), designed to further the

18. Aquinas's arguments are published in his *Quaestiones quodlibetales* (Turin and Rome: Marietti, 1949), Quodlibet VII, Q. 7, articles 1–2. James Weisheipl argues, however, that they were almost certainly the topic of his inaugural lecture and that their present position in his works is rather arbitrary: "It is hard to imagine that such a burning question would have been neglected by Thomas on the very occasion of his claim to the second Dominican chair in the university" (Weisheipl, *Friar,* 106). In a slightly later work, Aquinas again vehemently defends the mendicant orders: "Those, however, who adopt the opinions of these enemies of religious will blindly follow the blind, and with them will fall into the ditch" (St. Thomas Aquinas, *Against Those Who Attack the Religious Profession* [Contra impugnantes Dei cultum et religionem], epilogue, in *An Apology for the Religious Orders,* trans. John Proctor, OP [St. Louis, Mo.: B. Herder, 1902], 373).

19. Humbert of Romans, as cited in Weisheipl, *Friar,* 93.

20. *Epistola exhortatoria de modo studendi ad fratrem Joannem* [The Letter of Thomas Aquinas to Brother John on How to Study], *Opuscula Theologica* 1:451 (Rome: Marietti, 1954). The authenticity of this document is disputed, but James Weisheipl accepts it as "probably authentic" (Weisheipl, *Friar,* 397).

21. Early in the work, Aquinas remarks: "To proceed against the errors of individuals . . . is difficult because some of them, such as the Mohammedans and the pagans, do not agree with us in accepting the authority of any Scripture, by which they may be convinced of their error. . . . We must, therefore, have recourse to the natural reason, to which all men are forced to give their assent. However, it is true, in divine matters the natural reason has its failings" (*SCG* I, c.2.3). On the purpose of the *Summa contra Gentiles,* see Tugwell, *Albert and Thomas,* 252–53; Weisheipl, *Friar,* 130–34; Norman Kretzmann, *The Metaphysics of Theism: Aquinas's Natural Theology in "Summa contra Gentiles" I* (Oxford: Clarendon Press, 1997), 44; Brian Davies, OP, *Thomas Aquinas's "Summa contra Gentiles": A Guide and Commentary* (Oxford: Oxford University Press, 2016), 15; Torrell, *Saint Thomas,* 1:107; Rudi A. te Velde, "Natural Reason in the *Summa contra Gentiles,*" in *Thomas Aquinas: Contemporary Philosophical Perspectives,* ed. Brian Davies, OP (Oxford: Oxford University Press, 2002), 121.

pope's efforts to reunite the Eastern and Western churches.[22] In 1274 at the request of Pope Gregory X, he set out for the Second Council of Lyons in another effort to reunite the churches. As his party approached the abbey of Monte Cassino, the abbot asked him to settle a dispute among the monks about the nature of divine foreknowledge and human free will. His brief letter of response was to be "his last known writing."[23]

His theology sprang from a deep spirituality. As Fergus Kerr notes: "For Thomas, theological activity is a form of sharing in God's being, a form of union with God, an anticipation of the beatific vision."[24] We see the simplicity of his spiritual life in his words of December 6, 1273. When Christ appeared to him and asked what reward he might like for all of his theological labors, he replied: "Nothing but yourself, Lord." All of his writings suddenly seemed a very poor thing next to that vision: "Everything I have written seems to me as straw in comparison with what I have seen."[25] A few months later on March 7, 1274, Thomas died in the Cistercian abbey of Fossanova, still on his journey to the Second Council of Lyons.

Miracles were attributed to Aquinas from the moment of his death, and pilgrimages were soon arriving at his tomb.[26] In 1323, he was canonized by Pope John XXII.[27] His relics eventually found their way to the Dominican church in Toulouse in 1369, after what Jean-Pierre Torrell calls "the incredible and hardly appetizing detail of their tribulations during a good part of the fourteenth century."[28] The Dominican pope Pius V declared him a Doctor of the Church on April 15, 1567.

22. St. Thomas Aquinas, *Contra errores Graecorum*, in *Opuscula theologica*, 1:315–46 (Turin and Rome: Marietti, 1954).

23. See Torrell, *Saint Thomas*, 1:14–15, 290–91, 356–57; St. Thomas Aquinas, *Epistola ad Bernardum abbatem casinensem*, vol. 42 of *Opera omnia* (Rome: Typographia polyglotta, 1979), 413–15.

24. Fergus Kerr, OP, *After Aquinas: Versions of Thomism* (Oxford: Blackwell, 2002), 158.

25. Torrell, *Saint Thomas*, 1:285, 289. "St. Thomas's first recorded question was, What is God? and it was when he had found the answer with a fullness not given to most men that he spoke of his writings as straw" (Vann, *Saint Thomas*, 184).

26. Torrell, *Saint Thomas*, 1:297. "Pope John XXII, when questioned if there were enough miracles for Thomas's canonization, is alleged to have responded, 'He performed as many miracles as articles he wrote'" (McGinn, *Thomas*, 220n18).

27. Torrell, *Saint Thomas*, 1:321.

28. Ibid., 1:298. Not so discreet as Torrell, Bernard McGinn adds some details: "Afraid that the Dominicans might steal or commandeer the body with papal approval, they [the Cistercians of Fossanova] moved it several times and may have cut off the head to keep it should this happen. We

Aquinas's Doctrine of God

Aquinas never got an answer to his childhood question, "What is God?" We might say he founded his whole theology on that missing answer: "We cannot know what God is, but rather what he is not."[29] In many ways, his theology is a sustained defense of that unfathomable mystery.[30] Yet his theology does not consist entirely of *not*-statements. Our words can truly "signify the divine substance."[31] Although our statements merely point to the divine reality, the pointing is true.[32] Aquinas's remarkable achievement is to have developed a most comprehensive theology, while never pretending to comprehend the God about whom he speaks.[33]

---

know that at one exhumation, Thomas's hand was removed and given to one of the saint's sisters, though the thumb was later presented to the Dominicans. As ghastly as this all sounds, it fits medieval reverence for the relics of holy men and women. At some time after Thomas's canonization, the remains were boiled down, and the more transportable bones were eventually given to the Dominicans, who laid them to rest in their church in Toulouse in 1369" (McGinn, *Thomas*, 39–40). See also Tugwell, *Albert and Thomas*, 234–35. Lest we think that such disputes are a thing of the past, we might note the recent legal proceedings between the dioceses of New York and Peoria over the relics of Fulton J. Sheen. His niece, Joan Sheen Cunningham, suggests a solution with a familiar ring to those acquainted with the story of Aquinas: "Let the body go to Peoria for a few months, and then bring back some of the relics to New York and leave some in Peoria. It's just too bad it can't just be settled without all this fuss" ("Archbishop Sheen's Body to Stay in New York, for Now," *The New York Times*, February 7, 2018). The case was resolved on June 8, 2018, when the Superior Court of New York ruled "in favor of Joan Sheen Cunningham, who had petitioned to move the body of her uncle, Venerable Fulton Sheen, to the Cathedral of St. Mary in Peoria" ("Civil Court Rules Fulton Sheen's Remains Can Go to Peoria," *Catholic News Agency*, June 9, 2018).

29. *ST* I, 3, prologue. We are, as Anton Pegis says, to "reach him by unsaying progressively all the things in the universe that the human mind can know and know also that they are not God" (Anton C. Pegis, *St. Thomas and Philosophy* [Milwaukee, Wisc.: Marquette University Press, 1964], 72).

30. "In the work of St. Thomas all ways of creaturely knowing have been followed to the very end—to the boundary of mystery. And the more intensely we pursue these ways of knowledge, the more is revealed to us—of the *darkness*, but also of the *reality* of mystery" (Josef Pieper, *The Silence of Saint Thomas*, trans. John Murray and Daniel O'Connor [Chicago: Henry Regnery, 1966], 38).

31. *ST* I, 13, 2, co. "Moreover the idea of negation is always based on an affirmation: as evinced by the fact that every negative proposition is proved by an affirmative: wherefore unless the human mind knew something positively about God, it would be unable to deny anything about him. And it would know nothing if nothing that it affirmed about God were positively verified about him. Hence following Dionysius we must hold that these terms signify the divine essence, albeit defectively and imperfectly" (*De pot.* 7, 5, co.).

32. See *ST* I, 3, 4, ad 2; *ST* I, 13, 3, co.

33. "Because we cannot know what God is, but rather what he is not, we have no means for considering how God is, but rather how he is not" (*ST* I, 3, prologue).

Aquinas's Method

The word "method," coming from the Greek words *meta* (in quest of) and *hodos* (way), means "a way of procedure." Early in his career, Aquinas explained the division and methods of the sciences of his day.[34] A brief look at his distinctions will help us understand the difference between philosophy and theology.

Method of Philosophy

Philosophy, or "love of wisdom," is a work of human reason. In the tradition of Aquinas, to philosophize is "to concentrate our gaze upon the totality of encountered phenomena and methodically to investigate the coherency of them all and the ultimate meaning of the Whole."[35] As human knowledge begins with sensation, philosophy begins with a consideration of material things (perceptible to the senses) and studies their universal properties and principles (not always perceptible to the senses). Like empirical science, philosophy studies the natural world. Unlike empirical science, however, philosophy does not limit its account to what is quantifiable. It includes the philosophy of nature (Aristotle's *Physics*), which seeks the ultimate causes of change in material things, and philosophical anthropology (Aristotle's *On the Soul*), which looks for the ultimate causes of living material things, including human beings. Through its consideration of material things, philosophy eventually comes to the conclusion that material beings and their activities are not self-explanatory but require an immaterial ground or source (God). A reasoned reflection on reality must therefore include not only material being but also immaterial being. The judgment that being is not necessarily material opens a new realm of inquiry: the study of being as such or "being as being" (whether material or immaterial). This is the realm of metaphysics. It studies being

34. The basic speculative sciences are "physics or natural science," "mathematics," and "metaphysics." They are differentiated "according to their degree of separation from matter and motion." The objects of physics (material things) depend on matter "both for their being and for their being understood." The objects of mathematics (e.g., lines, numbers), "although dependent upon matter for their being, do not depend upon it for their being understood, because sensible matter is not included in their definition." The objects of metaphysics (e.g., God and angels) "do not depend upon matter for their being, because they can exist without matter" (*Super de trin.* 5, 1, co.).

35. Pieper, *Guide*, 131.

as being and considers God as the ultimate principle of being. Aquinas calls this "divine science" or "metaphysics" or "philosophical theology."[36] Today it is often called "natural theology."

Method of Theology

With the discovery of God in metaphysics, human reason reaches its limit. Beyond the boundaries of reason, however, and beyond all human expectation, God has revealed himself to us. God can therefore be known not only as the reasoned conclusion of philosophy but also as he actively reveals himself to us: "There is, however, another way of knowing beings of this kind, not as their effects reveal them, but as they reveal themselves."[37] This constitutes a distinct science of God. Accordingly, "there are two kinds of theology." The one pursued by philosophers is named "metaphysics"; the other, based on revelation, is called "the theology taught in Sacred Scripture [*theologia, quae in sacra Scriptura traditur*]."[38] There can be no fundamental conflict between the truth that God reveals and the truth that reason discovers: "Although the truth of the Christian faith ... surpasses the capacity of reason, nevertheless that truth that the human reason is naturally endowed to know cannot be opposed to the truth of the Christian faith."[39]

36. "Philosophers, then, study these divine beings only insofar as they are the principles of all things. Consequently, they are the objects of the science that investigates what is common to all beings, which has for its subject being as being. The philosophers call this divine science [*scientia divina*].... This is the kind of theology pursued by the philosophers and that is also called metaphysics [*metaphysica*].... Thus philosophical theology [*theologia philosophica*] investigates beings separate in the second sense as its subjects [i.e., beings that can exist without, but are sometimes found in, matter and motion], and beings separate in the first sense as the principles of its subject [i.e., beings that can in no way exist in matter and motion]" (*Super de trin.* 5, 4, co.).

37. *Super de trin.* 5, 4, co. "Still, one might say that Thomas proceeds from a basic theological assumption, consisting in the claim that God has made known his truth to man through revelation and that, consequently, the truth claim of Christian faith—the 'system of revealed truth'—is warranted by God himself" (Rudi A. te Velde, *Aquinas on God: The "Divine Science" of the "Summa Theologiae"* [Aldershot: Ashgate, 2006], 3).

38. *Super de trin.* 5, 4, co. "Sciences are differentiated according to the various means through which knowledge is obtained.... Hence theology included in sacred doctrine differs in kind from that theology which is part of philosophy" (*ST* I, 1, 1, ad 2). "This process of the emancipation of natural reason has as its implication that, for the first time in the history of Christian thought, theology was conceived as an independent 'science,' formally distinguished from the philosophical disciplines" (Te Velde, *Aquinas on God*, 4).

39. *SCG* I, c.7.1. "What is divinely taught to us by faith cannot be contrary to what we are endowed with by nature. One or the other would have to be false, and since we have both of them

God's revelation is never purely speculative; it is a practical necessity for human salvation: "It was necessary for man's salvation that there should be a knowledge revealed by God besides philosophical science built up by human reason.... Hence it was necessary for the salvation of man that certain truths which exceed human reason should be made known to him by divine revelation."[40]

For Aquinas theology is a science.[41] It begins with *Sacra Doctrina*, the word of God received in faith.[42] This means that the theologian is es-

---

from God, he would be the cause of our error, which is impossible. Rather, since what is imperfect bears a resemblance to what is perfect, what we know by natural reason has some likeness to what is taught to us by faith. Now just as sacred doctrine is based on the light of faith, so philosophy is based on the natural light of reason. So it is impossible that the contents of philosophy should be contrary to the contents of faith, but they fall short of them" (*Super de trin.* 2, 3, co.). For Aquinas, "faith presupposes natural knowledge, even as grace presupposes nature, and perfection presupposes something to be perfected" (*ST* I, 2, 2, ad 1). "Himself a theologian, St. Thomas had asked the professors of theology never to prove an article of faith by rational demonstration, for faith is not based on reason, but on the word of God, and if you try to prove it, you destroy it. He had likewise asked the professors of philosophy never to prove a philosophical truth by resorting to the words of God, for philosophy is not based on Revelation, but on reason, and if you try to base it on authority, you destroy it. In other words, theology is the science of those things which are received by faith from divine revelation, and philosophy is the knowledge of those things which flow from the principles of natural reason. Since their common source is God, the creator of both reason and revelation, these two sciences are bound ultimately to agree; but if you really want them to agree, you must first be careful not to forget their essential difference. Only distinct things can be united; if you attempt to blend them, you inevitably lose them in what is not union, but confusion" (Etienne Gilson, *The Unity of Philosophical Experience* [Westminster, Md.: Christian Classics, 1982], 62).

40. *ST* I, 1, 1, co. "Thus *sacra doctrina* always has a soteriological purpose.... To put it differently: no talk of God can belong to genuine knowledge of him which cannot aid in the attainment of God as life's final aim. Aquinas does, of course, argue that *sacra doctrina* is a contemplative (*speculativa*) as well as a practical science, indeed that it is primarily contemplative. By this he does not mean, however, that this teaching may ever be divorced from the purpose which alone justifies its existence, which is human salvation" (Bruce D. Marshall, "*Quod sit una uetula*: Aquinas on the Nature of Theology," in *The Theology of Thomas Aquinas*, ed. Rik Van Nieuwenhove and Joseph Wawrykov [Notre Dame, Ind.: University of Notre Dame Press, 1995], 5).

41. "Sacred doctrine is a science. We must bear in mind that there are two kinds of sciences. There are some which proceed from a principle known by the natural light of intelligence, such as arithmetic and geometry and the like. There are some which proceed from principles known by the light of a higher science: thus the science of perspective proceeds from principles established by geometry, and music from principles established by arithmetic. So it is that sacred doctrine is a science because it proceeds from principles established by the light of a higher science, namely, the science of God and the blessed. Hence, just as the musician accepts on authority the principles taught him by the mathematician, so sacred science is established on principles revealed by God" (*ST* I, 1, 2, co.). See Geoffrey Turner, "St. Thomas Aquinas on the 'Scientific' Nature of Theology," *New Blackfriars* 78, no. 921 (1997): 464–76.

42. "Consequently, the definition of *sacra doctrina* is simply wisdom (art. 6), about God (art. 7) in faith, derived from divine revelation (art.1)" (James A. Weisheipl, OP, "The Meaning

sentially a believer. One can certainly study the Bible "as literature," as a branch of "religious studies," as an aspect of "world religions," or as part of the "philosophy of religion," but none of these is theology, which begins with faith in the revealed Word of God. Although the theologian is a believer, theology is not simply faith in God, but "faith seeking understanding" (to use St. Anselm's phrase).[43] It is faith using reason to penetrate the depth of God's revelation.[44] It begins with scripture, but it's not about scripture: it's about God. As Aquinas says: "In sacred science, all things are treated of under the aspect of God: either because they are God himself or because they refer to God as their beginning and end. Hence it follows that God is in very truth the object of this science."[45] Here God is

---

of *Sacra Doctrina* in *Summa Theologiae* I, q. 1," *Thomist* 38, no. 1 [1974]: 75). "It is remarkable that he [Aquinas] seems to use the notions of *sacra Scriptura* and *sacra doctrina* interchangeably in his mature reflections on theological method. This indicates that whenever Aquinas wants to account for his theological activities, he chooses a term that has the connotations of both 'Scripture' and 'scholarship.' *Sacra doctrina* might be translated as 'the instruction in faith' or as 'holy teaching': it is a dual process of teaching. In the first place, God instructs humankind through revelation recorded in the Scriptures. Because of this first aspect, *sacra doctrina* is sometimes translated as 'Revelation.' In the second place, in the course of history, this instruction has been transmitted by the Saints and the Doctors of the Church as teachers of faith. Theology is one of the means by which the instruction in faith is received and transmitted to others; preaching and pastoral care are some other means" (Wilhelmus G. B. M. Valkenberg, *Words of the Living God: Place and Function of Holy Scripture in the Theology of St. Thomas Aquinas* [Leuven: Peeters, 2000], 9–10). See also Fáinche Ryan, *Formation in Holiness: Thomas Aquinas on Sacra doctrina* (Dudley, Mass.: Peeters, 2007).

43. Aquinas never uses the phrase *fides quaerens intellectum*, but he does seem to embrace the concept in quoting John Chrysostom: "Therefore, do not seek to understand in order that you may believe, but believe in order that you may understand: because unless you believe, you will not understand" (*Cat. aur. in joann.* VII, 3, lines 108–10). Also, "in his commentary on the *Sentences* he speaks of an act of thinking that 'presses on to understand that which is already believed' (*tendit ad intellectum eorum quae jam credit*). *Sent.* III, 23, 2, 2, qc. 1 ad 2" (Frederick Christian Bauerschmidt, *Thomas Aquinas: Faith, Reason, and Following Christ* [Oxford: Oxford University Press, 2013], 143n1).

44. See *ST* I, 1, 8, ad 2. "Thomas also holds that reason plays a vital role *within* theology. Indeed, it must have a role to play if *sacra doctrina* is to be *scientia*. Thomas is not willing to say that holy teaching is simply a matter of believing a collection of bits of information that God has revealed. If it is true *scientia*, then reason must have some role to play in this activity. It must be a process of, to use St. Anselm's phrase, 'faith seeking understanding' (*fides quaerens intellectum*), in which understanding involves some sort of seeing the whole by grasping the interrelatedness of the parts" (Bauerschmidt, *Thomas Aquinas*, 141).

45. *ST* I, 1, 7, co. "Sacred doctrine does not treat of God and creatures equally, but of God primarily, and of creatures only so far as they are referable to God as their beginning or end" (*ST* I, 1, 3, ad 1).

not simply the conclusion of some philosophical argument but the Living God who freely reveals himself.[46] He is the Triune Creator of all things, made manifest in all of creation but definitively revealed in the sending of the Son and in the gift of the Holy Spirit.

To explain the method of theology, Aquinas uses the analogy of astronomy. We can extend his analogy to all contemporary empirical science. Both theology and science start with a "given" and then invent a model to understand it. Though helpful, the model can't provide a complete explanation of the "given." In astronomy, for instance, the "given" is the data of astronomical observation. Aquinas notes that, while the Ptolemaic model is useful in explaining such observations, it does not provide a final or definitive explanation of them since other models are always possible: "In astronomy, the theory of eccentrics and epicycles is considered as established, because thereby the sensible appearances of the heavenly movements can be explained; not, however, as if this proof were sufficient, forasmuch as some other theory might explain them."[47]

In theology, the "given" is divine revelation, such as the revealed truth of the Trinity that the One God is Father, Son, and Holy Spirit. Theologians find ways to model this truth in order to penetrate its intelligibility, employing philosophy and the natural sciences as needed in this task.[48] So Bonaventure uses the notion of goodness as diffusive, Richard of St. Victor employs the model of love, and Augustine proposes the example of

46. "Sacred doctrine ... properly uses the authority of the canonical Scriptures as an incontrovertible proof.... For our faith rests upon the revelation make to the apostles and prophets, who wrote the canonical books" (*ST* I, 1, 8, ad 2).

47. *ST* I, 32, 1, ad 2. "Yet it is not necessary that the various suppositions which they hit upon be true for although these suppositions save the appearances, we are nevertheless not obliged to say that these suppositions are true, because perhaps there is some other way men have not yet grasped by which the things which appear as to the stars are saved" (*In de caelo.* II, lect. 17, no. 451).

48. "This science can in a sense depend upon the philosophical sciences, not as though it stood in need of them, but only in order to make its teaching clearer. For it accepts its principles not from other sciences, but immediately from God, by revelation. Therefore it does not depend upon other sciences as upon the higher, but makes use of them as of the lesser, and as handmaidens: even so the master sciences make use of the sciences that supply their materials, as political of military science. That it thus uses them is not due to its own defect or insufficiency, but to the defect of our intelligence, which is more easily led by what is known through natural reason (from which proceed the other sciences) to that which is above reason, such as the teachings of this science" (*ST* I, 1, 5, ad 2). On how theology employs philosophy, see Leo Elders, "Faith and Reason: The Synthesis of St. Thomas Aquinas," *Nova et Vetera* (English ed.) 8, no. 3 (2010): 527–52.

the mind knowing and loving itself. While all of these models are helpful, none can claim to give the proper reason why God is triune.[49] In theology as in science, other models are always possible.

Although science and theology invent models to help us understand the "given," neither may validly modify the "given" to fit the model. For instance, one may not change the data of astronomical observation to fit one's model. However fine the model, the data must prevail. So Thomas Henry Huxley laments "the great tragedy of science: the slaying of a beautiful hypothesis by an ugly fact."[50] Similarly, one may not distort God's revelation to fit one's theological model.[51]

A number of theologians have argued that the use of Greek philosophy by the Fathers of the Church involved just such a distortion and resulted in a "hellenization" or "Greekifying" of the gospel. So Adolf von Harnack argued: "Dogma in its conception and development is a work of the Greek spirit on the soil of the Gospel."[52] Recent theologians, however, have rejected his position. Quoting von Harnack, Jaroslav Pelikan argues:

It is even more a distortion when the dogma formulated by the catholic tradition is described as "in its conception and development a work of the Greek spirit on the soil of the gospel." Indeed, in some ways it is more accurate to speak of dogma

---

49. "We must not think that the trinity of persons is adequately proved by such reasons" (*ST* I, 32, 1, ad 2). "Now, the human reason is related to the knowledge of the truth of faith ... in such a way that it can gather certain likenesses of it, which are yet not sufficient so that the truth of faith may be comprehended as being understood demonstratively or through itself. Yet it is useful for the human reason to exercise itself in such arguments, however weak they may be, provided only that there be present no presumption to comprehend or to demonstrate. For to be able to see something of the loftiest realities, however thin and weak the sight may be, is, as our previous remarks indicate, a cause of the greatest joy" (*SCG* I, c.8.1).

50. Thomas Henry Huxley, "Biogenesis and Abiogenesis," Presidential Address for the British Association for the Advancement of Science, 1870, http://alepho.clarku.edu/huxley/CE8/B-Ab .html.

51. Still, theology may not ignore the exacting task of interpretation in determining the meaning of revelation, and science may not sidestep that same task in judging the validity of its observations, which always entail the presuppositions of a particular scientific paradigm and the complex relationship between "theory-laden" data and "data-laden" theory. Yet the starting point of the scientific method remains observation, and that of theology, revelation. On the complexities of interpretation in science, see Thomas S. Kuhn, *The Structure of Scientific Revolutions* (Chicago: University of Chicago Press, 1970), and John C. Polkinghorne, *One World: The Interaction of Science and Theology* (Princeton, N.J.: Princeton University Press, 1986).

52. Adolf von Harnack, *History of Dogma*, trans. Neil Buchanan (New York: Russell and Russell, 1958), 17.

as the "dehellenization" of the theology that had preceded it and to argue that "by its dogma the church threw up a wall against an alien metaphysic."[53]

Paul Gavrilyuk writes: "The 'Theory of Theology's Fall into Hellenistic Philosophy' must be once and for all buried with honors, as one of the most enduring and illuminating mistakes among the interpretations of the development of Christian doctrine."[54] There is now a greater appreciation of the critical judgment exercised by the Church Fathers in their employment of Greek ideas and of how the historical process of hellenization may be viewed as not only unavoidable but uniquely valuable.

Aquinas saw philosophy as the "handmaid" of theology and studiously avoided allowing the handmaid the upper hand: "Those who use the works of the philosophers in sacred doctrine, by bringing them into the service of faith, do not mix water with wine, but rather change water into wine."[55] Accepting the truth of Scripture as the "given," theology may turn to human reason (including empirical science) not to critique or modify that truth but to penetrate its depth: "Sacred doctrine makes use even of human reason, not, indeed, to prove faith ... but to make clear other things that are put forward in this doctrine.... Hence sacred doctrine makes use also of the authority of philosophers in those questions in which they were able to know the truth by natural reason."[56] Theology's use of philosophy and science cannot change revealed truth but may help us to understand it more deeply, resulting in a change, not in scripture but perhaps in our interpretation of it.[57]

53. Jaroslav Pelikan, *The Emergence of the Catholic Tradition* (Chicago: University of Chicago Press, 1971), 55, quoting Adolf von Harnack, *Lehrbuch der Dogmengeschichte* (Tübingen: Mohr, 1931), 1:20; and Werner Elert, *Der Ausgang der altkirchlichen Christologie* (Berlin: Lutherisches Verlagshaus, 1957), 14.

54. Paul L. Gavrilyuk, *The Suffering of the Impassible God: The Dialectics of Patristic Thought* (New York: Oxford University Press, 2004), 46. See also Robert Louis Wilken, *The Spirit of Early Christian Thought: Seeking the Face of God* (New Haven, Conn.: Yale University Press, 2003), 59–61; William V. Rowe, "Adolf von Harnack and the Concept of Hellenization," in *Hellenization Revisited: Shaping a Christian Response within the Greco-Roman World*, ed. Wendy E. Helleman (Lanham, Md.: University Press of America, 1994), 69–98.

55. *Super de trin.* 2, 3, ad 5.

56. *ST* I, 1, 8, ad 2.

57. "Whatsoever is found in other sciences contrary to any truth of this science must be condemned as false" (*ST* I, 1, 7, ad 2). For how Aquinas negotiates apparent conflicts between faith and science, see Michael J. Dodds, OP, *Unlocking Divine Action: Contemporary Science and Thomas Aquinas* (Washington, D.C.: The Catholic University of America Press, 2012), 7–9.

The *Summa Theologica*

St. Thomas began his *Summa Theologica* in 1266 and left it unfinished at his death in 1274.[58] It comprises three "parts," often designated by the Roman numerals I, II, and III. The second part is divided in two: the first part of the second part (I-II) and the second part of the second part (II-II). Part I considers God in the unity of the divine essence and the distinction of persons, as well as the procession of creatures from God.[59] Part II examines questions of moral theology. Part III considers the Incarnation and the sacraments. This last part was also to include a discussion of eschatology ("the end of immortal life to which we attain by the resurrection").[60] It breaks off midway through a consideration of the sacrament of Penance, when Aquinas stopped writing after his experience on December 6, 1273.[61]

Various theories have been proposed regarding the structure of this work. Aquinas himself said that the work would treat: "(1) of God; (2) of the rational creature's advance towards God; (3) of Christ, Who as man, is our way to God."[62] Picking up on this, Marie-Dominique Chenu proposed

58. Weisheipl, *Friar*, 361–62. The pedagogical and unfinished character of the *Summa* reflects the nature of theology itself: "Thomas invents rhetorical forms to keep inherited theology whole. On his account of the pilgrim state of the human mind within history, theology cannot possibly be whole as an accomplished system of propositions. Theology is the work of faith, and faith is restlessness on the way to beatitude. Thomas writes through forms that keep theology whole in the only way it can be: as pedagogy, as a curriculum of ascent" (Mark D. Jordan, *Rewritten Theology: Aquinas after His Readers* [Oxford: Blackwell, 2006], 193).

59. "In treating of God there will be a threefold division, for we shall consider: (1) Whatever concerns the Divine Essence; (2) Whatever concerns the distinctions of Persons; (3) Whatever concerns the procession of creatures from him" (*ST* I, 2, prologue). Aquinas has been criticized by theologians such as Karl Rahner and Catherine LaCugna for separating his consideration of "the One God" from his treatment of the Trinity. The result, they argue, is that "the One God" becomes a mostly philosophical discussion while trinitarian theology is divorced from history and isolated from the rest of theology. See Karl Rahner, "Remarks on the Dogmatic Treatise 'De Trinitate,'" in *Theological Investigations,* trans. K. Smyth (Baltimore, Md.: Helicon Press, 1966), 4:83–84; Catherine Mowry LaCugna, *God for Us: The Trinity and Christian Life* (San Francisco: Harper, 1992), 6, 10, 44, 145–69. Other theologians, however, noting Aquinas's theological as well as pedagogical intent, have defended his approach. See Declan Marmion and Rik Van Nieuwenhove, *An Introduction to the Trinity* (New York: Cambridge University Press, 2010), 114–16; Gilles Emery, OP, *The Trinitarian Theology of Saint Thomas Aquinas* (New York: Oxford University Press, 2007), 39–50.

60. *ST* III, Prologue.

61. Weisheipl, *Friar*, 361–63.

62. *ST* I, 2, prologue. "Early in his life's work, in the first book of his *Commentary on the*

the still-popular idea that the work is structured in an "*exitus/reditus*" pattern: the *exitus*, or procession of all things from God, and the *reditus*, or return of all things to God through Christ.[63] Rudi te Velde argues, however: "In spite of its initial plausibility, serious doubts begin to arise when one attempts a more detailed application of the *exitus-reditus* scheme to the programmatic divisions of the *Summa*."[64] Jean-Pierre Torrell suggests that the *Summa* reflects the distinction, found in the Fathers of the Church, between "theology" (*ST* I, 2–43) and "economy" (the rest of the *Summa*): "Complete and nuanced, this explanation seems to correspond well to what Saint Thomas did."[65]

If the broad sweep of the work is open to various interpretations, the structure of its individual arguments clearly reflects the scholastic method of teaching that was characteristic of the Middle Ages. Each of the three parts comprises a number of questions dealing with various theological topics. The questions, in turn, are divided into articles. Every article follows the same structure: a question is posed; various objections are raised; a counter-argument (*sed contra*) is offered; the question is resolved; and finally the individual objections are answered. Dialogue is the soul of this method, reflecting the public disputations of the medieval universities. Theology does not consist of easy answers but of rigorous argumentation.[66] If there were no questions to raise, there would be no

---

Sentences, Thomas himself declared (at the age of twenty-eight): 'In the emergence of creatures from their first Source is revealed a kind of circulation, *quaedam circulatio vel regiratio*, in which all things return, as to their end, back to the very place from which they had their origin in the beginning' (*Sent.* I, 14, 2, 2)" (Pieper, *Guide*, 93).

63. "Beyond the scientific world of Aristotle, Saint Thomas appeals to the Platonic theme of emanation and return. Since theology is the science of God, all things will be studied in their relation to God, whether in their production or in their final end, in their *exitus et reditus* [going-out-from and coming-back-to]. What a splendid source of intelligibility!" (Marie-Dominique Chenu, OP, *Toward Understanding Saint Thomas*, trans. A.-M. Landry, OP, and D. Hughes, OP [Chicago: H. Regnery Co., 1964], 304). "Most contemporary commentators agree with Chenu that the *Summa* is based upon a neo-Platonic scheme of *exitus-reditus* from God to creatures, although they disagree on the specifics of how the scheme develops in the work itself" (Anna Bonta Moreland, *Known by Nature: Thomas Aquinas on Natural Knowledge of God* [New York: Crossroad, 2010], 50).

64. Te Velde, *Aquinas on God*, 12.

65. Torrell, *Saint Thomas*, 1:152–53.

66. Aquinas maintains that "sacred doctrine is a matter of argument" (*ST* I, 1, 8). "In this procedure there emerges an element profoundly characteristic of St. Thomas' intellectual style: the spirit of the *disputatio*, of disciplined opposition; the spirit of genuine discussion which remains a

theology.[67] The objections are not straw men to be easily dismissed; they are fundamental to the question being posed. For instance, when Aquinas asks whether God exists, the objections he poses are the same as those still raised today: (1) the reality of evil negates the existence of a good God; and (2) the God hypothesis is not needed since nature (today we might say science) can explain everything.[68]

The dialogue itself is wide open. Theology certainly presupposes the truth of scripture, but objections to that truth as well as arguments to support it can come from all quarters. In our day, as we make tentative overtures to dialogue with Judaism and Islam and other world religions, it is bracing to see Aquinas employing Jewish and Islamic philosophers (Moses Maimonides, Averroes, Avicenna) as well as the pagan Aristotle in his theology.[69] Since theology is founded on revelation received in faith, its method requires that scripture be the fundamental authority in its arguments. Yet philosophical arguments may be used, even though they are not based on revelation and so are extrinsic to the method of theology. The arguments of the doctors of the Church may also be used. These are employed as proper to theology (since they are also based on faith), but as merely probable in comparison to the authority of scripture:

This doctrine is especially based upon arguments from authority, inasmuch as its principles are obtained by revelation: thus we ought to believe on the authority

---

dialogue even while it is a dispute. This spirit governs the inner structure of all St. Thomas' works. And I feel that in this generosity of spirit, too, the exemplary, the paradigmatic character of the *doctor communis* of Christendom is displayed" (Pieper, *Guide*, 73).

67. "For a person stops being a theologian just when he or she thinks there is nothing left to be argued about" (Turner, *Faith, Reason*, xi).

68. *ST* I, 2, 3.

69. Regarding Aquinas's sources, Brian Davies remarks: "The first, of course, was the Bible, followed by the so-called 'fathers' of the Christian church—figures such as Augustine.... Aquinas's intellectual debts are not just biblical and patristic, however. As we have seen, he knew a lot about Aristotle. But he also knew (and, with various qualifications, approved of) Plato, and philosophers writing in Plato's vein (commonly referred to as Neoplatonists). Aquinas also drew on Jewish and Islamic authors—notable examples being Moses Maimonides (1138–1204) and Avicenna (980–1037). Aquinas's thinking sometimes resembles that of Maimonides and Avicenna to a striking degree, and both authors are cited multiple times in the *Summa Theologiae*. This is not, of course, to say that Aquinas merely echoes his sources uncritically. He is never the slave of his philosophical forerunners, even those with whom he is most strongly in agreement" (Davies, "Introduction," xii–xiii). See also Gilles Emery, OP, and Matthew Levering, eds., *Aristotle in Aquinas's Theology* (Oxford: Oxford University Press, 2015).

of those to whom the revelation has been made.... Sacred doctrine makes use
also of the authority of philosophers in those questions in which they were able
to know the truth by natural reason.... Nevertheless, sacred doctrine makes use
of these authorities as extrinsic and probable arguments; but properly uses the
authority of the canonical Scriptures as an incontrovertible proof, and the authority of the doctors of the Church as one that may properly be used, yet merely as probable. For our faith rests upon the revelation made to the apostles and
prophets who wrote the canonical books, and not on the revelations (if any such
there are) made to other doctors.[70]

Thomas and Thomism(s)

After his death, as during his life, Aquinas's theology did not meet with
universal praise. On March 7, 1277, Stephen Tempier, the bishop of Paris, condemned 219 propositions. They included "some of Thomas's positions," although he was "not *directly* a target."[71] A few days later, Robert
Kilwardby, the Dominican archbishop of Canterbury, with the support
of the faculty of Oxford, took more direct aim at Aquinas by condemn-
ing a list of thirty propositions, some of which were clearly "of Thomist
inspiration."[72] The condemnations sparked fierce controversies between
theologians who remained suspicious of Aristotle and those who, like
Aquinas, had incorporated his thought. The censures also caused the Dominicans to rally around Aquinas and his teaching: "In 1309 the Dominican General Chapter made 'Thomism' the official doctrine of the Order,
bidding all lectors throughout the Order to follow the teaching of Thom-

70. *ST* I, 1, 8, ad 2. "[The *Summa Theologiae*] is complete too, and perhaps especially, in its
method, since it contains everything necessary for an integral theological approach: a listening to
revealed data in the form of Sacred Scripture, the presence of the tradition by an abundant use of
the Fathers of the Church and the great Councils, a constant attention to the wisdom of philosophers whatever be their origin, and finally a recourse to human experience in all of its complexity"
(Jean-Pierre Torrell, OP, *Aquinas's "Summa": Background, Structure, and Reception,* trans. Benedict M. Guevin, OSB [Washington, D.C.: The Catholic University of America Press, 2005], 133).

71. Torrell, *Saint Thomas,* 1:300.

72. Ibid., 1:304. "In Paris, Thomas was only condemned privately. In Oxford the Dominican
Archbishop of Canterbury, Robert Kilwardby, secured the agreement of the Masters and issued his
own list of condemned propositions on 18 March 1277, and this list did affect Thomas unambig-
uously, though he was not mentioned by name" (Tugwell, *Albert and Thomas,* 238–39). See also
Weisheipl, *Friar,* 337; Josef Pieper, *Scholasticism: Personalities and Problems of Medieval Philosophy*
(New York: McGraw Hill, 1960), 126–35.

as."[73] Only in 1325 would the condemnations involving Aquinas's teachings be annulled.[74]

In the centuries since then, many great philosophers and theologians have commented on Aquinas and incorporated his teaching into their thought.[75] Whether their efforts enhanced or distorted Aquinas is a "disputed question."[76] Pope Leo XIII famously revived interest in Aquinas with his encyclical *Aeterni Patris* in 1879. The encyclical had a double effect: a healthy new energy for the study of Aquinas known as Neothomism,[77] combined with a rather dismal succession of manuals on Aquinas (manualism) which often neglected the actual study of his writings and were especially imposed on Roman Catholic seminaries.[78]

73. Tugwell, *Albert and Thomas*, 243. This was perhaps a mixed blessing, as Tugwell notes: "The great intellectual adventure, which had begun his life's work, soon turned into an orthodoxy to be defended and propagated, instead of being carried on as a task that can never be completed" (ibid., 243). Josef Pieper concurs: "It began to degenerate from a fruitful controversy to a sterile wrangle, with the debaters more concerned with being right than in finding the truth" (Pieper, *Scholasticism*, 134).

74. Torrell, *Saint Thomas*, 1:324.

75. On this history see Romanus Cessario, OP, *A Short History of Thomism* (Washington, D.C.: The Catholic University of America Press, 2005); Romanus Cessario, OP, and Cajetan Cuddy, OP, *Thomas and the Thomists: The Achievement of Thomas Aquinas and His Interpreters* (Minneapolis: Fortress Press, 2017); Aidan Nichols, OP, *Discovering Aquinas: An Introduction to His Life, Work, and Influence* (Grand Rapids, Mich.: Eerdmans, 2002); Brian J. Shanley, OP, *The Thomist Tradition* (Dordrecht: Kluwer Academic, 2000); McGinn, *Thomas*; Gerald A. McCool, SJ, *Nineteenth-Century Scholasticism: The Search for a Unitary Method* (New York: Fordham University Press, 1989); Gerald A. McCool, SJ, *From Unity to Pluralism: The Internal Evolution of Thomism* (New York: Fordham University Press, 1989); Otto Hermann Pesch, "Thomas Aquinas and Contemporary Theology," in *Contemplating Aquinas: On the Varieties of Interpretation*, ed. Fergus Kerr (London: SCM, 2003), 185–216; Bauerschmidt, *Thomas Aquinas*, 291–316; Torrell, *Aquinas's "Summa,"* 86–130.

76. See William C. Placher, *The Domestication of Transcendence: How Modern Thinking about God Went Wrong* (Louisville, Ky.: Westminster John Knox Press, 1996), 21–36, 71–87, 113–16, 119–22, 148–52.

77. "Neothomism is the name given to the papally supported form of Thomism that developed in the second half of the nineteenth century.... Many of the documents, such as the papal encyclical *Aeterni Patris* of 1879, speak of the renewal of 'scholastic philosophy' (*philosophia scholastica*); hence the term 'Neoscholasticism' is often used to describe this movement in modern Catholic thought. In practice, however, Thomas Aquinas was seen as *the* Neoscholastic author.... Hence, the terms 'Neoscholasticism' and 'Neothomism' can be used interchangeably" (McGinn, *Thomas*, 163, 238n3).

78. "Resisted at its birth, and even condemned, Thomism, once made official, became a weapon in the hands of the authorities.... But the consequences here were disastrous. Imposed in an authoritarian way, Thomas's doctrine had nothing left of the creative force of the original. The Thomism that was diffused in the manuals no longer referred to Thomas except by the intermediary of second-rate commentators. Rarely sensitive to the biblical and patristic sources (held

Despite such vicissitudes, the study of Aquinas has survived and at times flourished.[79] It continues to receive papal encouragement.[80] Even through the Protestant Reformation, the tradition of Aquinas continued and is still evident in contemporary evangelical theology.[81] Some of

under suspicion because of anti-Modernism), and imbued with a rationalism of which they were unaware, their authors propagated a repetitious, narrow, and legalistic doctrine that was Thomist only in name. This explains the discredit into which Master Thomas fell in our own century" (Torrell, *Aquinas's "Summa,"* 110–11). "If 'Thomists' claim that they can reduce the doctrine of St. Thomas to a system of propositions that can be transmitted by the tradition of a school, then their 'Thomism' must be called a falsification. For they have suppressed the very feature in which, so it seems to me, lies the greatness of St. Thomas as a philosophical and theological thinker: his attitude of veneration toward everything that is—which veneration is revealed above all in his falling silent before the ineffability and incomprehensibility of Being" (Pieper, *Guide*, 140). See also Herbert McCabe, OP, *On Aquinas*, ed. Brian Davies, OP (New York: Continuum, 2008), 4–5; Kerr, *After Aquinas*, 16; Fernand Van Steenberghen, *Hidden God: How Do We Know That God Exists?* (St. Louis, Mo.: Herder, 1966), 146.

79. For a comprehensive review of the reception of Aquinas's thought over the centuries, see Matthew Levering, Marcus Plested, and Charles Raith II, eds., *Oxford Handbook of Reception of Aquinas* (Oxford: Oxford University Press, forthcoming).

80. "This is why the Church has been justified in consistently proposing Saint Thomas as a master of thought and a model of the right way to do theology. In this connection, I would recall what my Predecessor, the Servant of God Paul VI, wrote on the occasion of the seventh centenary of the death of the Angelic Doctor: 'Without doubt, Thomas possessed supremely the courage of the truth, a freedom of spirit in confronting new problems, the intellectual honesty of those who allow Christianity to be contaminated neither by secular philosophy nor by a prejudiced rejection of it'" (Pope John Paul II, *Fides et ratio: On the Relationship between Faith and Reason*, Encyclical Letter [September 14, 1998] [Washington, D.C.: United States Catholic Conference, 1998], 43).

81. "Obviously, Thomas and his *Summa theologiae* were mostly viewed in negative terms by the majority of the Reformers and their successors, but the rise of what has been called 'Protestant scholasticism' in the late sixteenth century represents a complicated adoption and rejection of medieval scholasticism in general and of Thomas in particular. Learned Protestant divines, both on the Continent and in England, could scarcely avoid Thomas and the *Summa*, though their degree of knowledge and use varied" (McGinn, *Thomas*, 151). "Today, however, the majority of scholars see the Thomist understanding of things as the prevailing position among early Protestants in important areas of philosophy and theology.... [W]e confidently believe that serious and accurate wrestling with the texts and legacy of Thomas Aquinas can only benefit Protestant intellectual life" (Manfred Svensson and David VanDrunen, *Aquinas among the Protestants* [Oxford: Wiley Blackwell, 2018], 11–12, 17). See also Otto Herman Pesch, *The God Question in Thomas Aquinas and Martin Luther* (Philadelphia, Fortress Press, 1972). For contemporary examples of Protestant scholars who have effectively incorporated Aquinas, see James E. Dolezal, *All That Is in God: Evangelical Theology and the Challenge of Classical Christian Theism* (Grand Rapids, Mich.: Reformation Heritage Books, 2017); Ron Highfield, *The Faithful Creator: Affirming Creation and Providence in an Age of Anxiety* (Downers Grove, Ill.: IVP Academic, 2015); Arvin Vos, *Aquinas, Calvin, and Contemporary Protestant Thought: A Critique of Protestant Views on the Thought of Thomas Aquinas* (Washington, D.C.: Christian University Press, 1985); Norman L. Geisler, *Thomas Aquinas: An Evangelical Appraisal* (Grand Rapids, Mich.: Baker Book House, 1991).

Aquinas's followers emphasize his philosophy.[82] Others argue that his philosophy is always inseparable from and at the service of his theology.[83] Some of his followers have enriched (or "adulterated," according to some critics) his thought with more recent philosophical traditions, leading to "transcendental Thomism" (which incorporates Kant)[84] and "analytical

82. "Aquinas is, I believe, one of the dozen greatest philosophers of the western world" (Anthony Kenny, "Introduction," in *Aquinas: A Collection of Critical Essays*, ed. Anthony Kenny [Notre Dame, Ind.: University of Notre Dame Press, 1976], 1). "The philosophy of Thomas Aquinas has in recent decades found an audience well beyond its traditional home in Catholicism" (Robert Pasnau and Christopher John Shields, *The Philosophy of Aquinas* [Boulder, Colo.: Westview Press, 2004], vii). "Thomas Aquinas never called himself a philosopher. But his contribution to philosophy is now widely viewed as outstanding" (Davies, "Introduction," vii). "Aquinas is a theologian by profession. It is, however, not the professional philosophers of the thirteenth century, but the theologian Thomas Aquinas who belongs among the outstanding figures in the history of philosophy" (Jan A. Aersten, "Aquinas's Philosophy in its Historical Setting," in *The Cambridge Companion to Aquinas*, ed. Norman Kretzmann and Eleonore Stump [Cambridge: Cambridge University Press, 1993], 35). "Thomists insist that Thomism is acceptable on its own merits as a philosophy.... [W]hatever uses it may be put to, Thomism is and remains a philosophy. Despite its *de facto* connection with Catholicism, it is not part of the Catholic faith; and if we wish to judge of its philosophical merits and its potentialities for fruitful development, we have to turn to those Thomists who have written as serious philosophers rather than to the somewhat slick statements of Thomist positions by popular apologists" (Frederick C. Copleston, SJ, *Aquinas* [Baltimore, Md.: Penguin Books, 1975], 247–48). See also Leo Elders, *The Philosophical Theology of St. Thomas Aquinas* (Leiden: Brill, 1990).

83. "The typical modern distinction between the 'God of reason' and the 'God of faith' is not, I think, particularly helpful in identifying Thomas' position with regard to Christian faith. It is certainly true to say that he approaches the question of God from within the Christian tradition. In my opinion, any attempt to construe a system of 'natural theology' from Thomas' writings will distort the proper theological focus of his thought" (Te Velde, *Aquinas on God*, 2). "Nothing occurs more spontaneously to the modern reader of Aquinas than to ask about the relations between his philosophy and his theology, and no question is more misleading.... Any appropriate formulation [of the question] must begin by recognizing that whatever philosophy there is in Aquinas can be approached only through his theology if it is to be approached as he intended it" (Mark D. Jordan, "Theology and Philosophy," in *The Cambridge Companion to Aquinas*, ed. Norman Kretzmann and Eleonore Stump [Cambridge: Cambridge University Press, 1993], 232). "Independently of distortions of precise points, it seems that the most common and damaging error was to have considered Thomas first of all as a philosopher and to have believed it possible to isolate certain parts of the *Summa* as 'philosophical.' This is a glaring error of perspective. The *Summa* is theological from beginning to end and its author is first and foremost a theologian" (Torrell, *Aquinas's "Summa,"* 133). "He [Thomas Aquinas] was first and always a theologian: in the university and in the Dominican *studium*, in the pulpit and in his room writing. Whether commenting on Scripture or assembling opinions from past philosophers and theologians to flesh out his original, systematic conception of Christianity, he wrote to help the Christian message address sympathetically new problems and thought-forms" (Thomas F. O'Meara, OP, *Thomas Aquinas: Theologian* [Notre Dame, Ind.: University of Notre Dame Press, 1997], xi).

84. On the roots of Transcendental Thomism in the thought of Joseph Maréchal, see Gerald A. McCool, SJ, *The Neo-Thomists* (Milwaukee, Wisc.: Marquette University Press, 1994), 117–33,

Thomism" (which incorporates philosophers such as Wittgenstein).[85] As a result, there are currently many brands of Thomism, having perhaps as their only common feature the fact that they respect and incorporate his thought.[86] Perhaps, the presence of such variety and controversy—so vividly evident in Aquinas's own day—is a good sign of the continued health of Thomism.

and McCool, *From Unity*, 87–113. On the transcendental theology of Karl Rahner, see Thomas Sheehan, "Rahner's Transcendental Project," in *The Cambridge Companion to Karl Rahner*, ed. Declan Marmion and Mary E. Hines (New York: Cambridge University Press, 2005), 29–42. For critiques, see Christopher M. Cullen, "Transcendental Thomism: Realism Rejected," in *The Failure of Modernism: The Cartesian Legacy and Contemporary Pluralism*, ed. Brendan Sweetman (Mishawaka, Ind.: American Maritain Association, 1999), 72–86; Robert J. Henle, SJ, "Transcendental Thomism: A Critical Assessment," in *One Hundred Years of Thomism: Aeterni Patris and Afterwards, A Symposium*, ed. Victor B. Brezik (Houston: Center for Thomistic Studies, 1981), 90–116.

85. For an overview of analytic Thomism, see Brian J. Shanley, OP, "Analytical Thomism," *Thomist* 63, no. 1 (1999): 125–37; John Haldane, "Analytical Thomism: How We Got Here, Why It Is Worth Remaining and Where We May Go to Next," in *Analytical Thomism: Traditions in Dialogue*, ed. Craig Paterson and Matthew S. Pugh (Burlington, Vt.: Ashgate, 2006), 303–10. See also Edward Feser, *Scholastic Metaphysics: A Contemporary Introduction* (Heusenstamm, Germany: Editiones Scholasticae, 2014), a work that, as the author describes it, "interacts heavily with the literature in contemporary analytic metaphysics" (ibid., 8).

86. "The label 'Thomist' can be applied broadly, describing anyone who takes Thomas as a significant dialogue partner and who finds him more often than not helpful on a variety of questions. Typically, however, the label is applied more narrowly to identify those who hold to some determinate set of positions that are found in or derived from what Thomas wrote. The exact content of these positions is continually under dispute, and consequently who counts as a genuine Thomist is similarly disputed" (Bauerschmidt, *Thomas Aquinas*, 292). On the varieties of Thomism, see Fergus Kerr, OP, ed., *Contemplating Aquinas: On the Varieties of Interpretation* (London: SCM, 2003); Benedict M. Ashley, OP, *The Way toward Wisdom: An Interdisciplinary and Intercultural Introduction to Metaphysics* (Notre Dame, Ind.: University of Notre Dame Press, 2006), 44–54.

CHAPTER 1

THE EXISTENCE OF GOD

We might wonder why Aquinas begins his *Summa Theologica* with the question of God's existence when theology presupposes it and the "beginners" for whom he's writing are already convinced of it. Why, then, ask whether God exists? Perhaps he asks the question precisely *because* he's doing theology. If theology is "faith seeking understanding" and reason is our tool for understanding, then the question of God's existence may be a means to unlocking that tool. The question not only leads to several ways of showing that God exists, but also opens avenues for knowing and speaking of God that are all grounded in the different ways that reason discovers God's existence as the cause of creatures. Here we find the theological purpose of Aquinas's famous "Five Ways." They provide a language for thinking and talking about God that Aquinas will employ in subsequent questions about God's nature and attributes.[1] Not only are the Five

---

1. "Such demonstrations based on God's effects do not give us a firm grasp on the nature of God..., nor can they tell us why God should produce *this* effect rather than *that*. Fact-demonstrations allow us to know how properly to employ the word 'God' in discourse, as well as to know that our language is referring to something, but they offer no basis for grasping the *quidditas* of God" (Bauerschmidt, *Thomas Aquinas,* 94).

Ways or "proofs" philosophically valid, but they also have a special theological purpose.[2]

In this chapter, we will first consider whether reason is a powerful enough tool to get us to God's existence simply by reflecting on the idea of God. For this, we will examine Anselm's ontological argument. Then we will investigate whether it is at all possible to establish God's existence through rational argument and will review Aquinas's Five Ways of doing this. Finally, we will mention some other possible arguments for God's existence and say a brief word about the atheist critique of belief in God.

Anselm's Argument

St. Anselm (1033–1109) formulated what has traditionally been called the "ontological argument."[3] He frames it as a theological exercise of faith seeking understanding: "And so, O Lord, since thou givest understanding to faith, give me to understand . . . that thou dost exist."[4] Although it was in some ways a devotional exercise, Anselm also saw his argument as a valid philosophical proof.[5] It runs like this:

Now we believe that thou are a being than which none greater can be thought. . . . But clearly that than which a greater cannot be thought cannot exist in the understanding alone. For if it is actually in the understanding alone, it can be thought of as existing also in reality, and this is greater. Therefore, if that than which a greater cannot be thought is in the understanding alone, this same thing than which a greater cannot be thought is that than which a greater can be thought.

2. On the theological purpose of the Five Ways, see John R. Wilcox, "Our Knowledge of God in *Summa Theologiae, Prima Pars, Quaestiones 3–6*: Positive or Negative?" *Proceedings of the American Catholic Philosophical Association* 72 (1998): 201–11.

3. "St. Anselm did not use the expression 'ontological argument.' . . . It is everywhere now used to refer, however, to an argument first developed in St. Anselm's *Proslogion*. . . . He was . . . undoubtedly the first author of the ontological argument and his name is rarely omitted from any discussion of it" (Richard Taylor, "Introduction," in *The Ontological Argument from St. Anselm to Contemporary Philosophers*, ed. Alvin Plantinga [Garden City, N.Y.: Doubleday, 1965], viii).

4. St. Anselm, *Proslogion*, chap. 2, in *The Existence of God*, ed. John Hick (New York: Macmillan, 1964), 25.

5. "St. Anselm set forth his argument as an address to God. It is obvious, then, that he was not attempting to discover whether God exists. . . . On the other hand, he makes it perfectly clear that it is intended to be a philosophical proof and not merely an expression of pious persuasion. His argument presupposes no belief in the existence of God. It presupposes only the concept of God, that is to say, the concept of an absolutely supreme being, and for this no religious faith at all is required" (Taylor, "Introduction," viii–ix).

But obviously this is impossible. Without doubt, therefore, there exists, both in the understanding and in reality, something than which a greater cannot be thought.[6]

The argument implies that the existence of God is self-evident. In the same way that once we know the meaning of the word "triangle," it is self-evident that every triangle has three sides, so once we know the meaning of the word "God," it becomes self-evident that God exists. The idea of God leads us directly to the ontology (being) of God. The argument has intrigued philosophers and theologians for centuries.[7]

Aquinas considers the argument in his discussion of whether the existence of God is self-evident. He summarizes it in this way:

Those things are said to be self-evident which are known as soon as the terms are known.... Thus, when the nature of a whole and of a part is known, it is at once recognized that every whole is greater than its part. But as soon as the signification of the word "God" is understood, it is at once seen that God exists. For by this word is signified that thing than which nothing greater can be conceived. But that which exists actually and mentally is greater than that which exists only mentally. Therefore, since as soon as the word "God" is understood it exists mentally, it also follows that it exists actually. Therefore the proposition "God exists" is self-evident.[8]

The validity of the argument hinges on whether the argument allows us to move from the way we think about God to the fact that God is. For example, the fact that I think about a chocolate brownie as existing doesn't imply that it actually exists. In Anselm's argument, however, thinking about a brownie (or any creature) is not the same as thinking about God. You can always think of something greater than a brownie, but you can't think of anything greater than God, since God is defined as "that than which nothing greater can be thought." So if you find yourself thinking of something greater than God, it simply means that you weren't really thinking about God in the first place. More to the point, if you think of God as

---

6. St. Anselm, *Proslogion*, chap. 2, 25–26.

7. "This argument has held a profound fascination for men since it was first so thoroughly and beautifully formulated by St. Anselm of Canterbury in the eleventh century. Few philosophical arguments have been the target of more attacks, and yet it finds new defenders among the ablest thinkers in every generation" (Taylor, "Introduction," vii).

8. *ST* I, 2, 1, obj. 2.

not existing, you're not really thinking of God, since an existent God is greater than a nonexistent God. So you can't *think* about God without *thinking* that God exists. But does this limitation on your thinking imply that God *really* exists? Aquinas doesn't think so. One can accept Anselm's definition of God without admitting "that there actually exists something than which nothing greater can be thought."[9] Anselm's argument by itself does not allow us to cross over from thought to reality.

Aquinas argues that, although God's existence is self-evident *in itself*, it is not self-evident *to us*. That a triangle has three sides may be self-evident in itself (by definition), but it will not be self-evident to us if we don't know what a triangle is. So it may be self-evident in itself that God exists (since God's essence is his existence), but it is not self-evident to us since we do not know God's essence: we do not know what God is. Since we do not know God by his essence but only through his effects, we can show that God exists only through his effects.[10]

Natural Theology and the Existence of God

As a philosopher, Aquinas argues that we can demonstrate God's existence from his effects. Such arguments belong to natural theology, which is based on reason alone.[11] As a theologian, however, Aquinas notes that scripture also affirms the possibility of such a demonstration: "The invisible things of him are clearly seen, being understood by the things that are made."[12] The First and Second Vatican Councils and the *Catechism of the Catholic Church* also assert that God's existence can be demonstrated through rational argument.[13] Still, the question of whether and how

9. *ST* I, 2, 1, ad 2.

10. *ST* I, 2, 1, co.

11. "Aquinas's ambitious project in *Summa contra gentiles* Books I–III is the most fully accomplished and most promising natural theology I know of" (Norman Kretzmann, *Metaphysics*, 2). See also Thomas Joseph White, OP, *Wisdom in the Face of Modernity: A Study in Thomistic Natural Theology* (Naples, Fla.: Sapientia Press of Ave Maria, 2009); William Norris Clarke, SJ, "Is a Natural Theology Still Possible Today?" in *Physics, Philosophy, and Theology: A Common Quest for Understanding*, ed. Robert J. Russell, William R. Stoeger, and George V. Coyne (Vatican City and Berkeley, Calif.: Vatican Observatory and Center for Theology and the Natural Sciences, 1988), 103–23.

12. Rom 1:20, as quoted in *ST* I, 2, 2, sed contra.

13. "If anyone says that the One, true God, our Creator and Lord, cannot be known with

God's existence can be demonstrated by reason remains highly controversial.[14]

Aquinas argues that although we cannot know *what* God is (the divine essence), we can show *that* God is.[15] In empirical science, we often know *that* something is before we know *what* it is. Astronomers recognized, for instance, *that* something was causing anomalies in the behavior of the planet Uranus long before they were able to observe the planet Neptune as *what* was causing them.[16] In an analogous way, we can begin with creatures and come to recognize *that* God exists as their cause without knowing *what* God is.[17] God is known simply as the cause of this effect, and "since every effect depends upon its cause, if the effect exists,

---

certainty with the natural light of human reason through the things that have been created, *anathema sit*" (Vatican Council I, *Dei Filius*, canons on chap. 2, no. 1 [April 24, 1870], in *The Christian Faith in the Doctrinal Documents of the Catholic Church*, 5th ed., ed. J. Neuner, SJ, and J. Dupuis, SJ [New York: Alba House, 1990]). "The sacred Synod professes that 'God, the first principle and last end of all things, can be known with certainty from the created world, by the natural light of human reason' (cf. Rom. 1:20)" (Vatican Council II, *Dei verbum*, no. 6 [November 18, 1965], in *The Documents of Vatican II*, ed. Austin P. Flannery, OP [New York: Pillar Books, 1975]). Cf. *Catechism of the Catholic Church* (Mahwah, N.J.: Paulist Press, 1994), no. 36. "It is in the nature of faith that it is *quaerens intellectum*; but an *intellectus* which is not allowed to press its own *quaestio* to that limit which is in fact the unlimited mystery of creation can be partner only to an impoverished and much diminished faith. And that is why the first Vatican Council declares it to be a matter of *faith* that reason can know God. And I think Thomas agrees" (Turner, *Faith, Reason*, xv–xvi).

14. For a helpful review of arguments against the possibility of proving God's existence from reason, see Turner, *Faith, Reason*, 6–168. On the possibility and need for natural theology, see Lawrence Dewan, OP, "The Existence of God: Can It Be Demonstrated?" *Nova et Vetera* (English ed.) 10, no. 3 (2012): 731–56; and Moreland, *Known by Nature*.

15. "There is a twofold mode of truth in what we profess about God. Some truths about God exceed all the ability of the human reason. Such is the truth that God is triune. But there are some truths which the natural reason also is able to reach. Such are that God exists, that he is one, and the like. In fact, such truths about God have been proved demonstratively by the philosophers, guided by the light of the natural reason" (*SCG* I, c.3.2).

16. "Thus the existence of the planet Neptune, even before it was actually observed, was discovered by its effects on the motion of the planet Uranus, and similarly the existence of 'black holes' can be known only through their effects" (Ashley, *The Way*, 94). For other examples, see Paul Weingartner, *God's Existence: Can It Be Proven? A Logical Commentary on the Five Ways of Thomas Aquinas* (Frankfurt: Ontos Verlag, 2010), 32–33. On the consonance of the Five Ways and contemporary science, see Keith Ward, *The God Conclusion: God and the Western Philosophical Tradition* (London: Darton, Longman and Todd, 2009), 14–28.

17. "The point of insisting that argument for God's existence is required is, then, not to convince hypothetical open-minded atheists, or even to persuade 'fools,' so much as to deepen and enhance the mystery of the hidden God. From the start, the 'theistic proofs' are the first lesson in Thomas's negative theology. Far from being an exercise in rationalistic apologetics, the purpose of arguing for God's existence is to protect God's transcendence" (Kerr, *After Aquinas*, 58)

the cause must pre-exist."[18] Through creatures, we can know *that* God is, while *what* God is remains utterly unknown.[19]

The Five Ways

Aquinas argues that "the existence of God can be proved in five ways." Each begins with some ordinary aspect of the world and shows that it depends on a first cause that "everyone understands to be God."[20] These arguments, given in five short paragraphs, have sparked unending philosophical and theological controversies.[21] In Aquinas's *Summa Theologica*, the context is certainly theological. The very title of the work implies this, and the arguments themselves stand immediately under a *sed contra* that invokes revealed truth: "It has been said in the person of God: 'I am Who am' (Ex 3:14)."

18. *ST* I, 2, 2, co. Such reasoned conclusions about God are not themselves "articles of faith," but rather "preambles to the articles" (*ST* I, 2, 2, ad 1). See Ralph McInerny, *Praeambula fidei: Thomism and the God of the Philosophers* (Washington, D.C.: The Catholic University of America Press, 2006); Guy Mansini, OSB, *Fundamental Theology* (Washington, D.C.: The Catholic University of America Press, 2018), 143–83.

19. *ST* I, 2, 2, ad 3. "The most important thing we can know about the first cause is that it surpasses all our knowledge and power of expression. For that one knows God most perfectly who holds that whatever one can think or say about Him is less than what God is" (*Super de causis* 6 [Guagliardo, 46]). "For Thomas, to prove the existence of God is to prove the existence of a mystery..., to show God to exist is to show how, in the end, the human mind loses its grip on the meaning of 'exists'; such a demonstration is therefore designed to show that within creation itself, within our deepest human experience of the world, that mystery of unknowable existence is somehow always present within the world simply in its character of being created" (Turner, *Faith, Reason*, xiv). "The philosophical theology of St. Thomas presupposes at the same time the metaphysics of realism and the trustworthiness of reason. While reductive empiricism is discarded, rationalism is also excluded: the philosopher finds himself standing before the mystery of God which he cannot penetrate; the negative aspect of all our knowledge about God is constantly stressed" (Elders, *Philosophical Theology*, 4).

20. *ST* I, 2, 3, co.

21. On the Five Ways, see Robert Arp, ed., *Revisiting Aquinas' Proofs for the Existence of God* (Leiden: Brill, 2016); Etienne Gilson, *The Christian Philosophy of St. Thomas Aquinas*, trans. L. K. Shook (Notre Dame, Ind.: University of Notre Dame Press, 2006), 59–95; Victor White, OP, "Prelude to the Five Ways," in *Aquinas's "Summa Theologiae": Critical Essays*, ed. Brian Davies, OP (Lanham, Md.: Rowman and Littlefield, 2006), 25–44; John F. Wippel, "The Five Ways," in *The Metaphysical Thought of Thomas Aquinas: From Finite Being to Uncreated Being* (Washington, D.C.: The Catholic University of America Press, 2000), 442–500; Timothy Pawl, "The Five Ways," in *The Oxford Handbook of Aquinas*, ed. Brian Davies, OP, and Eleonore Stump (New York: Oxford University Press, 2011), 115–31; Lubor Velecky, *Aquinas' Five Arguments in the Summa Theologiae 1a 2,3* (Kampen, The Netherlands: Kok Pharos, 1994).

We have seen that Aquinas allows theology to employ philosophical arguments.[22] Here we have five such arguments, each valid in its own right, that Aquinas employs for theological purposes. This usage will become evident as we notice how often he refers back to them in his discussion of God's attributes.[23] Although God's essence (what God is) remains utterly unknown to us, we can still speak of God as long as we keep our eyes on creatures (the effects of the Creator). By showing different modes of creaturely dependence, the Five Ways provide a language for speaking about God, their unknown cause.[24]

Before presenting the Five Ways, Aquinas first considers two arguments that seem to negate God's existence. These two "objections" accord with the dialogical method of his theology. By no means antiquated, these arguments remain in the vanguard of contemporary atheism.[25]

The first objection is the problem of evil: if a God of infinite goodness

22. *ST* I, 1, 8, ad 2.

23. "The proof of God's existence is crucial in Thomas because it begins that movement from below, from man to God, which is essential to theology. The proof stands at the beginning but it is not a ladder which is then pushed away; it remains present in the content and structure of what follows" (Wayne Hankey, "The Place of the Proof for God's Existence in the *Summa Theologiae* of Thomas Aquinas," *Thomist* 46, no. 3 [1982]: 393). On the theological significance of the Five Ways, see Fergus Kerr, OP, "Theology in Philosophy: Revisiting the Five Ways," *International Journal for Philosophy of Religion* 50, no. 1 (2001): 115–30; William W. Young, "From Describing to Naming God: Correlating the Five Ways with Aquinas's Doctrine of the Trinity," *New Blackfriars* 85, no. 999 (2004): 527–41; O'Meara, *Thomas Aquinas*, 90–95; Simon Oliver, *Philosophy, God and Motion* (New York: Routledge, 2005), 105–7; Wayne Hankey, *God in Himself: Aquinas' Doctrine of God as Expounded in the "Summa Theologiae"* (New York: Oxford University Press, 1987).

24. "They [the Five Ways] each specify a dimension of contingency and then proceed to conclude the existence of the corresponding causing non-contingent. The arguments themselves ... do not bother to spell out any implications of the denial of limitation or dependency to this unmoved, first, necessary, maximal, and intelligent being. We are simply left with a relational claim between finite beings and their non-finite causal source. This relation is, in fact, the subject matter of the entire *Summa*. Thomas will first spell out what it is to be non-finite, and then elaborate on the nature of the finite creation, especially of persons in God's image. In just that sense, the Five Ways form the starting point of Thomas's argument in *ST* (also see *ST* I.1.1–10). And just so, we can say it is the starting point of any realist theology" (David Beck, "A Fourth Way to Prove God's Existence," in *Revisiting Aquinas' Proofs for the Existence of God*, ed. Robert Arp [Leiden: Brill, 2016], 165–66).

25. "After having studied Aquinas for many years, and taught philosophy of religion courses for many years, I was struck by the fact that atheists and hard agnostics today still appeal to these objections [*ST* I, 2, 3, obj. 1 and 2] as the most convincing reasons why the kind of god countenanced by Aquinas does not (atheists) or probably does not (hard agnostics) exist" (Robert Arp, "Introduction," in *Revisiting Aquinas' Proofs for the Existence of God*, ed. Robert Arp [Leiden: Brill, 2016], 1).

existed, there would be no evil; since evil does exist, God cannot exist. Aquinas's brief response does not "solve" the problem of evil but points instead to the mystery of divine goodness, which, he asserts with St. Augustine, is able "to bring good even out of evil." It is "part of the infinite goodness of God, that he should allow evil to exist, and out of it produce good."[26] This response admittedly leaves many questions unanswered, such as *how* God brings good out of evil and *why* God allows evil in the first place. Aquinas will address the problem of evil in greater detail later.[27] For now, he simply suggests a way of seeing that the presence of evil need not negate the existence of God.

The second objection also has a contemporary ring: we don't need God because the world explains itself. As Aquinas puts it, "all natural things can be reduced to one principle, which is nature," and "all voluntary things can be reduced to one principle, which is human reason or will."[28] A contemporary materialist might phrase the objection this way: since all of physics can be explained by the laws of science, and since all human consciousness can be reduced to the physics of brain activity, there is no need and no place for a divine cause. In response, Aquinas invokes the First and Fifth Ways: human reason and will must (like all changeable things) depend on an unchanging being, and all natural things (which are seen to act purposefully despite their lack of intelligence) must be directed to their ends by a transcendent intelligence who is God.[29]

The First Way

The first and more manifest way is the argument from motion. It is certain, and evident to our senses, that in the world some things are in motion. Now whatever is in motion is put in motion by another, for nothing can be in motion except it is in potentiality to that towards which it is in motion; whereas a thing moves inasmuch as it is in act. For motion is nothing else than the reduction of something

---

26. *ST* I, 2, 3, ad 1.

27. See *ST* I, 48–49, and chapter 7 of this book.

28. *ST* I, 2, 3, ad 2.

29. "Since nature works for a determinate end under the direction of a higher agent, whatever is done by nature must needs be traced back to God, as to its first cause. So also whatever is done voluntarily must also be traced back to some higher cause other than human reason or will, since these can change or fail; for all things that are changeable and capable of defect must be traced back to an immovable and self-necessary first principle" (*ST* I, 2, 3, ad 2).

from potentiality to actuality. But nothing can be reduced from potentiality to actuality, except by something in a state of actuality. Thus that which is actually hot, as fire, makes wood, which is potentially hot, to be actually hot, and thereby moves and changes it. Now it is not possible that the same thing should be at once in actuality and potentiality in the same respect, but only in different respects. For what is actually hot cannot simultaneously be potentially hot; but it is simultaneously potentially cold. It is therefore impossible that in the same respect and in the same way a thing should be both mover and moved, i.e., that it should move itself. Therefore, whatever is in motion must be put in motion by another. If that by which it is put in motion be itself put in motion, then this also must needs be put in motion by another, and that by another again. But this cannot go on to infinity, because then there would be no first mover, and, consequently, no other mover; seeing that subsequent movers move only inasmuch as they are put in motion by the first mover; as the staff moves only because it is put in motion by the hand. Therefore it is necessary to arrive at a first mover, put in motion by no other; and this everyone understands to be God.[30]

Aquinas calls this the "more manifest way [*manifestior via*]."[31] Since the First Way is about motion and movers, there's a temptation to visualize it mechanically as a fantastic Rube Goldberg machine, in which we trace an ingenious series of mechanisms until we come to the first (mechanical) mover. Unfortunately, many Thomists have succumbed to this temptation.[32] All such analogies leave us with the question of how to get to God from the first mechanical mover. They show that it's a fundamental mistake to interpret the First Way mechanically or to think that a philosophy of mechanism can accommodate it. Why? Because in a philosophy of mechanism you have pushers and pullers that are all of the same

---

30. *ST* I, 2, 3, co.

31. *ST* I, 2, 3, co. Elsewhere, he calls an argument similar to the Fifth Way the "most efficacious way [*via efficacissima*]" (*Super ev. ioann., prologus*, [§3]). On the context of these different claims, see Lawrence Dewan, "The Existence of God," 753n61. For a summary of contemporary discussions on the validity of the First Way, see John Wippel, "Five Ways," 444–59.

32. "Many Thomists throughout the centuries have followed precisely this line of thought. That is why they tend to exemplify Aquinas' idea of an essentially subordinated series of movers with mechanical linkages, any one of which moves only because the previous one has moved it" (William A. Wallace, OP, "Aquinas and Newton on the Causality of Nature and of God: The Medieval and Modern Problematic," in *Philosophy and the God of Abraham: Essays in Memory of James A. Weisheipl, O.P.,* ed. R. James Long [Toronto: Pontifical Institute of Mediaeval Studies, 1991], 275).

type—like cogs in a machine.[33] To get to God, we must find a cause that transcends all the others and is utterly different from them.[34]

We have a better chance of understanding the argument if we begin not with wheels and levers but with potency and act, which characterize motion and change in a more general sense.[35] To do so, we must move beyond the realm of empirical science to the philosophy of nature.[36] We need not transform the argument, however, from one based on the physics of motion and change to one grounded on the metaphysics of existence.[37] We start with the fact that "in the world some things are in

33. "For Aristotle and St. Thomas, 'to move' or to cause motion, is not primarily a mechanical function, such that the First Mover, as it were, pushes the material universe around in a circle. Rather, the immaterial mover is the source of material 'nature,' the cause of the mobile object's own principles of motion—matter and form. The Aristotelian-Thomistic world of nature is not a static universe of material bodies pushed here and there by immaterial souls or intelligences—it is a dynamic universe, filled with natural, physical beings that spontaneously and regularly exhibit specific, characteristic behavior. This spontaneous and characteristic activity springs from 'nature,' from matter and form, that is, from the constituents of natural, physical substances—mobile beings" (Eric A. Reitan, OP, "Aquinas and Weisheipl: Aristotle's Physics and the Existence of God," in *Philosophy and the God of Abraham: Essays in Memory of James A. Weisheipl, O.P.,* ed. R. James Long [Toronto: Pontifical Institute of Mediaeval Studies, 1991], 186).

34. "Aquinas does not have in mind a first mover who acts only to set off a kind of 'domino effect.' He is seeking to describe a cosmology in which any motion at any time is unintelligible without a fully actual first mover who is the source of motion for all things in the present" (Oliver, *Philosophy,* 107). "If the *per se* subordinated series of movers and moveds is likened to the fall of dominoes, the fall of the first domino could be temporally quite distant from that of the last. Applying this to the *prima via,* one could interpret this to hold that the argument does not prove that God exists here and now, but only that he existed some time ago—perhaps a very long time ago, say, at the 'Big Bang' fifteen billion years into the distant past. Clearly this is not what St. Thomas had in mind" (Wallace, "Aquinas and Newton," 275).

35. On the nature of motion and change, see "Motion" in appendix 1.

36. The philosophy of nature, as exemplified by Aristotle's *Physics,* broadly studies change in material things and its ultimate causes. It is distinct from, but complementary to, the investigations of empirical science: "When one uses the terminology of modern science one invariably interprets this causal agency through the concepts of force, mass, energy, and the like.... But when one absorbs motor causality totally into these terms, and regards them as logical constructs that have no reference to the real world apart from some theoretical system of which they form a part, the proof quickly loses its persuasive power. In effect, one suppresses any intimations of transcendence that are to be found in the movement of material objects. That is why, for many of our contemporaries, physical arguments for the existence of God are terminated before they start, or at least become so insulated from philosophical inquiry as to nullify their value as valid starting points" (Wallace, "Aquinas and Newton," 276–77). See also Edward Feser, "Natural Theology Must Be Grounded in the Philosophy of Nature, Not in Natural Science," in *Neo-Scholastic Essays* (South Bend, Ind.: Saint Augustine's Press, 2015), 61–83.

37. The First Way, in its argument for a First Mover, does not presuppose metaphysics but rather provides the foundation for metaphysics: "Far from reserving to metaphysics the proof for

motion." This is "certain and evident to our senses." But although such motion is evident, the nature of motion is not.[38] Aquinas provides a compact definition: "Motion is nothing else than the reduction of something from potentiality to actuality."[39] Motion is not fundamentally about mechanical pushers and pullers but about the more basic principles of potency and act.[40]

The thing that is moving or changing must be in potency to some new actuality. The fact that the change is happening tells us that some potency is presently being actualized (as water that has the potential to be hot actually becomes hot). But potency (the mere possibility of being) can't actualize itself. So the present influence of some being in act is required.[41] If that being accounts for its own actuality, we have arrived

---

a Prime Mover, the philosophy of St. Thomas requires such a proof as the necessary approach to metaphysics without which metaphysics, as a science, cannot come into existence. And should this verdict be accepted, then it is supremely necessary to rehabilitate the philosophy of nature not only to provide a porchlight for modern science but also to build the very portals of metaphysics itself" (Vincent E. Smith, "The Prime Mover: Physical and Metaphysical Considerations," *Proceedings of the American Catholic Philosophical Association* 28 [1954]: 79–80). As David Twetten notes: "The familiar proof of God's existence through motion has frequently been represented in more metaphysical terms so as to address contemporary conceptions of motion and causality. The resulting arguments, however cogent, inevitably lose the original's status as 'the first and most manifest way'" (David B. Twetten, "Why Motion Requires a Cause: The Foundation for a Prime Mover in Aristotle and Aquinas," in *Philosophy and the God of Abraham: Essays in Memory of James A. Weisheipl, O.P.*, ed. R. James Long [Toronto: Pontifical Institute of Mediaeval Studies, 1991], 239). For a critique of those (including Etienne Gilson, Joseph Owens, and John Knasas) who have interpreted the First Way in terms of "being" rather than "motion," see David B. Twetten, "Clearing a 'Way' for Aquinas: How the Proof from Motion Concludes to God," *Proceedings of the American Catholic Philosophical Association* 70 (1996): 259–78.

38. To understand the First Way, we need to understand the nature of motion: "This thorough investigation of 'mobile being,' the principles of 'nature,' and the reality of 'motion' is necessary for understanding the argument [for the unmoved mover] of books seven and eight [of Aristotle's *Physics*]. Only by grasping these preliminary principles can we perceive the need for an immaterial, immobile, and indivisible First Mover who 'moves' the whole universe for all eternity. Only by understanding natural beings, precisely in terms of their own natural principles, can we then identify the reasons for positing a being that is neither physical nor subject to change—a being upon whom the physical world depends for its physical existence, considered precisely as physical, that is, as natural and changeable" (Reitan, "Aquinas and Weisheipl," 184).

39. *ST* I, 2, 3, co. Cf. *Phys.* III, 1 (201b 5–6).

40. For a brief explanation of potency, act, and motion, see appendix 1.

41. "The *process* of coming-to-be requires the continued and simultaneous causation of the agent—since, '... removing a cause is to remove that of which it is a cause' (*SCG* I, c.13)" (Dennis Bonnette, *Aquinas' Proofs for God's Existence. St. Thomas Aquinas on: "The Per Accidens Necessarily Implies the Per Se"* [The Hague: Martinus Nijhoff, 1972], 100).

at the cause we're looking for. But if that being is itself dependent (right now) on something else for its own actuality (and so also for its capacity to move another), we must continue the search.

The next stage in the argument is to consider the series of dependent movers (or actualizers). The first thing to notice is that the series Aquinas has in mind is not "accidentally" but "essentially" ordered. In an accidental series of causes, one does not depend on another for the exercise of its causality. In Agatha Christie's *Murder on the Orient Express*, for instance, the passengers who stab the malevolent Samuel Ratchett (in an ordered succession and one after the other) are an accidental series of causes, since, although the passengers collectively cause his death, one passenger does not depend upon the others in doing the dastardly deed. Aquinas, by contrast, proposes an "essentially" ordered series of causes, as is evident in his example of the hand that moves a stick that moves a stone. The motion of the stone depends on the present action of the stick, which in turn depends on the present action of the hand.[42]

The second thing to notice is that an essentially ordered series of causes cannot be infinite.[43] This step is tricky, since infinity is a somewhat confounding concept. It conjures up the ghost of Zeno and his paradoxes of infinite division: before you can traverse the whole race track, you must cross the first half, and before that, the first half of that half, etc., until, sad to say, you find that in your limited lifetime, you'll never make it all the way across.[44] Still, it's important to spend a moment reflecting on infinity since the notion plays an essential role in the first three Ways. (But beware: before you can spend a moment, you must first spend half a moment, and before that, half of that, etc.)

Aquinas defines such infinity as "that beyond which there is always

---

42. See *ST* I, 2, 3, co.; *ST* I, 46, 3, ad 7.

43. "In efficient causes it is impossible to proceed to infinity *per se*—thus, there cannot be an infinite number of causes that are *per se* required for a certain effect; for instance, that a stone be moved by a stick, the stick by the hand, and so on to infinity. But it is not impossible to proceed to infinity *accidentally* as regards efficient causes; for instance, if all the causes thus infinitely multiplied should have the order of only one cause, their multiplication being accidental, as an artificer acts by means of many hammers accidentally, because one after the other may be broken" (*ST* I, 46, 3, ad 7).

44. For Zeno's paradoxes, see Milton C. Nahm, *Selections from Early Greek Philosophy* (New York: Appleton-Century-Crofts, 1964), 98–103.

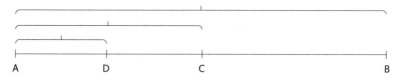

A   D   C   B

Figure 1-1. Infinity by Division

1   2   3   n   n+1

Figure 1-2. Infinity by Extension

something."[45] As regards division, for instance, no matter how many times you divide a line AB in half to AC, and then divide the half in half to AD, and so on, there will always be another division to be made. Almost by definition, there can be no "first" division, since there is always a division before whichever division you make, as illustrated in figure 1-1. The same is true of extension. An infinite line has no end, since no matter how far you extend it, "there is always something" beyond that. We can represent this mathematically: $1, 2, 3, \ldots n, (n + 1)$, as shown in figure 1-2.

This notion of infinity works well in mathematics but not so well in the physics of causality, where the "+ 1" that we can never attain is exactly what we need to explain the motion that's happening right before our eyes. In Aquinas's argument, what we need is a first mover, a first actualizer that doesn't owe its actuality to another. A mere series of actualizers in which each one depends on the next won't do the trick—even if you extend it to infinity, since the very notion of infinity requires that there is no first. So reference to infinity doesn't give us the actualizer we're looking for.[46] Aquinas therefore cuts to the chase and argues that "it is neces-

45. *In phys.* III, lect. 11, no. 383. Aquinas has a different way to define divine infinity (*ST* I, 7, 1).

46. "Taking the principle that if you remove the cause then you remove the effect, we can apply it to the essentially ordered series of causes and observe that if there were no primary cause in such a series, then the intermediate and the ultimate causes would be causally inefficacious with respect to the causal property of the series, since in an essentially ordered series of causes, the intermediate and ultimate causes depend on some primary cause not only for their existence but also for their causality.... But ... then there could not be an infinite series of such causes, since

sary to arrive at a first mover, put in motion by no other" (a first actualizer not actualized by another). This is not just a theoretical necessity but a practical one to explain the motion that's happening right in front of us. Aquinas concludes that the first mover is what "everyone understands to be God."[47]

We should add three caveats. First, this argument might appear hopelessly medieval.[48] It seems to conjure up the concentric celestial spheres of ancient cosmology, centered on the earth and imparting motion one to the next, all derived from the motion of the outermost sphere, which is itself moved by its desire for the unmoved mover.[49] The crystalline

---

an infinite series is infinite precisely insofar as it has no primary cause" (Gaven Kerr, OP, "The Relevance of Aquinas' Uncaused Cause Argument," in *Revisiting Aquinas' Proofs for the Existence of God,* ed. Robert Arp [Leiden: Brill, 2016], 80). See also Gaven Kerr, OP, "Essentially Ordered Series Reconsidered Once Again," *American Catholic Philosophical Quarterly* 91, no. 2 (2017): 155–74; Caleb Cohoe, "There Must Be a First: Why Thomas Aquinas Rejects Infinite, Essentially Ordered, Causal Series," *British Journal for the History of Philosophy* 21, no. 5 (2013): 838–56; Michael Rota, "Infinite Causal Chains and Explanation," *Proceedings of the American Catholic Philosophical Association* 81 (2007): 109–22.

47. *ST* I, 2, 3, co. "The point to note here is that Aristotle and St. Thomas, thinking as natural philosophers, are concerned not only with isolating individual agents of physical change, but also with tracing universal lines of natural causality, which account for the activities and characteristics proper to entire species of natural substances.... [T]his preserves the spontaneous dynamism of natural substances and avoids considering physical causality as merely some version of mechanical push or pull.... This immaterial being is not simply some created intelligence that pushes or pulls an independently existing material world; rather, this immaterial being is the active source and origin of the material world. It 'moves' that world by being the cause and foundation of all the material and formal principles of motion within that world.... [A]n analysis of Aristotle's fundamental principles of natural philosophy, including a notion of universal equivocal cause, as well as a dynamic understanding of nature and motion, leads the mind to God, that is, to the First Unmoved Mover, upon which the physical universe depends for its entire natural, physical, and material existence. Of course, this discovery leads to an expanded notion of 'existence,' which can no longer be restricted to the natural, physical, and material. This discovery leads to a new science, 'metaphysics,' which then leads us to a more profound understanding of God and his intimate relationship to the whole of material and immaterial creation. However, the roots of this more profound understanding lie in the philosophy of nature, in an understanding of the natural principles at work in the physical world, and in a recognition of the explanatory limits of those principles. It is in Aristotle's 'argument from motion,' in St. Thomas' *prima via,* that philosophy—'natural philosophy'—first encounters (albeit in a limited and hidden way) the God of Abraham" (Reitan, "Aquinas and Weisheipl," 188–90).

48. "The Five Ways fail, I shall argue, principally because it is much more difficult than at first appears to separate them from their background in medieval cosmology" (Anthony Kenny, *The Five Ways: Saint Thomas Aquinas' Proofs of God's Existence* [Notre Dame, Ind.: University of Notre Dame Press, 1980], 3).

49. On the celestial spheres, see Michael J. Dodds, OP, *The Unchanging God of Love: Thom-*

spheres have, of course, long since disappeared from the cosmos, and it might seem the validity of the First Way went with them. Here we should remember that the argument is to be understood not in terms of mechanisms (whether medieval or modern) but in terms of potency and act. The potential cannot actualize itself: it depends on the actual. The series of actualizers need not be crystalline spheres, but the need for a first actualizer remains.

So, given our cosmology and science, together with the philosophy of nature, how do we get to that first actualizer? We can start with Aquinas's simple example: "the staff moves only because it is put in motion by the hand." The next question, of course, is what moves the hand. Here we might get into all the complexity of physiology and neuroscience and, if we choose a human example, the added complications of free will, the immortal soul, and so on. To simplify things a bit, let's think of an ape who uses a stick to poke a juicy termite out of a log. The stick is moved by the ape's hand, which is moved by its arm, which is moved by its nerves and brain, which somehow entail its desire for food, etc. Ultimately, though, the ape exhibits all of this activity because it's an ape, and it is an ape in virtue of its substantial form, which, as its nature, is the source of its characteristic activities.[50] But the ape is not itself the cause of its own substantial form (it does not cause itself to be an ape); nor are its parents the proper cause of the form of ape as such (otherwise, they would cause themselves to be apes since they are apes in virtue of having that same kind of substantial form).[51] Our search for the first cause must therefore lead us beyond the parents to the cause of the form as such, and ultimately to God.[52] Here we have, of course, gone beyond the limits of empirical

---

as *Aquinas and Contemporary Theology on Divine Immutability* (Washington, D.C.: The Catholic University of America Press, 2008), 19–25.

50. On substantial form (nature) as the source of activity, see appendix 1.

51. On the cause of the substantial form as such, see "Causality" in appendix 1. "The doctrine of the nature of univocal causality (dogs producing dogs and cats cats) should be taken into consideration. A univocal cause presupposes the common nature which it communicates in causing individuals of that nature. The dogs which reproduce are not causes of doghood as doghood, but of doghood-in-this-or-that. To say that they cause doghood would be to make them causes of themselves, and thus prior to themselves, a contradiction in terms. The cause of doghood as doghood must have a nature nobler than doghood" (Lawrence Dewan, OP, "St. Thomas's Fourth Way and Creation," *Thomist* 59, no. 3 [1995]: 376).

52. "Accordingly this or that individual thing cannot by its action produce another individual

science, but we are still within the philosophy of nature where this argument finds its home. The First Way does not require a medieval cosmos or a metaphysical interpretation—only an account of motion in terms of potency and act, which is the business of the philosophy of nature.[53]

Second, the argument seems to ignore the principle of inertia as described in Newton's First Law of Motion: "Every body continues in its state of rest, or of uniform motion in a right line, unless it is compelled to change that state by forces impressed upon it."[54] According to the principle, it seems that a body does not require a cause for its state of motion, but only for a change in its state of motion. As Isaac Asimov explains, "A body remains at rest or, if already in motion, remains in uniform motion with constant speed in a straight line, unless it is acted on by an unbalanced external force."[55] Inertia describes the motion of a body mathematically, but it does not explain why such a body bothers to move in accord with that mathematical description—or bothers to move at all. The philosophical answer is that the body acts in a certain way "because it is a certain kind of body." If we ask why it is a certain kind of body, the philosophical explanation is "because of its substantial form, by which it

---

of the same species except as the instrument of that cause which includes in its scope the whole species and, besides, the whole being of the inferior creature.... Therefore God is the cause of every action, inasmuch as every agent is an instrument of the divine power operating" (*De pot.* 3, 7, co.). "Now not only is every motion from God as from the First Mover, but all formal perfection is from him as from the First Act. And thus the act of the intellect or of any created being whatsoever depends upon God in two ways: first, inasmuch as it is from him that it has the form whereby it acts; secondly, inasmuch as it is moved by him to act. Now every form bestowed on created things by God has power for a determined act, which it can bring about in proportion to its own proper endowment" (*ST* I-II, 109, 1, co.). See also *ST* I, 104, 1, ad 1; *ST* I, 44, 3, co.; *SCG* II, c.21.5.

53. Were we to use a human example and trace the motion of the stick to an act of human free will, we would find that, although the human, as a secondary cause, is the authentic source of its own free acts, it is not the *first* cause of them. Here too we will find the need for God as primary cause to account for the action of the will as secondary cause: "Besides, as natural inclination in an inanimate thing, which is also called natural appetite, is related to its proper end, so also is the will, which is also called intellectual appetite, in an intellectual substance. Now, to give natural inclinations is the sole prerogative of him who has established the nature. So also, to incline the will to anything is the sole prerogative of him who is the cause of the intellectual nature. Now, this is proper to God alone, as is evident from our earlier explanations. Therefore, he alone can incline our will to something" (*SCG* III, c.88.4).

54. Sir Isaac Newton, *Mathematical Principles of Natural Philosophy*, in *Sir Isaac Newton's Mathematical Principles of Natural Philosophy and His System of the World,* trans. Andrew Motte and Florian Cajori (Berkeley, Calif.: University of California Press, 1946), 13.

55. Isaac Asimov, *Understanding Physics* (London: Bracken Books, 1966), 24.

is the kind of thing that it is." To explain its substantial form as such, however, we must again look to a transcendent cause, and ultimately to God. As Dennis Bonnette explains: "[We] do not wish to challenge Newton's law which simply describes the fact that a body in motion tends to remain in motion. Yet, we do demand an explanation as to why this fact is so.... It is our suggestion that, since the conventional physical agent as well as the 'law of inertia' have proven to be insufficient as a total explanation, it is possible that some transcendental cause beyond the range of natural science may be posited as the only adequate cause for the phenomena of inertia."[56]

Third, it might seem that the argument robs all other causes of their proper causality: if they all depend on God as first cause it might seem that God alone is the only true cause of whatever happens in the world.[57] Here we must remember the notions of primary and secondary causality. A secondary cause *does* exercise its own proper causality, but not without the influence of the primary cause.[58]

The Second Way

The second way is from the nature of the efficient cause. In the world of sense we find there is an order of efficient causes. There is no case known (neither is it, indeed, possible) in which a thing is found to be the efficient cause of itself; for so it would be prior to itself, which is impossible. Now in efficient causes it is not possible to go on to infinity, because in all efficient causes following in order, the

56. Bonnette, *Aquinas' Proofs*, 100–2. "Further, far from the principle of inertia disproving the existence of God, the more one tries to verify this principle, the more one is led to affirm the existence of an infinite Mover. If all the idealized concepts that have been discussed be granted, and the idealized case be considered as physically real, then not only is *some* extrinsic mover required, but also one of infinite power, and this can only be God" (William A. Wallace, OP, "Newtonian Antinomies against the Prima Via," *Thomist* 19, no. 2 [1956]: 184). See also Antonio Moreno, OP, "The Law of Inertia and the Principle *'Quidquid movetur ab alio movetur,'" Thomist* 38, no. 2 (1974): 306–31; James A. Weisheipl, OP, "The Principle *'Omne quod movetur ab alio movetur'* in Medieval Physics," in *Nature and Motion in the Middle Ages*, ed. William E. Carroll (Washington, D.C.: The Catholic University of America Press, 1985), 75–97.

57. Leonard Eslick argues, for instance, that the divine causality envisioned by Aquinas "eliminates from the divine effects any real contingency and freedom, any creaturely share (however modest) in divine causality" (Leonard Eslick, "From the World to God: The Cosmological Argument," *Modern Schoolman* 60, no. 3 [1983]: 153).

58. For a brief account of primary and secondary causality, see appendix 1. These ideas with respect to divine causality will be further developed in chapters 5 and 10 of this book.

first is the cause of the intermediate cause, and the intermediate is the cause of the ultimate cause, whether the intermediate cause be several, or only one. Now to take away the cause is to take away the effect. Therefore, if there be no first cause among efficient causes, there will be no ultimate, nor any intermediate cause. But if in efficient causes it is possible to go on to infinity, there will be no first efficient cause, neither will there be an ultimate effect, nor any intermediate efficient causes; all of which is plainly false. Therefore it is necessary to admit a first efficient cause, to which everyone gives the name of God.[59]

In the Second Way, Aquinas again starts with an observable feature of the natural world: "In the world of sense we find there is an order of efficient causes." This simple statement makes it clear how far we have come (or fallen) since his time. Ever since David Hume redefined causality as a "constant conjunction" of mental states and Immanuel Kant interpreted it as a transcendental idea rather than as an objective feature of nature, the whole philosophy of causation has become something of a wasteland.[60] A complete account of the Second Way would therefore require an extensive critique of contemporary accounts of causality (which seem to multiply like heads of the Hydra). For our purposes here, we will simply accept Aquinas's understanding of the efficient cause as the agent or source of change.[61]

---

59. *ST* I, 2, 3, co.

60. "Philosophers have been interested in the nature of causation for as long as there has been philosophy.... Despite the attention, there is still very little agreement on the most central question concerning causation: what *is* it? ... One reason for the lack of a consensus view is the sheer difficulty of the task; anyone familiar with the causation debate as it has been conducted in recent years will be familiar with a vast range of theories and counterexamples, which collectively can lead one to suspect that no univocal analysis of the concept of causation is possible" (Helen Beebee, Christopher Hitchcock, and Peter Menzies, "Introduction," in *The Oxford Handbook of Causation*, ed. Helen Beebee, Christopher Hitchcock, and Peter Menzies [Oxford: Oxford University Press, 2012], 1). For a magisterial account of the history of causality, see William A. Wallace, OP, *Causality and Scientific Explanation*, 2 vols. (Ann Arbor: University of Michigan Press, 1972). See also Mario Bunge, *Causality and Modern Science* (New York: Dover Publications, 1979); Lawrence Dewan, OP, "Saint Thomas and the Principle of Causality," in *Form and Being: Studies in Thomistic Metaphysics* (Washington, D.C.: The Catholic University of America Press, 2006), 61–80.

61. "That from which there is a beginning of motion or rest is in some way called a cause" (*In phys.* II, lect. 5, no. 180). "If one adopts a realist philosophy of science ... and particularly if one restores causality to its proper ontological category (instead of relegating it to some psychological projection on reality, following Hume or Kant), one can go far in readdressing Aquinas's *quinque viae* to the modern mind" (Wallace, "Aquinas and Newton," 277). See also Rosemary Lauer, "The Notion of Efficient Cause in the *Secunda Via*," *Thomist* 38, no. 4 (1974): 754–67.

Since the efficient cause is in some way prior to the effect, nothing can be the efficient cause of itself. One efficient cause may, however, depend on another in the exercise of its causality (as the mallet which moves the croquet ball depends on the hand that moves it). Such a series of dependent causes, however, cannot go on forever. As in the first way, Aquinas argues that positing an infinite series of efficient causes would yield no first efficient cause, and so no series, and ultimately no effect. So, there must be a first efficient cause "to which everyone gives the name of God."

The Third Way

The third way is taken from possibility and necessity, and runs thus. We find in nature things that are possible to be and not to be, since they are found to be generated, and to corrupt, and consequently, they are possible to be and not to be. But it is impossible for these always to exist, for that which is possible not to be at some time is not. Therefore, if everything is possible not to be, then at one time there was nothing in existence. Now if this were true, even now there would be nothing in existence, because that which does not exist only begins to exist by something already existing. Therefore, if at one time nothing was in existence, it would have been impossible for anything to have begun to exist; and thus even now nothing would be in existence—which is absurd. Therefore, not all beings are merely possible, but there must exist something the existence of which is necessary. But every necessary thing either has its necessity caused by another, or not. Now it is impossible to go on to infinity in necessary things which have their necessity caused by another, as has been already proved in regard to efficient causes. Therefore we cannot but postulate the existence of some being having of itself its own necessity, and not receiving it from another, but rather causing in others their necessity. This all men speak of as God.[62]

We might look at the Third Way as the proof from Murphy's law: "If it can fail, it will." It begins with the observable fact of contingency in nature. If contingency was evident to Aquinas, it seems even more obvious today when chance plays an essential role in evolution and the whole science of quantum physics is framed in terms of probability.[63] Aquinas takes contingency quite seriously, arguing not just that a contingent be-

---

62. *ST* I, 2, 3, co.
63. See Lydia Jaeger, "The Contingency of Creation and Modern Science," *Theology and Science* 16, no. 1 (2018): 54–78; Dodds, *Unlocking*, 53–104.

ing "might" fail, but that, given sufficient time, it "must" fail. Necessity implies everlasting existence, while contingency entails temporally limited existence. To predicate everlasting existence of a contingent being is therefore a contradiction: it implies that a contingent being is also a necessary being.[64] To allow enough time for the contingent being to fail, Aquinas assumes for the sake of argument that the world has always existed—that the past is infinite.

Having assumed an infinite amount of time, he argues "that which is possible not to be at some time is not." For example, as a "blinking light" that never blinks is not really a blinking light but an unblinking light, so a "contingent being" that never ceases to be is not really a contingent being but a necessary being.

If every being is contingent, then, in an infinite past time, every being would have ceased to be. If so, then at some time they would have all ceased to be, and so "at one time there was nothing in existence." If this were the case, then even now (since nothing comes from nothing) "there would be nothing in existence."[65] Since this is "absurd," our initial supposition must be wrong: not all beings are contingent, but some being must be necessary. That being either explains its own necessity or depends on another for its necessity. But, as already seen in the first two ways, a series of dependent beings cannot be infinite. So we must arrive at a being that explains its own necessity, and that "all speak of as God."

Listening to this rather exotic proof, we might ask: "Why can't you just have a series of contingent beings in which each one produces another as it ceases to be? Grass ceases to be when eaten by the bunny, which ceases to be when it dies and becomes a carcass, which ceases to be when it decays and becomes soil, which nourishes the grass, which is eaten by

64. As Francisco Muñiz explains: "The whole argument of Saint Thomas rests on a proposition, brief in expression, but profound in content: 'Nothing that has the potency not to be can have existed always.' The potency not to be necessarily imposes a limit in duration for the potency to be, or, what is the same thing, the potency not to be supposes a potency to be during a finite and limited duration. A natural potency to be always, and a natural potency not to be at some determined moment, are two contradictory things which can never be joined in the same subject" (Francisco Muñiz, OP, "Introducción a la cuestion 2," in Suma Teológica, by Tomás de Aquino, trans. Raimundo Suarez, OP [Madrid: Biblioteca de Autores Cristianos, 1964], 1:303).

65. See Martin J. De Nys, "If Everything Can Not-Be There Would Be Nothing: Another Look at the Third Way," Review of Metaphysics 56, no. 1 (2002): 99–122; Thomas Kevin Connolly, OP, "The Basis of the Third Proof for the Existence of God," Thomist 17, no. 3 (1954): 281–349.

another bunny, and so on in the great cycles of nature." This looks like a good argument, but it tacitly assumes the existence of a sort of necessary being, or at least a necessary principle. That principle is primary matter, which endures through all changes and so has a kind of necessity about it.[66] If it were also radically contingent and ceased to be when the substance ceased, then no new substance could be generated when a previous substance corrupted. The cessation of any substance would be absolute annihilation. But from annihilation (nothing), no new substance could arise.

On one hand, prime matter is a sort of necessary being or necessary principle since it cannot cease to exist. On the other hand, it does not explain its own necessity, since in itself it is only the mere possibility of being—always dependent on its coprinciple of substantial form. So, it may be primary matter that Aquinas is thinking of when he talks about a "necessary thing that has its necessity caused by another."[67] To get to the necessary thing that does not have its necessity caused by another, we have to mount up from prime matter (the lowest on the ontological chain since it is the mere possibility of being) through whatever necessary principles or substances there may be that also have their necessity caused by another until we come to "some being having of itself its own necessity." Only then would we arrive at what "all men speak of as God."

The Fourth Way

The fourth way is taken from the gradation to be found in things. Among beings there are some more and some less good, true, noble and the like. But "more" and "less" are predicated of different things, according as they resemble in their different ways something which is the maximum, as a thing is said to be hot-

66. For a brief explanation of primary matter, see appendix 1.

67. "It is immediately obvious, however, that matter qua matter cannot possibly have its necessity of itself, at least in an Aristotelian conception. For matter, considered apart from anything else, and in particular apart from form, is just 'prime matter' or pure potentiality; and pure potentiality, since by definition it has no actuality, has no reality either, necessary or otherwise" (Edward Feser, *Aquinas: A Beginner's Guide* [London: Oneworld Publications, 2009], 97). On primary matter as the necessary thing that has its necessity from another, see Toshiyoki Miyakawa, "The Value and the Meaning of the Tertia Via of St. Thomas Aquinas," *Aquinas* 6, no. 2 (1963): 250–51. Another possible candidate for this role is "the cause of the form as such [*causa formae inquantum huiusmodi*]" (*ST* I, 104, 1, co.). On this possibility, see John M. Quinn, OSA, "The Third Way to God: A New Approach," *Thomist* 42, no. 1 (1978): 50–68.

ter according as it more nearly resembles that which is hottest; so that there is something which is truest, and best, and noblest and, consequently, uttermost being [*verissimum, et optimum, et nobilissimum, et per consequens maxime ens*]; for those things that are greatest in truth are greatest in being, as it is written in Metaph. ii. Now the maximum in any genus is the cause of all in that genus; as fire, which is the maximum heat, is the cause of all hot things. Therefore there must also be something which is to all beings the cause of their being, goodness, and every other perfection; and this we call God.[68]

This proof begins again with an evident feature of the world: some things are better than others (as the Whopper is evidently better than the Big Mac). But how do we get from a better burger to a best being who is God? We have to admit that some of Aquinas's medieval examples are not especially helpful (such as positing fire as "the maximum of heat").[69] Rather than get too heated about old fashioned examples, we'll try to keep our eye on the being of the burger, remembering that this argument is all about being from beginning to end.[70]

The first thing to notice is the sorts of qualities Aquinas singles out, such as goodness, truth, nobility, and being. These are not generic qualities that belong to only one species of being (as dogness belongs only to dogs) or to one category of being (as redness belongs only to the category of quality). Rather, they are transcendental qualities or transcendental

---

68. *ST* I, 2, 3, co.

69. "A source of difficulty for moderns is that efforts by Aquinas to illumine obscure theological or philosophical insights with illustrations drawn from the natural science of his time become for a modern reader so many further puzzles to be solved. A particularly awkward instance of this is the use he made of 'fire' in his famous 'fourth way' to demonstrate that there is and must be what 'all men call God.' . . . The argument of the 'fourth way,' obscure in itself, is hardly elucidated by this reference to the elemental 'fire' of the classical physics; we have heard of the temperatures at the core of a star and find it hard to think of the Aristotelian-Thomistic 'fire' as 'maximum heat'" (Edward A. Synan, "Aquinas and the Children of Abraham," in *Philosophy and the God of Abraham: Essays in Memory of James A. Weisheipl, O.P.*, ed. R. James Long [Toronto: Pontifical Institute of Mediaeval Studies, 1991], 211).

70. "Every excellence in any given thing belongs to it according to its being. For man would have no excellence as a result of his wisdom unless through it he were wise. So, too, with the other excellences. Hence, the mode of a thing's excellence is according to the mode of its being. For a thing is said to be more or less excellent according as its being is limited to a certain greater or lesser mode of excellence" (*SCG* I, c.28.2). Grades of perfection (*nobilitas* in Latin) are in terms of grades of *being*, so, we're in the realm of being (not just ideas) throughout the Fourth Way. We therefore don't have to worry about how to cross over from the realm of ideas to the realm of being (the problem with Anselm's ontological argument).

modes of being that are not restricted to one genus of being, but coextensive with being itself.[71]

Generic and transcendental qualities are quite different. First, generic qualities are predicated univocally. (Spot has "dogness" just as much as Rover does.) Second, they are predicated of some beings only. (Only dogs have "dogness.") Third, they imply inherent limitation. (Spot is a great dog—but hey, he's only a dog!)[72] By contrast, transcendental qualities are, first, predicated analogously. (The burger is good, but not in the same way the dog is good.) Second, they are predicated of all beings. (Each thing, insofar as it has being, is good and true.) Third, they are not inherently limited. Though the goodness of one being or another may be limited, goodness as such is boundless: it implies no limitation.[73]

71. "Since *one* is a transcendental, it is both common to all, and adapted to each single thing, just as the good and the true" (*ST* I, 93, 9, co.). A "transcendental" (*transcendens*) may be defined as "that which because of the analogical nature of being cannot be determined to any category or predicament, or the *'modus generaliter consequens omne ens'* [the common mode following upon every being] (*De ver.* Q. 1, a. 1, co)" (Roy J. Deferrari, *A Latin-English Dictionary of St. Thomas Aquinas* [Boston: St. Paul Editions, 1960], 1046). "Understood in their Aristotelian/Thomistic sense, they are the properties of *all* things, of every item in the actual world. And so only they will allow the argument to go forward in the way Thomas intends. . . . So it is clear, as virtually all commentators agree, that Thomas here refers to *transcending* properties. These are the constituent properties of being" (Beck, "A Fourth Way," 155). On Aristotle's ten "categories" (substance and nine accidents), see Aristotle, *Categories* 4 (1b 25 – 2a 4), in *The Basic Works of Aristotle*, ed. Richard McKeon (New York: Random House, 1941).

72. "This order of things is the domain of univocity, and of beings, values or perfections confined within genera and categories" (Jacques Maritain, *Approaches to God* [New York: Macmillan, 1954], 54).

73. "There are some names which signify these perfections flowing from God to creatures in such a way that the imperfect way in which creatures receive the divine perfection is part of the very signification of the name itself as 'stone' signifies a material being, and names of this kind can be applied to God only in a metaphorical sense. Other names, however, express these perfections absolutely, without any such mode of participation being part of their signification as the words 'being,' 'good,' 'living,' and the like, and such names can be literally applied to God" (*ST* I, 13, 3, ad 1). "The whole force of the demonstration [in the Fourth Way] comes from the fact that it deals with transcendental values or perfections, which surpass every genus and every category, and by their very nature demand existence on ever higher levels of being" (Maritain, *Approaches*, 54). Fernand Van Steenberghen evidently misses this point when he uses the example of wealth, and then argues that "the richest man is obviously not the cause of wealth in others," and concludes that "the *quarta via* has not proved the existence of this absolute maximum" (Van Steenberghen, *Hidden God*, 69–70). Richard Dawkins seems to intentionally miss the point (if he ever saw it): "You might as well say, people vary in smelliness but we can make the comparison only by reference to a perfect maximum of conceivable smelliness. Therefore there must exist a pre-eminently peerless stinker, and we call him God" (Richard Dawkins, *The God Delusion* [London: Bantam Press, 2006], 79).

Types of qualities		Modes of possession	
		Essential	Accidental
	Generic (one category)	Dogness	Dog training
	Transcendental (all categories)	Divine goodness	Goodness in creatures

Figure 1-3. Types of Qualities and Modes of Possession

Once we've got a handle on generic and transcendental qualities, we also need to consider whether a given being possesses a certain quality essentially (because of its very essence or nature) or accidentally (because of the influence of something else). A dog, for instance, has the generic quality of "dogness" essentially, by its very nature. It is therefore never just "slightly" or "moderately" a dog, but is always "completely" a dog (from nose to tail) or otherwise it's not a dog at all.[74] The dog does not, however, possess the generic quality of obedience training essentially (by nature), but accidentally through the hard work of its trainer. While essential qualities do not admit of gradations, accidental qualities do—as one dog may have more training than another or the same dog may become better trained over time. These distinctions are illustrated in figure 1-3.

To sum up, the Fourth Way is always concerned with transcendental qualities rather than generic ones. Since it begins with "the gradation to be found in things," it is evidently starting with qualities that are possessed accidentally, to which alone gradation is possible. Its basic question is whether beings that possess transcendental qualities accidentally

74. "Whatever a thing possesses by its own nature, and not from some other cause, cannot be diminished and deficient in it. For, if something essential be subtracted from or added to a nature, another nature will at once arise, as in the case of numbers, where the addition or the subtraction of the unit changes the species of the number" (*SCG* II, c.15.3). "There are perfections that do not admit of grades of more or less: either they are possessed in all their fulness or they are not possessed at all. So it happens that a thing either is human or is not human; or is a plant or is not a plant, and so on; but it is not possible for it to be more or less human or more or less a plant" (Francisco P. Muñiz, "La 'quarta via' de Santo Tomás para demonstrar la existencia de Dios," *Revista de Filosofía* 3, no. 10 [1944]: 398). See also Angel Luis Gonzalez, *Ser y participación: Estudio sobre la cuarta vía de Tomás de Aquino* (Pamplona: Ediciones Universidad de Navarra, 1995), 96–98.

are able to account for their possession of such qualities or whether they depend on a being that possesses such qualities essentially.

Our next step, therefore, is to consider the difference between possessing a transcendental quality essentially and possessing it accidentally. We can use the example of goodness. A being that possesses the transcendental quality of goodness essentially, by its very nature, will be completely good—just as a dog that possesses the generic quality of dogness essentially, by its very nature, is completely *dog*. But since goodness and other transcendental qualities imply no limitation, a being that possessed goodness essentially would have boundless goodness. For instance, if a good dog possessed its goodness by its very nature, it would have unbounded goodness. This is evidently not the case since even the "best dog" (that obeys every command and wins the blue ribbon) can still sometimes be a "bad dog" (when it gets ornery and poops on the carpet). And however well it behaves, it always has only the limited goodness of a dog. We can therefore be sure that the dog does not possess its goodness essentially (by its very nature), but only accidentally through the influence of something else.[75] We can therefore find gradations of goodness in dogs. A moment's consideration will show us that all of creation is just like the dog in this respect: every creature and even creation as a whole has only limited goodness, manifested by the fact that we find degrees of goodness in things. All of creation therefore has its goodness accidentally, from another.

Continuing Aquinas's argument, as we look around the world, we find degrees of goodness in things. The very fact that things manifest degrees of goodness tells us that they do not possess goodness essentially, but only accidentally through the influence of another. They are said to share or "participate" in goodness.[76] Creatures participate or possess in part the qualities of goodness, truth, and being through the influence of a being that possesses such qualities essentially.

To account for the goodness of creatures, we must therefore affirm the

75. "Whatever does not belong to a thing as such appertains to it through some cause, as white to man" (*SCG* II, c.15.2).

76. "Just as that which has fire, but is not itself fire, is on fire by participation; so that which has existence but is not existence, is a being by participation" (*ST* I, 3, 4, co.). "As that which participates is posterior to that which is essential, so likewise is that which is participated; as fire in ignited objects is posterior to fire that is essentially such" (*ST* I, 3, 8, co.).

existence of a being that *does* possess goodness essentially and therefore boundlessly.[77] Although Aquinas does not explicitly mention the distinction between accidental and essential qualities in the Fourth Way, it is evident in the distinction he makes between beings that have "gradations of goodness" (goodness possessed accidentally) and "something which is truest, and best, and noblest, and, consequently, uttermost being" (goodness possessed essentially). It is also evident in his argument that "the maximum in any genus is the cause of all in that genus; as fire, which is the maximum heat, is the cause of all hot things," since the maximum in any genus is precisely the being that possesses the particular quality not accidentally but essentially—as, in his cosmology, fire has heat essentially while all other things have heat accidentally or by participation.[78] The most excellent being therefore requires no other to account for its existence and goodness, since it possesses (or rather "is") such qualities essentially and can therefore be the source of being, goodness, and all other transcendental qualities in all other things.[79] This being is "to all beings

77. "If, however, the nature or quiddity of a thing remains integral, and yet something in it is found to be diminished, it is at once clear that this diminution does not derive simply from that nature, but from something else, by whose removal the nature is diminished. Therefore, whatever belongs to one thing less than to others belongs to it not by virtue of its own nature alone, but through some other cause. Thus, that thing of which a genus is chiefly predicated will be the cause of everything in that genus. So we see that what is most hot is the cause of heat in all hot things; and what is most light, the cause of all illuminated things. But as we proved in Book I, God is being in the highest mode. Therefore, he is the cause of all things of which being is predicated" (*SCG* II, c.15.3). "The different limited realizations of the perfection of being are as many participations of that which the first is by essence, and there would be no degrees of being without a primary instance which is the fullness of being and from which the rest receive their perfection" (Bernard Montagnes, *The Doctrine of the Analogy of Being according to Thomas Aquinas*, trans. E. M. Macierowski [Milwaukee, Wisc.: Marquette University Press, 2004], 89).

78. See *ST* I, 3, 4, co. "Precisely because God is not determined to any species or genus, when it is said that God is the first in the genus of being, one must take the word *genus* in a broad sense, that is, analogously. If it is not understood in this way, one runs the risk of falling into univocity, a pitfall which Saint Thomas avoids at all cost.... God is a cause and principle analogously. This is the sense in which one ought to understand God as *primum* or *maximum* in the genus of being" (Gonzalez, *Ser y participación*, 184–85).

79. The Fourth Way involves both exemplar and efficient causality, but the latter has primacy: "Certainly similarity or imitation exists between graduated perfections and the maximum; nevertheless that exemplar causality be taken exclusively in the proof from grades of perfection and that there might be exemplarity that does not presuppose efficient causality in the philosophy of Thomas Aquinas, is contrary the thought of Aquinas. For him, extrinsic or exemplar formal causality is posterior and consequential to efficient causality.... The similarities existing in the whole dominion of the created order are similarities precisely because they proceed from or have been caused

the cause of their being, goodness, and every other perfection; and this we call God."

The Fifth Way

The fifth way is taken from the governance of the world. We see that things which lack intelligence, such as natural bodies, act for an end, and this is evident from their acting always, or nearly always, in the same way, so as to obtain the best result. Hence it is plain that not fortuitously, but designedly, do they achieve their end. Now whatever lacks intelligence cannot move towards an end, unless it be directed by some being endowed with knowledge and intelligence; as the arrow is shot to its mark by the archer. Therefore some intelligent being exists by whom all natural things are directed to their end; and this being we call God.[80]

Once again, Aquinas begins with a readily observable aspect of the world: things that lack intelligence act for an end. Of course, this phenomenon became less observable with the advent of modern science and the scientism that followed in its wake. While science quite rightly studies the world through measurement, scientism arbitrarily decrees that whatever is not measurable is not real.[81] In this way it eliminates purpose or acting for an end (since purpose is not measurable), and so eliminates the premise of the Fifth Way. If we ignore the ideology of scientism for a moment, however, we might notice that Aquinas sets the bar rather low in determining whether something is acting purposefully or "for an end." All we have to see is whether it acts "always, or nearly always, in the same way, so as to obtain the best result." We might consider the humble garden spider. With no degree in engineering, it regularly constructs its intricate web *in order to* catch flies *so that* it may survive.[82] In this, the spider fits

---

by God. . . . Efficient causality grounds exemplar causality" (Gonzalez, *Ser y participación*, 138–39). On the kinds of causality involved in the Fourth Way, see also Joseph Bobik, "Aquinas's Fourth Way and the Approximating Relation," *Thomist* 51, no. 1 (1987): 17–36; Monty De La Torre. "In Defense of the Fourth Way and Its Metaphysics" (PhD diss., Australian Catholic University, 2016).

80. *ST* I, 2, 3, co.

81. Scientism arbitrarily restricts truth to what is knowable to reason through empirical science. Aquinas warns against such a restriction: "Those, however, who use philosophy in sacred doctrine can err . . . by including the contents of faith within the bounds of philosophy, as would happen should somebody decide to believe nothing but what could be established by philosophy" (*Super de trin.* 2, 3, co.). On scientism and the rise of modern science, see Dodds, *Unlocking*, 51–56.

82. On other possible examples of final causality in contemporary science, see Benedict M. Ashley, OP, "Research into the Intrinsic Final Causes of Physical Things," *Proceedings of the*

Aquinas's requirements for acting purposefully: the spider generally acts in the same way to get "the best result" for itself (survival). Biology offers many such examples, so it's not surprising that contemporary biology has become not just reconciled with, but committed to recognizing, purposefulness in nature.[83]

Once we've admitted purposeful action in nature, we can continue with Aquinas's argument. Since purpose implies intelligence (knowledge of the logical relation of means to end), and since unintelligent beings are found to act purposefully, Aquinas concludes that "some intelligent being exists by whom all natural things are directed to their end; and this being we call God." His conclusion is correct, but it might seem a bit abrupt, leaving some questions unanswered.

First, *how* are natural things directed to their end? Aristotle's answer was simply that nature itself possesses a kind of intelligence allowing it to act without deliberation.[84] Aquinas goes beyond Aristotle to ask about the source of this intelligence that is built into nature. His answer is God.[85] God acts within nature as the source of the substantial form

American Catholic Philosophical Association 26 (April 1952): 185–94; Robert L. Faricy, SJ, "The Establishment of the Basic Principle of the Fifth Way," *New Scholasticism* 31, no. 2 (1957): 189–208.

83. As biologist Francisco Ayala says, "teleological explanations in biology are not only acceptable but indeed indispensable" (Francisco J. Ayala, "Teleological Explanations in Evolutionary Biology," in *Nature's Purposes: Analyses of Function and Design in Biology*, ed. Colin Allen, Marc Bekoff, and George Lauder [Cambridge, Mass.: MIT Press, 1998], 44). The terms "teleology" and "teleological" refer to explanations or arguments that employ final causality. See "Causality" in appendix 1.

84. "It is absurd to suppose that purpose is not present because we do not observe the agent [in nature] deliberating. Art does not deliberate. If the ship-building art were in the wood, it would produce the same result *by nature*. If therefore purpose is present in art, it is present also in nature" (*Phys.* II, 8 [199b 26–27]). On purpose among spiders, swallows, and ants, see *Phys.* II, 8 (199a 20–34).

85. "It must be pointed out that nature is among the number of causes which act for the sake of something. And this is important with reference to the problem of providence. For things which do not know the end do not tend toward the end unless they are directed by one who does know, as the arrow is directed by the archer. Hence if nature acts for an end it is necessary that it be ordered by someone who is intelligent. This is the work of providence" (*In phys.* II, lect. 12, no. 250). Robert Spaemann shows how Aquinas introduces a theological dimension into Aristotle's notion of purpose: "If we perceive teleological structures in nature, and teleology necessarily implies consciousness, then nature requires us to speak of God; teleology becomes an argument in the proof for the existence of God. Aristotle rejected the premise with the remark that in nature art works as non-deliberatively as in a perfect artist. Thomas qualifies this thought: indeed art is non-deliberative in things, but how did it get into them?" (Robert Spaemann and Reinhard Löw, *Die Frage Wozu? Geschichte und Wiederentdeckung des teleologischen Denkens* [The question,

by which nature itself acts intelligently: "Although God provides the external end of all things, nevertheless the divine is also the immediate and primary source of nature's substantial forms which are internal to substances. Although God moves all things to their requisite ends, he does so through the fulfilment of a formal nature in such a way that this motion becomes genuinely the creature's own."[86] Since the agent without intelligence is acting intelligently here and now by its form, and since here and now (not ages ago) God is the cause of the form as such, God is "the intelligent being," immanent in the natural world, "by whom all natural things are directed to their end."[87]

The Fifth Way reveals Aquinas's view of the natural world. It's not just stuff that gets shoved around by forces, as in Newton's world where "things have no universal point"—where things "just are" and changes "just happen, because other previous changes have happened."[88] For Aquinas, the world is rich with meaning, since nature itself manifests meaning, direction, and intelligence: "Since both intellect and nature act for an end ... , the natural agent must have the end and the necessary means predetermined for it by some higher intellect; as the end and definite movement is predetermined for the arrow by the archer. Hence the intellectual and voluntary agent must precede the agent that acts by nature."[89] The world is not just a chance happening but a place of intelligence and purpose.

For him [Aquinas] "just being" or "just happening" is in the last analysis unintelligible. Nothing can enter into being simply as a phenomenon. To exist, as St. Thomas sees it, is to have significance, to have point, to play out a role. Such an idea of being is indeed the seminal idea of his philosophical view of the world: an idea of being, that is, not just as an arbitrary thereness of things for sense-experience, but as a logical and significant thereness in a community of the universe revealed to man by knowledge and love. The model or image that St. Thomas uses to express this idea of being is the model of an action: being is playing out

'to what purpose?' History and rediscovery of teleological thinking] [München: Piper, 1985], 85).

86. Simon Oliver, "Aquinas and Aristotle's Teleology," *Nova et Vetera* (English ed.) 11, no. 3 (2013): 864.

87. *ST* I, 2, 3, co. Cf. *ST* I-II, 109, 1, co.

88. Timothy McDermott, OP, "Introduction," in *Summa Theologiae*, by St. Thomas Aquinas, ed. Timothy McDermott (London: Eyre and Spottiswoode, 1964), 2:xxiii–xxiv).

89. *ST* I, 19, 4, co.

a role, realizing a significant conception.... [S]ince action is in turn conceived as the expression and execution of some agent's desire (giving point to the action), the being of things is conceived as fulfilling a role desired by someone, as the expression of someone's love. So that this seminal idea of being leads almost immediately to the notion of a God whose intentions rule the world, the expression of whose intentions the world indeed is. Since St. Thomas's word for the community of the universe about which we have been talking is "nature," we may say that God enters into his philosophy as the one who conceives nature, as the "author" of nature.[90]

God's role in the Fifth Way is quite different from that of the designer proposed by William Paley (1743–1805) or by contemporary Intelligent Design (ID) arguments.[91] Neither of these begin with the present, apparently intelligent activity of evidently unintelligent creatures, but with complex structures in nature (like the bacterial flagellum) that were first instantiated sometime in the past. These arguments then posit an extrinsic "designer" who first put the complex structure together. The designer need not transcend the natural world (as does the cause of the form as such, who acts through the substantial form) but might be something like "space aliens from Alpha Centauri."[92] If given the name "God" (which ID folk are reluctant to do), the designer would be, at best, a deist God who acted long ago to produce some feature in organisms that could then be reproduced without any further influence of the designer.[93] This is not at

90. McDermott, "Introduction," xxiii–xxiv.

91. For the famous "watchmaker" analogy, see William Paley, *Natural Theology: Or, Evidences of the Existence and Attributes of the Deity, Collected from the Appearances of Nature* (Boston: Gould, Kendall and Lincoln, 1842). For ID arguments based on the bacterial flagellum, see Michael J. Behe, *Darwin's Black Box: The Biochemical Challenge to Evolution* (New York: Free Press, 1996). For critiques, see Glenn Siniscalchi, "Fine-Tuning, Atheist Criticism, and the Fifth Way," *Theology and Science* 12, no. 1 (2014): 64–77; William Newton, "A Case of Mistaken Identity: Aquinas's Fifth Way and Arguments of Intelligent Design," *New Blackfriars* 95, no. 1059 (2014): 569–78.

92. "Thus, while I argue for design, the question of the identity of the designer is left open. Possible candidates for the role of designer include: the God of Christianity; an angel—fallen or not; Plato's demiurge; some mystical new-age force; space aliens from Alpha Centauri; time travelers; or some utterly unknown intelligent being" (Michael J. Behe, "The Modern Intelligent Design Hypothesis: Breaking Rules," in *God and Design: The Teleological Argument and Modern Science*, ed. Neil A. Manson [London: Routledge, 2003], 277).

93. Behe points out that quite a "lesser god" might be sufficient for his purposes: "The fact that modern ID theory is a minimalist argument for design itself, not an argument for the existence of God, relieves it of much of the baggage that weighed down Paley's argument.... Per-

all like the God who must be immanently present in the world right now to account for the presently occurring intelligent activities of unintelligent creatures.

Although the Fifth Way employs final causality (which it finds in the activities of creatures), it does not establish God as the ultimate final cause, nor is this its intention. It does not invoke God's causality as the final cause, drawing all things to himself as the ultimate good. Such divine causality will be established only later.[94] Here Aquinas establishes God as the intelligent agent intimately acting in each thing, as the source of its nature or substantial form, to direct it to its end.

This intelligent agent is certainly not a mere mechanical agency that might act by pushing, pulling, or shoving things around. Nor is this an agent that steps in to provide features of the natural world (such as the bacterial flagellum), which nature is presumably incapable of achieving. This is rather the Transcendent Cause who acts most intimately, through the very natures of creatures, as the ultimate source of the intelligent effects naturally produced by creatures who evidently lack intelligence— the source of the intelligent action of nature as such: "At the beginning of all action, therefore, is the Word. All action in the universe is ultimately the expression, direct or mediated, of a Logos, an ordering Mind."[95]

---

haps the designer isn't omnipotent or very competent. More to the point, perhaps the designer was not interested in every detail of biology, as Paley thought, so that, while some features were indeed designed, others were left to the vagaries of nature. Thus the modern argument for design need only show that intelligent agency appears to be a good explanation for some biological features" (Behe, "Modern Intelligent," 277–78). For a critique of the God of ID in relation to the Christian God, see Chris Doran, "Intelligent Design: It's Just Too Good to Be True," *Theology and Science* 8, no. 2 (2010): 223–37.

94. This way is sometimes called "the proof from final cause" (Gilson, *Christian Philosophy*, 75). It is important to remember that the "final causality" it employs is that of creatures who act for an end. Only later will Aquinas argue that God is the final cause of all creation. See *ST* I, 6, 1; *ST* I, 44, 4.

95. William Norris Clarke, SJ, "What Is Most and Least Relevant in the Metaphysics of St. Thomas Today?" in *Explorations in Metaphysics: Being—God—Person* (Notre Dame, Ind.: University of Notre Dame Press, 1994), 24.

Other Ways

Aquinas never claims that his Five Ways exhaust all possible approaches to the existence of God. In fact, he seems to suggest other arguments in some of his writings. Some thinkers, for instance, have found an argument for God's existence in his distinction between essence and existence.[96] Others have discovered a proof from design.[97] Transcendental Thomism offers a proof, "first suggested by Joseph Maréchal, taken over and elaborated by Karl Rahner," in which God is "necessarily affirmed as the final cause of our intellectual dynamism."[98] Edith Stein offers a proof of God from consciousness,[99] and Jacques Maritain suggests a kind of prolegomenon to any proof for the existence of God that he calls "the primordial intuition of being."[100] Religious experience and miracles have also been presented as ways to establish the existence of God.[101] David Braine uses the reality of time and the consequent contingency of beings existing in time to show that God exists in an argument that is in many ways con-

96. See *De ente*, chap. 4. For a contemporary presentation of this argument, see Gaven Kerr, OP, *Aquinas's Way to God: The Proof in "De Ente et Essentia"* (New York: Oxford University Press, 2015); Edward Feser, *Five Proofs of the Existence of God* (San Francisco: Ignatius Press, 2017), 117–43; Stephen Pimentel, "Thomas's Elusive Proof: A Reconstruction of the 'Existential Argument' for the Existence of God," *Proceedings of the American Catholic Philosophical Association* 78 (2004): 93–105.

97. See Robert Faricy, "Establishment," 190–91, citing *SCG* I, c.13.35 and *De ver.* 5, 2.

98. Joseph Donceel, SJ, "Can We Still Make a Case in Reason for the Existence of God?" in *God Knowable and Unknowable*, ed. Robert J. Roth (New York: Fordham University Press, 1973), 165. See also Joseph Donceel, SJ, *The Searching Mind: An Introduction to a Philosophy of God* (Notre Dame, Ind.: University of Notre Dame Press, 1979), 55–92.

99. See Karl Schudt, "Edith Stein's Proof for the Existence of God from Consciousness," *American Catholic Philosophical Quarterly* 82, no. 1 (2008): 105–25.

100. "It appears, therefore, that the philosophic proofs of the existence of God, let us say the five ways of Thomas Aquinas, are a development and an unfolding of this natural knowledge, raised to the level of scientific discussion and scientific certitude.... If the preceding observations are true, it would be necessary, before proposing the philosophic proofs, to be assured ... that the minds to which one addresses oneself are alive to the primordial intuition of existence" (Maritain, *Approaches*, 23).

101. R. Douglas Geivett, "The Evidential Value of Religious Experience," in *The Rationality of Theism*, ed. Paul Copan and Paul K. Moser (New York: Routledge, 2003), 175–203; R. Douglas Geivett, "The Evidential Value of Miracles," in *In Defense of Miracles: A Comprehensive Case for God's Action in History*, ed. R. Douglas Geivett and Gary R. Habermas (Downers Grove, Ill.: Intervarsity Press, 1997), 178–95; Brian Davies, OP, *Thinking about God* (London: Geoffrey Chapman, 1985), 50–88; Richard Swinburne, *The Existence of God*, 2nd ed. (Oxford: Oxford University Press, 2004), 273–327.

sonant with Aquinas's Third Way.[102] Proofs for God's existence based on the discoveries of empirical science have also been suggested.[103] While we cannot review all of these arguments here, much less evaluate their merits, it does seem appropriate to say that Aquinas's theological method, given its openness, would allow for the discovery and formulation of new ways of arguing for God's existence.

Atheism

In discussing God's existence, we should say a brief word about atheism.[104] In 1965, the Second Vatican Council called it "one of the most serious problems of our time."[105] With the rise of the "New Atheism," the problem seems even more acute today.[106]

102. "The continuance of the very stuff of the Universe, the fact that it goes on existing, is not self-explanatory. It is incoherent to say that the very stuff of the Universe continues to exist by its very nature since it has to continue to exist in order for this nature to exist or to be operative. Hence, nature presupposes existence" (David Braine, *The Reality of Time and the Existence of God: The Project of Proving God's Existence* [New York: Oxford University Press, 1988], 10).

103. See Robert J. Spitzer, SJ, *New Proofs for the Existence of God: Contributions of Contemporary Physics and Philosophy* (Grand Rapids, Mich.: Eerdmans, 2010); Russell Stannard, *The God Experiment: Can Science Prove the Existence of God?* (London: Faber and Faber, 1999); John M. Shackleford, *Faith Seeking Understanding: Approaching God through Science* (New York: Paulist Press, 2007).

104. For more information on atheism from among the many available studies, see Bernardino M. Bonansea, OFM, *God and Atheism: A Philosophical Approach to the Problem of God* (Washington, D.C.: The Catholic University of America Press, 1979); Michael J. Buckley, SJ, *At the Origins of Modern Atheism* (New Haven, Conn.: Yale University Press, 1987); Michael J. Buckley, SJ, *Denying and Disclosing God: The Ambiguous Progress of Modern Atheism* (New Haven, Conn.: Yale University Press, 2004); Cornelio Fabro, *God in Exile: Modern Atheism,* trans. Arthur Gibson (New York: Paulist Press, 1968); Michael Martin, ed., *The Cambridge Companion to Atheism* (New York: Cambridge University Press, 2007); Julian Baggini, *Atheism: A Very Short Introduction* (New York: Oxford University Press, 2003); Alister McGrath, *The Twilight of Atheism: The Rise and Fall of Disbelief in the Modern World* (New York: Doubleday, 2004).

105. Vatican Council II, *Gaudium et Spes,* no. 19 (December 7, 1965), in *The Documents of Vatican II,* ed. Austin P. Flannery, OP (New York: Pillar Books, 1975).

106. For examples of the new atheism, see Richard Dawkins, *The God Delusion*; Sam Harris, *The End of Faith: Religion, Terror, and the Future of Reason* (New York: W. W. Norton, 2005); Daniel Clement Dennett, *Breaking the Spell: Religion as a Natural Phenomenon* (New York: Viking, 2006); Christopher Hitchens, *God Is Not Great: How Religion Poisons Everything* (New York: Warner Twelve, 2007). For critiques of the new atheism, see John F. Haught, *God and the New Atheism: A Critical Response to Dawkins, Harris, and Hitchens* (Louisville, Ky.: Westminster John Knox, 2008); Christopher R. Cotter, Philip Andrew Quadrio, and Jonathan Tuckett, eds., *New Atheism: Critical Perspectives and Contemporary Debates* (Cham, Switzerland: Springer,

We must first distinguish atheism from agnosticism. While atheism denies the existence of God, agnosticism simply suspends judgment. Atheism's denial of God can take many forms. These are not easily classified, however, since the notion of the "God" who is being denied, the character of the denial, and the reasons behind it vary considerably.[107] Still, some sorting out may be helpful.

Regarding the notion of God, we might distinguish genuine atheism from "pseudo-atheism." While genuine atheists have an idea of God that would also be accepted by believers, pseudo-atheists have a notion of God that is "inadequate or completely distorted."[108] The Second Vatican Council seems to refer to these when it notes, "Yet others have such a faulty notion of God that when they disown this product of the imagination their denial has no reference to the God of the Gospels."[109] There seem to be quite a few pseudo-atheists among New Atheists, who propose absurd notions of God, as David Bentley Hart notes:

Consider Richard Dawkins: he devoted several pages of *The God Delusion* to a discussion of the "Five Ways" of Thomas Aquinas but never thought to avail himself of the services of some scholar of ancient and mediaeval thought who might have explained them to him.... If one could conclusively show that the philosophical claims the major religions make about the nature and reality of God were fundamentally incoherent or demonstrably false, that would be a signifi-

---

2017); Alister McGrath and Joanna Collicutt McGrath, *The Dawkins Delusion? Atheist Fundamentalism and the Denial of the Divine* (Downers Grove, Ill.: IVP Books, 2007); Thomas Crean, OP, *God Is No Delusion: A Refutation of Richard Dawkins* (San Francisco: Ignatius Press, 2007); Edward Feser, *The Last Superstition: A Refutation of the New Atheism* (South Bend, Ind.: St. Augustine's Press, 2008); David Bentley Hart, *Atheist Delusions: The Christian Revolution and its Fashionable Enemies* (New Haven, Conn.: Yale University Press, 2009); Ian S. Markham, *Against Atheism: Why Dawkins, Hitchens, and Harris Are Fundamentally Wrong* (Malden, Mass.: Wiley-Blackwell, 2010).

107. The Second Vatican Council, for example, lists ten types of atheism and notes that "the word atheism is used to signify things that differ considerably from one another" (*Gaudium et Spes*, no. 19). For other ways of classifying atheism, see Cornelio Fabro, *God: An Introduction to Problems in Theology*, trans. Joseph T. Papa, ed. Nathaniel Dreyer (Cullum, Md.: IVE Press, 2017), 25–26; Jacques Maritain, *The Range of Reason* (New York: Charles Scribner's Sons, 1952), 83–85, 97–100, 103–5; Bonansea, *God*, 4–6.

108. Bonansea, *God*, 5. "There are *pseudo-atheists* who believe that they do not believe in God and who in reality unconsciously believe in him, because the God whose existence they deny is not God but something else.... There are *absolute atheists* who actually deny the existence of the very God in whom the believers believe" (Jacques Maritain, *Range*, 97).

109. *Gaudium et Spes*, no. 19.

cant achievement; but if one is content merely to devise images of God that are self-evidently nonsensical, and then proceed triumphantly to demonstrate just how infuriatingly nonsensical they are, one is not going to accomplish anything interesting. For the sake of harmony, I for one am more than willing to acknowledge that the God described by the new atheists definitely does not exist; but, to be perfectly honest, that is an altogether painless concession to make.[110]

Regarding the character of the "denial" of God, we might distinguish "theoretical atheism" from "practical atheism." The theoretical atheist sees the denial of God as the conclusion of rational arguments. For the practical atheist, however, the denial is a matter not so much of argumentation but of lifestyle. Practical atheism is marked by a basic lack of concern for the whole question of God. A practical atheist denies God implicitly by a simple indifference to God in one's way of life. As the Second Vatican Council notes, "There are also those who never enquire about God; religion never seems to trouble or interest them at all, nor do they see why they should bother about it."[111]

Within the realm of theoretical atheism, further distinctions can be made according to the kinds of arguments or reasons presented for denying the existence of God. Some arguments have an epistemological character. These invoke the limits of human knowledge and argue that God's existence is in principle unknowable. This is sometimes called "agnostic atheism."[112] It is very close to agnosticism, but while the agnostic simply suspends judgment on the question of God's existence, the agnostic atheist maintains that no judgment is possible.

Other arguments are more metaphysical. They are often based implicitly on the assumptions of materialism or scientism—that only that

---

110. David Bentley Hart, *The Experience of God: Being, Consciousness, Bliss* (New Haven, Conn.: Yale University Press, 2013), 21, 23. "Unless, dear atheist, you are denying what the true believer affirms, all you are doing is rejecting an idolatry that the true believer anyway rejects" (Denys Turner, "On Denying the Right God: Aquinas on Atheism and Idolatry," *Modern Theology* 20, no. 1 [2004]: 142). For Dawkins's arguments, see Richard Dawkins, *The God Delusion*, 77–79. See also Nicholas Lash, "Where Does the God Delusion Come From?" *New Blackfriars* 88 (2007): 507–21.

111. *Gaudium et Spes*, no. 19. Jacques Maritain includes, among practical atheists, those who profess faith in God but deny it by their lifestyle: "There are ... practical atheists, who believe that they believe in God, but who in actual fact deny his existence by their deeds and the testimony of their behavior" (Maritain, *Range*, 103).

112. Cornelio Fabro uses this term and gives Immanuel Kant's philosophy as an example. See Cornelio, *God: An Introduction*, 25, 40.

which is material or quantifiable (and so within the purview of empirical science) is real. Since God is neither material nor quantifiable, God must not be real. The assumptions of naturalism are also invoked: since the natural world can explain itself, there is simply no need to posit a supernatural being.[113]

Still other arguments have a moral character. The presence of evil and suffering in the world is a long-standing argument against the existence of a good and omnipotent God.[114] In addition, modern notions of human autonomy seem to require the negation of a supernatural creator.

With others it is their exaggerated idea of man that causes their faith to languish; they are more prone, it would seem, to affirm man than to deny God.... Among the various kinds of present-day atheism, that one should not go unnoticed which looks for man's autonomy through his economic and social emancipation. It holds that religion, of its very nature, thwarts such emancipation by raising man's hopes in a future life."[115]

However God is conceived, the secular currents of our age have made belief in God no longer a given but simply one option among others, as Charles Taylor points out:

The shift to secularity ... consists, among other things, of a move from a society where belief in God is unchallenged and, indeed, unproblematic, to one in which it is understood to be one option among others, and frequently not the easiest to embrace.... [T]he change I want to define and trace is one which takes us from a society in which it was virtually impossible not to believe in God, to one in which faith, even for the staunchest believer, is one human possibility among others.... Belief in God is no longer axiomatic. There are alternatives.[116]

Responding to the challenges of atheism and secularism requires something more than just philosophical arguments for God's existence—important as they are in their own context. It demands a deep understanding of the reality of God expressed not just in ideas but in the witness of life. This is the exhortation of the Second Vatican Council:

---

113. Aquinas seems to recognize such arguments in *ST* I, 2, 3, ad 2.
114. Aquinas addresses the argument from evil in *ST* I, 2, 3, ad 1.
115. *Gaudium et Spes*, nos. 19–20.
116. Charles Taylor, *A Secular Age* (Cambridge, Mass.: Harvard University Press, 2007), 3.

Atheism must be countered both by presenting true teaching in a fitting manner and by the full and complete life of the Church and of her members. For it is the function of the Church to render God the Father and his incarnate Son present and as it were visible, while ceaselessly renewing and purifying herself under the guidance of the Holy Spirit.... Lastly, what does most to show God's presence clearly is the brotherly love of the faithful who, being all of one mind and spirit, work together for the faith of the Gospel and present themselves as a sign of unity.[117]

117. *Gaudium et Spes*, no. 21. "A decorative Christianity is henceforth not enough. A living Christianity is necessary to the world. Faith must be actual, practical, existential faith. To believe in God must mean to live in such a manner that life could not possibly be lived if God did not exist. For the practical believer, gospel justice, gospel attentiveness to everything human must inspire not only the deeds of the saints, but the structure and institutions of common life, and must penetrate to the depths of terrestrial existence" (Maritain, *Range*, 100). "In the face of the radical challenge to the Christian faith, help will come not from a feeble, general and vague theism but only from a decisive witness to the living God of history who has disclosed himself in a concrete way through Jesus Christ in the Holy Spirit" (Walter Kasper, *The God of Jesus Christ*, trans. Matthew J. O'Connell [New York: Crossroad, 1984], 315).

CHAPTER 2

DIVINE ATTRIBUTES

Having shown that God exists, Aquinas then uses the modes of divine causality uncovered in the Five Ways to discuss the divine attributes. As his arguments for God's existence maintain God's incomprehensibility, so his discussion of divine attributes continues to treat of the God who utterly exceeds our understanding: "Because we cannot know what God is, but rather what he is not, we have no means for considering how God is, but rather how he is not."[1] Aquinas first considers things we must deny of God (*ST* I, 3–11) and then uses that discussion as a kind of object lesson to reflect on how we know and speak of God (*ST* I, 12–13).

Simplicity, Perfection, and Goodness

The discussions of God's simplicity and perfection are in a sense mutually corrective. We first affirm God's simplicity by denying any kind of composition in him. But because simplicity in creatures is frequently a sign of imperfection (as simple creatures are often less perfect than more complex ones), we must then deny that God is simple in the same way as

1. *ST* I, 3, prologue.

creatures.[2] This dialectic of a denial followed by a denial of the denial will mark the whole discussion of the divine attributes.

Simplicity

To establish God's simplicity, we deny the various modes of composition found in creatures.[3] Bodily composition is the first consideration. Such composition is incompatible with God's primacy in being, established in the Five Ways, where God was shown to be "the First Mover" (First Way), "the First Being," and "the most noble of beings" (Fourth Way). Since God has absolute primacy, and since act is prior to potency, "it is impossible that in God there should be any potentiality." But every body has potency insofar as it has matter. We must therefore deny that God is a body.[4]

The Five Ways are further employed to show that in God there can be no composition of (1) form and matter, (2) substance and accident, (3) nature and suppositum, or (4) essence and existence. God cannot be composed of form and matter (1) because matter implies potency and God is pure act (First and Fourth Ways). Also, God was shown to be the first agent (Second Way). Since every agent acts in virtue of its form, the first agent must be essentially form, not form and matter.[5] Nor can God be composed of substance and accidents (2), since a substance is related to its accidents as potency to act (as an apple may be actualized by red or green color), but there is no potency in God (First Way).[6]

Likewise, God cannot be composed of nature and suppositum (3). In

2. "Now it can be shown how God is not, by denying of him whatever is opposed to the idea of him, viz. composition, motion, and the like. Therefore (1) we must discuss his simplicity, whereby we deny composition in him; and because whatever is simple in material things is imperfect and a part of something else, we shall discuss (2) his perfection; (3) his infinity; (4) his immutability; (5) his unity" (*ST* I, 3, prologue).

3. For a penetrating discussion of divine simplicity, see James E. Dolezal, *God without Parts: Divine Simplicity and the Metaphysics of God's Absoluteness* (Eugene, Ore.: Pickwick Publications, 2011). See also Matthew Levering, *Engaging the Doctrine of Creation: Cosmos, Creatures, and the Wise and Good Creator* (Grand Rapids, Mich.: Baker Academic, 2017), 73–107.

4. *ST* I, 3, 1, co. On the contemporary discussion of whether bodiliness should be attributed to God, see Sallie McFague, *The Body of God: An Ecological Theology* (Minneapolis: Fortress Press, 1993); Sallie McFague, *Models of God: Theology for an Ecological, Nuclear Age* (Philadelphia: Fortress Press, 1987); Grace Jantzen, *God's World, God's Body* (Philadelphia: Westminster, 1984).

5. *ST* I, 3, 2.

6. *ST* I, 3, 6.

every material being, we can distinguish the suppositum (the individual, existing thing) from its nature (the kind of thing it is). No individual material thing is identical with its nature. No individual human being, for instance, is identical with its nature (humanity). I can say, "I am Michael Dodds," but not "I am humanity." In material things, the nature or form is individuated by matter, and can therefore exist in many individuals of the same species. No individual is identical with its nature since no individual is the whole species. The case is different for immaterial beings (such as angels), who have no individuating matter and whose forms are "individualized of themselves."[7] In such beings, the suppositum (the existing thing) is identical with its form or nature. So even though we use the same word "angel" for all angels, each one is really its own distinct form or nature or type.[8] Since God is immaterial, God is also identical with his nature: "He must be his own Godhead, his own Life, and whatever else is thus predicated of him."[9]

Finally, God is not composed of essence and existence (4). To show the difference between divine simplicity and that of other spiritual beings (angels), a further distinction is needed. This is the famous distinction between essence, which accounts for *what* something is, and existence or *esse*, which accounts for the fact *that* something is.[10] Although essence and existence are distinct in every creature, they are identical in God. To show this, Aquinas employs three arguments, each of which relies on what we have discovered about God in the Five Ways. First, he argues that whatever a being possesses in addition to its essence must be caused in it either by its essence or by something else. The color and temperature of iron, for instance, are distinct from its essence. Its characteristic gray color is caused by its essence. (It's gray because it's iron.) Its temperature, however, is the result of some external agency, such as the surrounding environment. So, if the essence of something differs from its existence, its existence must be caused either by its essence or by something else. But a thing's essence can't be the cause of its existence if its existence is caused: it cannot bring itself into existence. Such a being must have its existence

7. *ST* I, 3, 3, co.
8. See *ST* I, 50, 2; *ST* I, 50, 4.
9. *ST* I, 3, 3, co.
10. On the distinction between essence and existence, see appendix 1.

caused by another. God's existence, however, cannot be caused by another since God is himself the "first efficient cause" (Second Way). So essence and existence are identical in God.

Second, when essence and existence are distinct, essence is actualized by existence. Fido's "dogness," for instance, is actualized or made existent by Fido's act of existence (*esse*). In such cases, essence is a principle of potency in relation to *esse*. Since there is no potency in God (First Way), his essence cannot be actualized by his *esse* and therefore cannot be distinct from his *esse*.

Third, if God's essence were distinct from his *esse*, he would not have *esse* essentially but through participation in some other being that does have *esse* essentially. This cannot be the case, however, since God is the First Being (Fourth Way). So in God, essence and *esse* are the same: "God is his own existence, and not merely his own essence."[11]

God is thus shown to be both utterly simple (since there is no composition in him) and absolutely perfect (since God is essentially *esse*, and *esse* is "the act of all acts and the perfection of all perfections").[12] Since essence and *esse* are the same in God, Aquinas calls God "subsistent being itself [*ipsum esse subsistens*]."[13] The infinitive verb form (*esse*, to be) indicates the perfection of God, not as a static essence but as the dynamic summit of all actuality, in whom essence and *esse* (to-be) are one.[14]

Perfection

To establish God's perfection, Aquinas employs the Second Way, which shows that God is the first efficient cause. Since every efficient cause must be in a state of actuality in order to act, and since God is the first efficient cause, God "must be most actual." And since "a thing is perfect in propor-

---

11. *ST* I, 3, 4, co.

12. *De pot.* 7, 2, ad 9. "With us composite things are better than simple things, because the perfections of created goodness cannot be found in one simple thing, but in many things. But the perfection of divine goodness is found in one simple thing" (*ST* I, 3, 7, ad 2).

13. "God is the essentially self-subsisting Being [*ipsum esse per se subsistens*]" (*ST* I, 44, 1, co.). Cf. *Sent.* I, 37, 1, 1, co.; *De ver.* 5, 8, ad 9; *SCG* III, c.65.3; *ST* I, 3, 4, co.; *ST* I, 4, 2, co.

14. "If such be the God of natural theology, true metaphysics does not culminate in a concept, be it that of Thought, of Good, of One, or of Substance. It does not even culminate in an essence, be it that of Being itself. Its last word is not *ens*, but *esse*; not *being* but *is*" (Etienne Gilson, *God and Philosophy* [New Haven, Conn.: Yale University Press, 1941], 143).

tion to its state of actuality," God must therefore be "most perfect."[15] As such, God contains all the perfections of creatures, since the perfection of an effect must exist somehow in its cause, as the artistry that one finds in a painting must first be present in the skill of the artist.[16] Therefore God is not only the efficient cause of creatures but also the exemplar cause. As a sculptor produces a statue in accordance with the idea (exemplar) in her mind, so God produces creatures in accordance with the exemplars in the divine mind.[17]

The presence of all creaturely perfections in God does not jeopardize God's simplicity since all exist in the unity of the one divine essence: "All things in a kind of natural unity pre-exist in the cause of all things; and thus things diverse and in themselves opposed to each other, pre-exist in God as one, without injury to his simplicity."[18] Since God's essence is his existence, God is pure actuality, which "precludes any addition."[19] What would be accidental in us is simply the divine essence in God: "Virtue and wisdom are not predicated of God and of us univocally. Hence it does not follow that there are accidents in God as there are in us."[20] Rather, God simply *is* his own wisdom and goodness. In Aquinas's famous phrase, "Whatever is in God is God."[21]

Every creature is in some way like God, since an effect is in some way like its cause.[22] This similitude between God and creatures does not reduce God to the level of a creature. Although we must say that creatures

---

15. *ST* I, 4, 1, co.

16. *ST* I, 4, 2.

17. "It is absolutely true that there is first something which is essentially being and essentially good, which we call God.... Hence from the first being, essentially such, and good, everything can be called good and a being, inasmuch as it participates in it by way of a certain assimilation which is far removed and defective.... Everything is therefore called good from the divine goodness, as from the first exemplary, effective and final principle of all goodness" (*ST* I, 6, 4, co.). On God's exemplar causality, see Gregory T. Doolan, *Aquinas on the Divine Ideas as Exemplar Causes* (Washington, D.C.: The Catholic University of America Press, 2008); Vivian Boland, OP, *Ideas in God according to Saint Thomas Aquinas: Sources and Synthesis* (Leiden: Brill, 1996); John F. Wippel, *Thomas Aquinas on the Divine Ideas* (Toronto: Pontifical Institute of Mediaeval Studies, 1993); Levering, *Engaging*, 29–71.

18. *ST* I, 4, 2, ad 1.

19. *ST* I, 3, 4, ad 1.

20. *ST* I, 3, 6, ad 1.

21. "Quidquid est in Deo, est Deus" (*ST* I, 27, 3, ad 2). See also *ST* I, 28, 2, co.; *ST* I, 40, 1, ad 1.

22. *ST* I, 4, 3.

are like God, we may not say that God is like creatures: "Although it may be admitted that creatures are in some way like God, it must nowise be admitted that God is like creatures."[23] While the effect resembles its cause, the cause is not said to resemble the effect. We might say, for instance, that a picture resembles its subject, but we don't tend to say that the subject resembles its picture.[24] As we will see, the likeness of creatures to God forms the foundation of all of our talk about God when we use creaturely words to speak of him. At the same time, the "unlikeness" of God to creatures ensures that we are really speaking about God and not reducing God to the level of a creature.

Goodness

Goodness is defined philosophically as "that which all desire."[25] As such, goodness is the final cause, "that for the sake of which something is done."[26] The Fourth Way shows that God is the supreme good and the efficient cause of goodness in creatures, but it does not consider God as the final cause. The Fifth Way refers to final causality in the actions of creatures (as when the spider weaves a web *in order to* catch flies), but it does not establish God as the ultimate final cause. Since the Five Ways do establish that God is the first efficient cause, Aquinas now argues from God's efficient causality to his final causality as the ultimate good.

Each thing acts in accordance with its nature to attain its fulfillment, which is a good. That good is proportionate to its nature and so in some way like its nature. Its nature, however, bears some likeness to God, since God is the cause of its nature and every effect resembles its cause. Since the good that it is seeking is somehow like its nature, which is in turn somehow like God, the good that it is seeking must also be in some way like God. So we can conclude that God is good, since each thing, in seeking its own good, is also implicitly seeking divine goodness: "All things, by desiring their own perfection, desire God himself, inasmuch as the perfections of all things are so many similitudes of the divine being."[27] This

---

23. *ST* I, 4, 3, ad 4.

24. "We say that a statue is like a man, but not conversely, so also a creature can be spoken of as in some way like God; but not that God is like a creature" (*ST* I, 4, 3, ad 4).

25. *ST* I-II, 8, 1, co. See *Nicomach.* I, 1 (1094a 3).

26. *Phys.* II, 3 (1094b 33).

27. *ST* I, 6, 1, ad 2. "To be good belongs pre-eminently to God. For a thing is good according

66   DIVINE ATTRIBUTES

desire takes various forms in different types of creatures: "Of those things which desire God, some know him as he is himself, and this is proper to the rational creature; others know some participation of his goodness, and this belongs also to sensible knowledge; others have a natural desire without knowledge, as being directed to their ends by a higher intelligence."[28]

Infinity, Transcendence, and Immanence

Aquinas puts the questions of God's infinity and immanence together: "We must consider the divine infinity and God's existence in things: for God is everywhere, and in all things, inasmuch as he is boundless and infinite."[29]

Infinity

Infinity is a difficult concept, and divine infinity so much more so. It's helpful to remember that we're still under the umbrella of Aquinas's negative theology—saying what God is not. Infinity means simply that God is "*not* finite." But having said that, we must immediately add that he is also "not infinite" in the way that the word is sometimes used mathematically to describe, for instance, a line that goes on forever or can be divided forever. This notion of infinity implies potency through the very language of our definition: the line *can be* extended ever farther or *can be* divided ever more minutely. Since this idea of infinity implies potency, it cannot be attributed to God.

There is a way to understand infinity, however, that implies neither potency nor imperfection. To grasp it, we have to understand something about the relationship between actuality and potency. Each of these no-

---

to its desirableness. Now everything seeks after its own perfection; and the perfection and form of an effect consist in a certain likeness to the agent, since every agent makes its like; and hence the agent itself is desirable and has the nature of good. For the very thing which is desirable in it is the participation of its likeness. Therefore, since God is the first effective cause of all things, it is manifest that the aspect of good and of desirableness belong to him; and hence Dionysius attributes good to God as to the first efficient cause, saying that, God is called good 'as by whom all things subsist'" (*ST* I, 6, 1, co.).

28. *ST* I, 6, 1, ad 2.

29. *ST* I, 7, prologue

tions, considered in itself, suggests a kind of boundlessness. Potency is boundless in the sense that something can always be added to it: it can always be actualized in new ways. Pure potency would be devoid of perfection in itself, but infinitely perfectible according to the many ways it might be actualized. Taken in this sense, infinity is "that beyond which there is always something."[30] (One more segment can always be added to the line; one more division can always be made.) Infinity of this sort cannot be used to describe God.

Actuality or form, considered apart from potency, is also boundless in the sense that it is not restricted to any particular matter. The form of circularity, considered in itself, is not limited to any one circular thing. As instantiated in a pie pan, however, it is limited or contracted by the matter of the pan. In general, we can say that actuality is not limited except by potency.[31] Pure actuality would be in no way restricted and so would possess unbounded perfection. We might characterize it as "that beyond which there is nothing." No further actuality or perfection could be added to it since there would be no perfection that it did not already possess in boundless fullness.

We have seen that existence (*esse*) is the highest actuality. As found in creatures, it is always limited by the essence of the particular creature to a particular mode of existence, since in creatures essence stands in relation to existence as potency to act. In God, however, existence is not limited by essence, since God's essence simply *is* his own existence. God's existence therefore has a kind of boundlessness or lack of limitation—not in the sense of a potency to which something more could always be added or actualized, but in the sense of an actuality which is complete, an actuality to which nothing can be added since nothing is missing. This is the infinity not of potency but of actuality and perfection. Since this type of infinity implies no imperfection, it may be attributed to God.[32]

---

30. *In phys.* III, lect. 11, no. 383.

31. William Norris Clarke, SJ, "The Limitation of Act by Potency: Aristotelianism or Neoplatonism?" in *Explorations in Metaphysics: Being—God—Person* (Notre Dame, Ind.: University of Notre Dame Press: 1994), 65–88.

32. "Since therefore the divine being is not a being received in anything, but he is his own subsistent being, ... it is clear that God himself is infinite and perfect" (*ST* I, 7, 1, co.).

Transcendence and Immanence

Contemporary theology often makes the mistake of viewing God's transcendence and immanence as a zero-sum game: the more God is said to be transcendent, the less he can be called immanent, and vice versa.[33] Rightly understood, however, God's utter immanence in creation can be affirmed precisely because of God's absolute transcendence.[34]

Since God's essence is his existence (*esse*), God utterly transcends the realm of creatures in which existence is distinct from and limited by essence. Only the transcendent God, who is essentially *esse*, can be the source of existence in creatures. Yet as the source of creaturely existence, God is utterly immanent in creation since nothing is more intimate to the creature than its own existence.[35] God's transcendence, therefore, does not contradict his immanence but is in a sense its ground: "God is in all things, and innermostly."[36]

God is not divorced from and indifferent to the world (as deism proposes). Rather, God is present in the world. Yet God is not identical with the world (as pantheism teaches), nor is God simply a part of the world or

33. William Placher points out, for instance, that process theologians "tend to define the issues in terms of a debate between rival metaphysical systems, with the utterly transcendent, omnipotent God of classical theism set against the more immanent, collaborative God of process thought" (Placher, *Domestication*, 9).

34. "God is above all things by the excellence of his nature; nevertheless, he is in all things as the cause of the being of all things" (*ST* I, 7, 8, ad 1). "The very transcendence of God ... is itself the ground of the divine immanence in everything that partakes of being. The total otherness of God explains that he is not present and operative in any one place but simultaneously in all places giving them their very powers of location; he is not present to any one order of being but to everything whatsoever that participates in being" (William J. Hill, OP, "The Implicate World: God's Oneness with Mankind as a Mediated Immediacy," in *Beyond Mechanism: The Universe in Recent Physics and Catholic Thought*, ed. David L. Schindler [Lanham, Md.: University Press of America, 1986], 88). "Such an extreme of divine involvement requires, one could say, an extreme of divine transcendence" (Kathryn Tanner, *God and Creation in Christian Theology: Tyranny or Empowerment?* [New York: Basil Blackwell, 1988], 46).

35. "Now since God is very being by his own essence, created being must be his proper effect; as to ignite is the proper effect of fire. Now God causes this effect in things not only when they first begin to be, but as long as they are preserved in being; as light is caused in the air by the sun as long as the air remains illuminated. Therefore as long as a thing has being, God must be present to it, according to its mode of being" (*ST* I, 8, 1, co.).

36. *ST* I, 8, 1, co. In addition to his presence as the cause of being, God is also present in human beings through grace (*ST* I, 8, 3, co.; *ST* I, 43, 3, co.; *ST* I-II, 110), and in Christ through the hypostatic union (*ST* I, 8, 3, ad 4; *ST* III, 2–6).

the world a part of God (as panentheism maintains).[37] God is not "present in things in the sense of being combined with them as one of their parts," but rather "in the fashion of an agent cause."[38] Nor are God and the world together part of a greater whole.[39] And yet it can be truly said that God is in the world and the world is in God.[40]

Panentheism is especially prevalent in contemporary theology.[41] It has been defined as "the belief that the Being of God includes and penetrates the whole universe, so that every part of it exists in him, but . . . that his being is more than, and is not exhausted by, the universe."[42] A key feature of panentheism is its teaching that God is in some way dependent upon the world.[43] It is often presented as an alternative to deism (transcendence to the exclusion of immanence) and pantheism (immanence to

37. "Thus one must never separate God's immanence and transcendence in speaking of God's relationship to the world and the world's to God. Unless these two modes of acting are held together when one speaks of God, we fall either into deism, for which God is far from the world and indifferent to it, or into pantheism, which confuses God and the world: two fatal errors to avoid in speaking of God!" (Pierre-Marie Emonet, *God Seen in the Mirror of the World: An Introduction to the Philosophy of God* [New York: Crossroad, 2016], 57).

38. *SCG* III, c.68.11.

39. "It is not possible for God to enter into the composition of anything . . . because no part of a compound can be absolutely primal among beings" (*ST* I, 3, 8, co.).

40. "Although corporeal things are said to be in another as in that which contains them, nevertheless, spiritual things contain those things in which they are; as the soul contains the body. Hence also God is in things as containing them; nevertheless, by a certain similitude to corporeal things, it is said that all things are in God; inasmuch as they are contained by him" (*ST* I, 8, 1, ad 2).

41. See John W. Cooper, *Panentheism: The Other God of the Philosophers: From Plato to the Present* (Grand Rapids, Mich.: Baker Books, 2006); Michael W. Brierley, "The Potential of Panentheism for Dialogue between Science and Religion," in *The Oxford Handbook of Religion and Science*, ed. Philip Clayton and Zachary Simpson (Oxford: Oxford University Press, 2006), 635–51; Owen C. Thomas, "Problems in Panentheism," in *The Oxford Handbook of Religion and Science*, ed. Philip Clayton and Zachary Simpson (Oxford: Oxford University Press, 2006), 652–64; Philip Clayton, "Panentheism in Metaphysical and Scientific Perspective," in *In Whom We Live and Move and Have Our Being: Panentheistic Reflections on God's Presence in a Scientific World*, ed. Philip Clayton and Arthur R. Peacocke (Grand Rapids, Mich.: Eerdmans, 2004), 73–91; Mariusz Tabaczek, OP, "Hegel and Whitehead: In Search for Sources of Contemporary Versions of Panentheism in the Science-Theology Dialogue," *Theology and Science* 11, no. 2 (2013): 143–61.

42. Frank Leslie Cross and Elizabeth A. Livingstone, eds., *The Oxford Dictionary of the Christian Church*, 3rd rev. ed. (Oxford: Oxford University Press, 2005), 1221–22.

43. "[Panentheism is] defined as a doctrine which constitutes divinity as neither identical with the world (pantheism) nor as autonomous from it (classical theism), but as in a state of dependence upon it" (William J. Hill, OP, "Does Divine Love Entail Suffering in God?" in *God and Temporality*, ed. Bowman L. Clarke and Eugene T. Long [New York: Paragon, 1984], 57). According to panentheism, "God is not identical with the world but is still present in the world in such a way that he is changed by it" (Feser, *Five Proofs*, 234).

the exclusion of transcendence), and is frequently contrasted with "traditional theism."[44]

Panentheism, however, leans towards pantheism. Its teaching that God's being is "more than and not exhausted by the universe" implies that God and the universe are univocal, for only in that case could one be described as "more" than the other. It is pantheistic to think that God's being and the being of the world are the same—even if one posits "more" of that univocal being in God than in the world.

When Aquinas affirms that "God is in things," and "all things are in God," he does not mean that things are part of God, that God is part of things, or both are part of some larger whole.[45] In Herbert McCabe's pithy phrase, "God is not what is left over when you remove creatures."[46] Rather, the transcendent God, precisely as wholly other, is wholly present in each creature as the source of its being. Neither a pantheistic God nor a panentheistic God can be wholly present in each part of the universe. The pantheistic God (identical with the whole universe) is only partly in each part, and the panentheistic God (including the universe and more) is only partly in and partly out of the universe. The transcendent God is therefore more immanent than the God of either pantheism or panentheism.

God is in all things, not indeed as part of their essence, nor as an accident; but as an agent is present to that upon which it works.... Therefore as long as a thing has being, God must be present to it, according to its mode of being. But being is innermost in each thing and most fundamentally inherent in all things since it is formal in respect to everything found in a thing.... Hence it must be that God is in all things and innermostly.[47]

---

44. The term "theism" denotes "a philosophical system which accepts a transcendent and personal God who not only created but also preserves and governs the world, the contingency of which does not exclude miracles and the exercise of human freedom" (Cross and Livingstone, *Oxford Dictionary*, 1608).

45. *ST* I, 8, 1, ad 2; *ST* I, 3, 7, co.

46. Herbert McCabe, OP, *God and Evil in the Theology of St. Thomas Aquinas*, ed. Brian Davies, OP (New York: Continuum, 2010), 129.

47. *ST* I, 8, 1, co. "Whatever number of places be supposed to exist, God must be in all of them, not as to a part of him, but as to his very self" (*ST* I, 8, 4, co.).

Immutability and Eternity

For Aquinas, immutability and eternity are closely related, since one is the logical consequence of the other: "We next consider divine immutability and eternity which follows from immutability."[48]

Immutability

Divine immutability has become a hot topic in contemporary theology. The immutable God is often presented as deistic, distant, and indifferent to creation.[49] Aquinas sees no contradiction between God's immutability and his loving intimacy in creation. In fact, the immutable God is found to be more truly loving than a changeable God.[50] Here, we will look at Aquinas's arguments for God's immutability and then review three ways in which he also attributes motion to God. Later, in our discussion of divine compassion, we will consider the related question of divine impassibility—whether and how God can be said to suffer.[51]

Aquinas established divine immutability initially in his arguments for the existence of God: "All things that are changeable and capable of defect must be traced back to an immovable and self-necessary first principle."[52] Yet immutability is an ambiguous term, since creaturely immobility (like creaturely simplicity) can be a sign of imperfection.[53] Just as the discussion of divine simplicity required a complementary discussion

---

48. *ST* I, 9, prologue. "The idea of eternity follows immutability, as the idea of time follows movement" (*ST* I, 10, 2, co.).

49. Alfred North Whitehead, the founder of "process philosophy," laments the traditional doctrines of God's immutability and transcendence: "The notion of God as the 'unmoved mover' is derived from Aristotle, at least so far as Western thought is concerned. The notion of God as 'eminently real' is a favorite doctrine of Christian theology. The combination of the two into the doctrine of an aboriginal, eminently real, transcendent creator, at whose fiat the world came into being, and whose imposed will it obeys, is the fallacy which has infused tragedy into the histories of Christianity and of Mahometanism" (Alfred North Whitehead, *Process and Reality* [New York: Free Press, 1978], 342). Jürgen Moltmann finds the unchanging God to be "as cold and hard and unfeeling as cement" (Jürgen Moltmann, *History and the Triune God: Contributions to Trinitarian Theology* [New York: Crossroad, 1992], 123).

50. See Dodds, *Unchanging God*.

51. See chapter 6 of this book.

52. *ST* I, 2, 3, ad 2.

53. On how "immutability" may imply imperfection in creatures, see Dodds, *Unchanging God*, 5–45.

of divine perfection lest divine simplicity be mistaken for the imperfect simplicity of creatures,[54] so divine immutability must be established as a mode of divine perfection.

As subsistent being (*ipsum esse subsistens*), God is purely actual, absolutely simple, and wholly perfect. God's actuality, simplicity, and perfection are the premises Aquinas uses in his arguments for divine immutability.[55] Far from attributing to God the imperfection that is often part of creaturely immutability, he intends to show that divine immutability is a sign of God's perfection.

In his first argument, Aquinas alludes to the Fourth Way, which establishes God's perfection as "uttermost being," who is "to all beings the cause of their being, goodness and every other perfection."[56] Since God is the first being and since act is prior to potency, God must be pure act with no admixture of potency. Since change implies potency and since God has no potency, God must be absolutely unchangeable.

Aquinas's second argument is based on God's absolute simplicity. He has already shown that divine simplicity is a sign of divine perfection. But all change implies composition or complexity since it always entails an enduring subject that attains a new actuality.[57] Since God is absolutely simple, he must be unchangeable.

The third argument begins with God's infinite perfection in being, with God "comprehending in himself all the plenitude of perfection of all being."[58] Because God is subsisting being itself (*ipsum esse subsistens*), "nothing of the perfection of being can be wanting to him."[59] Changeable things, on the contrary, always lack some actuality that they then acquire through change. Since there is nothing that God can acquire— nothing that he does not eternally possess in infinite fullness—he must be completely immutable. God's immutability distinguishes him from creatures since God alone is utterly unchangeable.[60]

54. See *ST* I, 3, prologue.
55. On the premises of Aquinas's arguments for divine immutability, see Dodds, *Unchanging God,* 125–26.
56. *ST* I, 2, 3, co.
57. On how change implies complexity, see "Motion" in appendix 1.
58. *ST* I, 9, 1, co.
59. *ST* I, 4, 2, co.
60. See *ST* I, 9, 2, co.

Having established God's immutability, Aquinas surprisingly goes on in his replies to the objections to show three ways in which God can be said to "move." The first objection concerns immanent motion (such as knowing and loving).[61] It arises from Augustine's statement that God "moves himself." Thomas explains that Augustine is speaking of immanent motion, which implies no imperfection and may therefore be predicated of God.

Far from suggesting imperfection, the immanent actions of knowing and loving denote the summit of perfection. Aquinas can therefore use them in modeling the Trinity.[62] He likens the procession of the Son (the Word) from the Father to the procession of the mental word (the concept) in the act of human knowing. As the procession of the mental word in itself implies no potency, neither does the procession of the Son. As the mental word proceeds from and yet remains in the knower, so the Son proceeds from and yet remains in the Father. As the intellect in its act of understanding is one with the object understood, so the Son is one with the Father. As the mental word is a likeness of the object conceived, so the Son is the likeness of the Father, and his procession may be called "generation."

Aquinas compares the procession of the Holy Spirit to the human activity of willing or loving. The one loved is in the lover as a certain inclination or impulse in that the lover is inclined toward the beloved. So the divine person who proceeds according to love is called "spirit," since this name "implies a certain vital movement and impulse."[63] Using the analogy of immanent motion, Aquinas is able to characterize the blessed Trinity as a never-ceasing yet ever-unchanging life of unbounded wisdom and love. As Thomas Merton says, evoking Aquinas's theology, "The One God Who exists only in Three Persons is a circle of relations in which His infinite reality, Love, is ever identical and ever renewed, always perfect and always total, always beginning and never ending, absolute, everlasting and full."[64]

The second objection entails transient motion considered on the part

61. On the nature of immanent and transient motion, see appendix 1.
62. See *ST* I, 27, 1–4; *ST* I, 42, 5.
63. *ST* I, 27, 4, co.
64. Thomas Merton, *New Seeds of Contemplation* (New York: New Directions, 2007), 68.

of the agent. It arises from a scriptural passage: "Wisdom is more movable than all movable things."[65] Since God is wisdom itself, it seems that God must be movable. Aquinas explains that such motion is predicated of divine wisdom insofar as it is the efficient and exemplar cause of all things. Since every agent "effects something similar to itself to the extent that it is an agent," divine wisdom produces creatures that are similar to itself, "diffusing its similitude even to the most remote things."[66] Since creatures participate in divine being and goodness in varying degrees, there is said to be a sort of procession or motion of divine wisdom into all things from the highest to the lowest. Since such motion implies neither imperfection nor potency, it may be attributed to God.

Thomas uses this kind of motion to model God's causality in creating and governing the universe. The missions of the Son and the Holy Spirit, especially the sending of the Son in the Incarnation, are also framed in terms of this motion.[67] Using this analogy, Aquinas agrees with Pseudo-Dionysius that God can be said "to be moved [*moveri*]" and to be made "outside himself [*extra seipsum*]" in his ecstatic love for creatures.[68]

The third objection concerns transient motion considered on the part of the receiver. The objection is again based on a scriptural passage that seems to attribute motion to God: "Draw near to God and he will draw near to you."[69] Aquinas explains that, although such motion implies imperfection, it really belongs to the creature and is said of God only metaphorically or "by transference." In our relationship with God, we are the ones who change—growing colder or warmer, wandering away and returning. Such motion on our part is sometimes described as a change in God. Here we find the rich metaphorical language of religious experience. As metaphor, however, it implies no imperfection when predicated of God.

In showing God's perfection, Aquinas gives three arguments for de-

65. Wis 7:24.
66. *ST* I, 4, 3, co.; *ST* I, 9, 1, ad 2.
67. *ST* I, 43, 1–3 and 5; *ST* III, 1, 1, ad 1; *Sent.* I, 15, 1, 1, ad 1 and ad 4; *Sent.* I, 4, 1, co.; *Sent.* I, 16, 1, 1, ad 1; *SCG* II, c.1.2–3; *SCG* IV, c.23.4. See also Thomas G. Weinandy, OFM Cap., *Does God Change? The Word's Becoming in the Incarnation* (Still River, Mass.: St. Bede's Publications, 1985).
68. *In de div. nom.* IX, lect. 4, nos. 840–41; *In de div. nom.* IV, lect. 10, no. 437; *ST* I, 20, 2, ad 1.
69. Jas 4:8.

nying divine motion and three ways of affirming it. Here, he agrees with Pseudo-Dionysius that "not only do theologians attribute motion to God, but it is also granted us that we may fittingly praise the motion of the immovable God."[70]

Eternity

The attribute of eternity follows logically on immutability.[71] Aquinas agrees with Boethius in defining eternity as "the simultaneously whole and perfect possession of interminable life."[72] To get a handle on this definition, we have to do another of those mind-bending theological exercises in which we deny one thing, then deny the denial, and finally affirm whatever is left!

Boethius's definition involves a tension between "interminable" and "simultaneously whole." "Interminable" conjures up images of unending extension—like an infinite line. "Simultaneously whole" suggests completion and self-containment with no succession—like a dot. So, to picture eternity, we have to imagine an infinitely extended (yet unextended) dot, or an unending succession that has no succession: "Thus eternity is known from two sources: first, because what is eternal is interminable—that is, has no beginning nor end (that is, no term either way); secondly, because eternity has no succession, being simultaneously whole."[73] If you have no idea of what an infinitely extended dot might look like, or what it could possibly mean to speak of an unending succession that has no succession, then you probably have a pretty good idea of eternity—since we really have no idea what eternity is.

Still, we can at least point in the direction of eternity if we begin with motion—a phenomenon that is mysterious enough in itself but at the same time more familiar to us than eternity. Suppose you throw a rock. You can ask, "How far did it go?" This is a distance question. You'll get an answer in terms of distance—perhaps the rock went "ten feet." But what's a foot? It's an arbitrary measurement of distance that we still hang onto in the United States while the rest of the world has gone metric. Returning

70. *In de div. nom.* IX, lect. 4, no. 841.
71. *ST* I, 9, prologue.
72. *ST* I, 10, 1.
73. *ST* I, 10, 1, co.

to the rock, you might also ask, "How long did the motion of the rock last?" This is a time question. You'll get an answer in terms of time. Perhaps the motion of the rock lasted "three seconds." But what's a second? It's again an arbitrary measurement, but luckily one that the whole world seems to agree on. It's associated with some particular motion—generally a division of the daily rotation of the earth on its axis, or the yearly rotation of the earth around the sun, or the energy levels of the cesium atom in an atomic clock. Aristotle defines time as the "measure of motion."[74] To measure time, you choose the duration of some arbitrary motion and use it as your unit to measure the duration of all other motions.

Now that we know what time is, we can use it to get a clue about eternity. We set up a kind of proportion: as motion is to time, so immutability is to eternity:

motion : time :: immutability : eternity

As time is the measure of the duration of motion, so eternity is the corresponding (*quasi*) measure of the "duration" of that which has no motion: "As therefore the idea of time consists in the numbering of before and after in movement; so likewise in the apprehension of the uniformity of what is outside of movement, consists the idea of eternity."[75]

Now that we have a notion of eternity, we can make short work of affirming divine eternity: "The idea of eternity follows immutability, as the idea of time follows movement.... Hence, as God is supremely immutable, it supremely belongs to him to be eternal."[76] Though we conceive of eternity as a kind of "measure" of the immutable, corresponding to time as the measure of motion, we must remember that such ideas, however helpful, are only in our minds, and that in reality God is in no way measured: "Eternity is nothing else but God himself. Hence God is not called eternal, as if he were in any way measured; but the idea of measurement is there taken according to the apprehension of our mind

---

74. "For time is just this—number of motion in respect of 'before' and 'after'" (*Phys.* IV, c. 11 [2019b 1–2]).

75. *ST* I, 10, 1, co.

76. *ST* I, 10, 2. co.

alone."[77] By his eternity, God is again absolutely distinguished from creatures.[78]

One caveat is needed here: it is very easy to mistake the eternal for the everlasting.[79] What is everlasting belongs to time: it just happens to go on forever and ever in the past and the future. To think of God as simply existing forever and ever in the past and the future is to subject God to time and understand him as an everlasting temporal being rather than as an eternal being.[80] As eternal, God is utterly outside of time—present to all of time at once, and not subject to a moment-by-moment existence. Since it is much easier on the brain to think of God as everlasting rather than eternal, this has become a common theological mistake.[81]

Unity

Today, monotheism is challenged by the reappearance of polytheism. Neopaganism is becoming more popular in certain circles, while religious pluralism sometimes asserts that the gods of all religions are somehow the same.[82] Of course, Christians are also capable of turning something oth-

77. *ST* I, 10, 2, ad 3.

78. "Eternity truly and properly so called is in God alone, because eternity follows on immutability.... But God alone is altogether immutable" (*ST* I, 10, 3, co.).

79. See Brian J. Shanley, OP, "Eternity and Duration in Aquinas," *Thomist* 61, no. 4 (1997): 525–48.

80. "It is manifest that time and eternity are not the same. Some have founded this difference on the fact that eternity has neither beginning nor an end; whereas time has a beginning and an end. This, however, makes a merely accidental, and not an absolute difference because, granted that time always was and always will be, according to the idea of those who think the movement of the heavens goes on for ever, there would yet remain a difference between eternity and time ... arising from the fact that eternity is simultaneously whole; which cannot be applied to time: for eternity is the measure of a permanent being; while time is a measure of movement" (*ST* I, 10, 4, co.).

81. For arguments for and against introducing a temporal dimension into God, see Christian Tapp and Edmund Runggaldier, eds., *God, Eternity, and Time* (Burlington, Vt.: Ashgate, 2011); William Lane Craig, *Time and Eternity: Exploring God's Relationship to Time* (Wheaton, Ill.: Crossway Books, 2001); Eleonore Stump and Norman Kretzmann, "Eternity," *Journal of Philosophy* 78, no. 8 (1981): 429–58.

82. John Hick argues that different religions "constitute different ways of experiencing, conceiving, and living in relation to an ultimate divine Reality which transcends all our varied visions of it" (John Hick, *An Interpretation of Religion: Human Responses to the Transcendent,* 2nd ed. [New Haven, Conn.: Yale University Press, 2004], 235–36). On neopaganism, see Hugh B. Urban, *New Age, Neopagan, and New Religious Movements: Alternative Spirituality in Contemporary America* (Oakland, Calif.: University of California Press, 2015); Carl E. Braaten and Robert W. Jenson, eds., *Either/Or: The Gospel or Neopaganism* (Grand Rapids, Mich.: Eerdmans, 1995).

er than God into their supreme good: "For many, of whom I have often told you and now tell you even with tears, live as enemies of the cross of Christ. Their end is destruction, their god is the belly, and they glory in their shame, with minds set on earthly things."[83]

Aquinas's brief discussion of divine unity remains, therefore, quite timely. He founds his argument theologically on the scriptural passage which grounds Jewish monotheism: "It is written: 'Hear, O Israel, the Lord our God is one Lord.'"[84] Aquinas has already shown that God contains all perfection of being. But if there were many gods, they would have to differ from one another. One would therefore have some perfection or quality the other lacked. The one lacking it would be less than perfect and therefore less than God. So it is impossible for there to be many gods.[85] Aquinas sees divine unity as both good theology and good philosophy: "Hence also the ancient philosophers, constrained as it were by truth, when they asserted an infinite principle, asserted likewise that there was only one such principle."[86] God's absolute unity again distinguishes him from creatures:

Since *one* is an undivided being, if anything is supremely *one* it must be supremely being, and supremely undivided. Now both of these belong to God. For he is supremely being, inasmuch as his being is not determined by any nature to which it is adjoined; since he is being itself, subsistent, absolutely undetermined. But he is supremely undivided inasmuch as he is divided neither actually nor potentially, by any mode of division; since he is altogether simple.... Hence it is manifest that God is *one* in the supreme degree.[87]

83. Phil 3:18–19.
84. Dt 6:4. See *ST* I, 11, 3, sed contra.
85. *ST* I, 11, 3, co.
86. *ST* I, 11, 3, co.
87. *ST* I, 11, 4, co.

KNOWING AND NAMING GOD

Aquinas's pedagogy in writing for "beginners" seems to involve a certain amount of "learning by doing." As a teacher, he firmly believes in the power of examples.[1] We might look at Questions 2–11 as a sustained example or practical exercise in knowing and speaking about God.[2] Once his students have been engaged in this activity for some time, he then explains the principles behind it. First, he considers how we can know God (*ST* I, 12) and then how we name or speak of him, since "everything is named by us according to our knowledge of it."[3]

---

1. "Anyone can experience this of himself, that when he tries to understand something, he forms certain phantasms to serve him by way of examples, in which as it were he examines what he is desirous of understanding. For this reason it is that when we wish to help someone to understand something, we lay examples before him, from which he forms phantasms for the purpose of understanding" (*ST* I, 84, 7, co.). See also *ST* I, 89, 1, co.; *ST* I, 117, 1, co.

2. "The questions that follow in this part of the *Summa* are exercises in the logic of speaking about the unknowable God" (McGinn, *Thomas*, 82).

3. *ST* I, 13, prologue.

Knowing God

In discussing the divine attributes, Aquinas uses the perspective of our present life in which "we cannot know what God is, but rather what he is not."[4] When he begins his formal consideration of our knowledge of God, he shifts to an eschatological perspective and asks whether a created intellect can ever see the essence of God. This was a hotly debated question that the medievals inherited from the Greek and Latin Church Fathers.[5] To say that humans can know the ineffable God sounds presumptuous, but denying it seems to defeat the deepest desire of our hearts. The Bible offers little direct help in resolving the issue since it says both that "no one has ever seen God" and that "we shall see him as he is."[6] St. Albert the Great struggled with the question and came up with a different answer from Aquinas's.[7] Emphasizing the way of negation, he concludes that, even in the life to come, "God is seen precisely in our ignorance of him."[8] Aquinas, however, is convinced that the next life will answer his haunting childhood question: "What is God?"

Reading Aquinas's serene response to the question of whether any created intellect can see the essence of God, one would never guess that such a controversy was boiling beneath the surface. He answers the question affirmatively, drawing again upon what we know of God through the Five Ways. The First Way taught us that, as the ultimate cause of motion, "God is pure act without any admixture of potency." As pure act, God is "supremely knowable" since "everything is knowable according as it is actual."[9] Yet something knowable in itself may not be knowable to a particular intellect. In our present state, we cannot know the divine essence, but in the life to come we will know not only *that* God is but also *what* God is:

4. *ST* I, 3, prologue.
5. See Torrell, *Saint Thomas*, 2:27–31; Tugwell, *Albert and Thomas*, 39–95.
6. Jn 1:18; 1 Jn 3:2.
7. Tugwell, *Albert and Thomas*, 94–95.
8. Albert the Great, *Commentary on the First Epistle of Dionysius*, as quoted in Tugwell, *Albert and Thomas*, 92.
9. *ST* I, 12, 1, co.

The statements of Dionysius and of Damascene should be understood as referring to the vision had in this life, in which a person sees God through some form or other. Since this form falls short of representing the divine essence, the latter cannot be seen through it. All that is known is that God transcends this intellectual representation of him. Consequently, that which God is remains hidden; and this is the most exalted mode of knowledge that we can attain while we are in this life. Hence, we do not know what God is, but only what he is not. But the divine essence represents itself sufficiently, and therefore, when it becomes, as it were, the form of the intellect, the intellect knows not only what God is not, but also what he is.[10]

To say that the human intellect can never see God would not only disappoint Thomas's boyhood wish; it would also contradict both the revealed truth—that our beatitude is found in God—and the truth of reason—that our natural desire can find its fulfillment only in the first cause, who is God.[11]

Having established that it is possible for the human intellect to see the divine essence, Aquinas makes a number of qualifications. Although we will see God, we will not "comprehend" him.[12] Also, the divine essence will not be seen through any created similitude or concept but only through union with the divine essence itself. Such union, however, requires "the light of glory" whereby "the intellect is made capable of seeing God."[13] The created intellect cannot see the divine essence by its own natural powers.[14] Although many may see the divine essence, some will see more perfectly than others, not because of their intellectual acumen but because of their capacity to love: "He will have a fuller participation of the light of glory who has more charity; because where there is the greater charity, there is the more desire; and desire in a certain degree makes the one desiring apt and prepared to receive the object desired. Hence he who possesses the more charity, will see God the more perfectly, and will be the more beatified."[15]

10. *De ver.* 8, 1, ad 8.
11. See *ST* I, 12, 1, co.
12. "It does not follow that [God] cannot be known at all, but that he exceeds every kind of knowledge; which means that he is not comprehended" (*ST* I, 12, 1, ad 3). See also Torrell, *Saint Thomas*, 2:29–30.
13. *ST* I, 12, 2, co.
14. *ST* I, 12, 4.
15. *ST* I, 12, 6, co.

While affirming that humans may enjoy the vision of God in heaven, Aquinas makes it clear that no one can see the divine essence in this life. His reason is founded on his conviction that we are bodily beings—even our soul, "as long as we live in this life, has its being in corporeal matter." Since "the mode of knowledge follows the mode of the nature of the knower," our soul (intellect) "knows only what has a form in matter, or what can be known by such a form." Since the divine essence "cannot be known through the nature of material things," it is "impossible for the soul of man in this life to see the essence of God."[16]

Still, it is possible to know God in this life by natural reason. Here again, Aquinas invokes revelation to ground his claim: "It is written (Rom 1:19), 'That which is known of God,' namely, what can be known of God by natural reason, 'is manifest in them.'"[17] Moving swiftly from the heights of revelation, Aquinas does not hesitate to acknowledge that humans, although capable of reason, are mere animals and that our knowledge begins, like that of other animals, with sensation. It is remarkable how far he allows our knowledge, although beginning with sensation, to take us.

Our natural knowledge begins from sense. Hence our natural knowledge can go as far as it can be led by sensible things. But our mind cannot be led by sense so far as to see the essence of God; because the sensible effects of God do not equal the power of God as their cause. Hence from the knowledge of sensible things the whole power of God cannot be known; nor therefore can his essence be seen. But because they are his effects and depend on their cause, we can be led from them so far as to know of God "whether he exists," and to know of him what must necessarily belong to him, as the first cause of all things, exceeding all things caused by him. Hence we know of him his relationship with creatures so far as to be the cause of them all; also that creatures differ from him, inasmuch as he is not in any way part of what is caused by him; and that creatures are not removed from him by reason of any defect on his part, but because he superexceeds them all.[18]

Here we have the key to our knowledge of God in this life. Without mentioning Pseudo-Dionysius, Aquinas has listed his three ways by which

16. *ST* I, 12, 11, co.
17. *ST* I, 12, 12, sed contra.
18. *ST* I, 12, 12, co.

we know God: causality, negation, and eminence.[19] Beginning with creatures, we come to know God as "the cause of them all" (the way of causality), and that "creatures differ from him" (the way of negation), and that he "superexceeds them all" (the way of eminence).

As a theologian, Aquinas readily allows that even in this life we can know God more perfectly by grace than natural reason. The light of reason may be "strengthened by the infusion of gratuitous light," and our imagination may be given "prophetic visions," and our senses may perceive phenomena that are "divinely formed to express some divine meaning; as in the Baptism, the Holy Spirit was seen in the shape of a dove."[20] In Aquinas's discussion, we find an ongoing dialectic of knowing and unknowing, affirming and denying. In this life "we cannot know of God what he is, and thus are united to him as to one unknown." Yet "we know him more fully according as many and more excellent of his effects are demonstrated to us, and according as we attribute to him some things known by divine revelation, to which natural reason cannot reach, as, for instance, that God is Three in One."[21] Still, our limitations remain: "Neither a Catholic nor a pagan knows the very nature of God as it is in itself; but each one knows it according to some idea of causality, or excellence, or remotion."[22]

Naming God

Since we cannot know what God is, Aquinas will be concerned here not so much with what God *is,* but with what we can *say* about him. His concern is to show how what we say may be true, even when we do not comprehend what we are saying.[23] Since we use nouns, verbs, pronouns, and

19. For the many places where Aquinas refers to the threefold ways of Pseudo-Dionysius, see Dodds, *Unchanging God,* 116n238; Fran O'Rourke, *Pseudo-Dionysius and the Metaphysics of Aquinas* (Leiden: Brill, 1992), 31–41.

20. *ST* I, 12, 13, co. In addition, God may always act miraculously to raise a human being, even in this life, to a vision of himself: "As God works miracles in corporeal things, so also he does supernatural wonders above the common order, raising the minds of some living in the flesh beyond the use of sense, even up to the vision of his own essence" (*ST* I, 12, 11, ad 2).

21. *ST* I, 12, 13, ad 1.

22. *ST* I, 13, 10, ad 5.

23. We know that our statement is true when we say, "God is good," even though we cannot comprehend divine goodness, just as we know that our statement is true when we say, "God

participles to say things, much of his discussion will be concerned with grammatical issues.[24]

He follows Aristotle's epistemology, in which human knowledge begins with things that are perceived by the senses, which in turn give rise to concepts of our understanding, which are then expressed in words. Since our words are related to things through the medium of our concepts, "it follows that we can give a name to anything in as far as we can understand it."[25] Although we cannot know the divine essence, we do know God from creatures by the ways of causality, negation, and eminence. So we can name or speak about God without pretending to know God's essence.[26]

The next question is whether our words can really apply to the divine substance (essence) even though it remains unknown to us.[27] Since we have three ways of naming God, we can consider how far each of them gets us. The ways of causality and negation are focused on creaturely qualities and either name God as the cause of such qualities (way of causality) or deny that such qualities are found in God (way of negation). Important as these ways are, they don't get us to the divine essence. Consideration of the way of eminence brings us back to the Fourth Way, where God was discovered as "truest, best, noblest, and uttermost being" and consequently "the cause of being, goodness, and every other perfection to all other beings."[28] Since the effect must in some way resemble the agent, "all created things, so far as they are beings, are like God as the first and

---

is," even though we do not comprehend the being or "is" of God: "*To be* can mean either of two things. It may mean the act of essence, or it may mean the composition of a proposition effected by the mind in joining a predicate to a subject. Taking *to be* in the first sense, we cannot understand God's existence nor his essence; but only in the second sense. We know that this proposition which we form about God when we say *God is,* is true; and this we know from his effects" (*ST* I, 3, 4, ad 2). "In this chapter, however, I shall explain how the *Summa Theologiae*'s teaching on God is shot through with the conviction that those who speak about God do not know what they are talking about regardless of whether they say 'God exists' or 'God does not exist'" (Brian Davies, OP, "The *Summa Theologiae* on What God Is Not," in *Aquinas's "Summa Theologiae": A Critical Guide,* ed. Jeffrey Hause [Cambridge: Cambridge University Press, 2018], 47).

24. See, for example, *ST* I, 13, 1, ad 3.

25. *ST* I, 13, 1, co.

26. The very name "God" is said by way of causality, negation, and eminence. See *ST* I, 13, 8, ad 2.

27. *ST* I, 13, 2.

28. *ST* I, 2, 3, co.

universal principle of all being."[29] So every creature is like God "insofar as it possesses some perfection" and represents God "as the excelling principle of whose form the effects fall short, although they derive some kind of likeness thereto."[30] Our names for such creaturely perfections therefore "signify the divine substance, but in an imperfect manner, even as creatures represent it imperfectly."[31] So, when we say that God is good, we don't just mean that God is not bad (way of negation), or that God is the cause of goodness in creatures (way of causality), but that "whatever good we attribute to creatures pre-exists in God in a more excellent and higher way" (way of eminence).[32]

So the way of eminence allows us to name the divine substance, but there are still a couple of qualifications. Our words (or "names") signify perfections, such as goodness, but only according to the way we know them. When we apply them to God, therefore, we have to take into account both "the thing signified" by the name (the perfection as it exists in God) and the "mode of signification" (our limited human way of knowing that perfection as we find it in creatures). However true our assertion is when we say things like "God is good" and however much we know that we are speaking the truth, we can never get out of our own heads to know what divine goodness is: we know it only according to our limited way of knowing goodness in creatures. As Aquinas explains: "As regards what is signified by these names, they belong properly to God, and more properly than they belong to creatures, and are applied primarily to him. But as regards their mode of signification, they do not properly and strictly apply to God; for their mode of signification applies to creatures."[33]

Names such as "goodness" that imply no imperfection regarding the thing signified may be applied literally to God. Sometimes, however, the thing signified by the name (e.g., "rock") also implies imperfection. Such names may be applied to God only metaphorically, as when we say, "Be my rock and refuge."[34] Still, metaphorical statements often lead us closer

29. *ST* I, 4, 3, co.
30. *ST* I, 13, 2, co.
31. *ST* I, 13, 2, co.
32. *ST* I, 13, 2, co.
33. *ST* I, 13, 3, co.
34. Ps 71:3.

to the truth about God than our dowdy prosaic formulations do.[35] The upshot is that we can speak of the divine substance, that not all our names are metaphorical, and that some can be applied to God literally.[36]

Analogy

Once we know *that* we can name God, we have to consider *how* we name him. What do our words mean when we take them from the realm of creatures and move them to the divine context—when, instead of saying, "the burger is good," we say, "God is good"? There are three possibilities. They might mean (1) exactly the same thing (univocal meaning), (2) something totally different (equivocal meaning), or (3) something that is in some ways the same and in some ways different (analogous meaning).[37] We can rule out univocity since God is certainly not "good" in the same way as the Whopper.[38] We can also rule out equivocation unless we want to reduce our God-talk to babble and confusion. Just as the "bark" of a tree is totally different from and tells us nothing about the "bark" of a dog, so the "goodness" of the creature would tell us nothing about the "goodness" of God if the terms were equivocal.

The third possibility is that names are used of God and creatures "in an

35. "It is befitting Holy Writ to put forward divine and spiritual truths by means of comparisons with material things. For God provides for everything according to the capacity of its nature. Now it is natural to man to attain to intellectual truths through sensible objects, because all our knowledge originates from sense. Hence in Holy Writ, spiritual truths are fittingly taught under the likeness of material things. . . . It is also befitting Holy Writ, which is proposed to all without distinction of persons . . . that spiritual truths be expounded by means of figures taken from corporeal things, in order that thereby even the simple who are unable by themselves to grasp intellectual things may be able to understand it" (*ST* I, 1, 9, co.).

36. See *ST* I, 13, 3, ad 1; *ST* I, 13, 6. Some contemporary theologians argue that all theological language is only metaphorical. For instance, Sallie McFague argues that "no language about God is adequate and all of it is improper," and that "no authority—not scriptural status, liturgical longevity, nor ecclesiastical fiat—can decree that some types of language, or some images, refer literally to God while others do not. None do" (McFague, *Models*, 35). On the merits and limits of metaphorical language, see Dodds, *Unchanging God*, 139–42.

37. "Univocal terms mean absolutely the same thing, but equivocal terms absolutely different; whereas in analogical terms a word taken in one signification must be placed in the definition of the same word taken in other senses; as, for instance, . . . 'healthy' applied to animal is placed in the definition of healthy as applied to urine and medicine. For urine is the sign of health in the animal, and medicine is the cause of health" (*ST* I, 13, 10, co.).

38. At least we *should* be able to rule out univocity, but we will find that it keeps cropping up in contemporary theology, in which God's knowledge, love, compassion, and action are often assumed to be fundamentally the same as ours, as we will see in succeeding chapters.

analogous sense, that is, according to proportion."[39] Names are used analogously in two basic ways. The first way is "according as many things are proportionate to one."[40] Here there is an analogy among the names applied to many things because of their various relationships to one thing. In Aquinas's example, "healthy" may be applied to medicine and urine since both are related in some way to one thing: the "healthy" animal.[41] Note that the many things don't have to be related in the same way to the one. Medicine is called healthy as the cause of health in the animal, while urine is the sign of health. The word "healthy" is analogous among all the things that may be said to be healthy in relation to the animal, as illustrated in figure 3-1. Note that one thing (the healthy animal) is our key to understanding the word "health" as applied to the others. What health means as applied to the animal is contained in its meaning as applied to medicine and urine: "Thus *healthy* as applied to animals comes into the definition of *healthy* as applied to medicine, which is called healthy as being the cause of health in the animal; and also into the definition of *healthy* which is applied to urine, which is called healthy in so far as it is the sign of the animal's health."[42]

39. *ST* I, 13, 5, co. On analogy in Aquinas, see Ralph McInerny, *Aquinas and Analogy* (Washington, D.C.: The Catholic University of America Press, 1996); David B. Burrell, CSC, *Analogy and Philosophical Language* (New Haven, Conn.: Yale University Press, 1973); William J. Hill, OP, *Knowing the Unknown God* (New York: Philosophical Library, 1971); Gregory P. Rocca, *Speaking the Incomprehensible God: Thomas Aquinas on the Interplay of Positive and Negative Theology* (Washington, D.C.: The Catholic University of America Press, 2004); Steven A. Long, *Analogia Entis: On the Analogy of Being, Metaphysics, and the Act of Faith* (Notre Dame, Ind.: University of Notre Dame Press, 2011); Brian Davies, OP, "Aquinas on What God Is Not," in *Thomas Aquinas: Contemporary Philosophical Perspectives*, ed. Brian Davies, OP (Oxford: Oxford University Press, 2002), 227–42; Reinhard Hütter, "Attending to the Wisdom of God—from Effect to Cause, from Creation to God: A *Relecture* of the Analogy of Being according to Thomas Aquinas," in *The Analogy of Being: Invention of the Antichrist or the Wisdom of God?* ed. Thomas Joseph White, OP (Grand Rapids, Mich.: Eerdmans, 2011), 209–45.

40. *ST* I, 13, 5, co.

41. Although the "four humors" of medieval medicine have disappeared along with the crystalline spheres, urine is still seen as a sign of health or pathology. See "Urine Color," Mayo Clinic, last modified October 27, 2017, https://www.mayoclinic.org/diseases-conditions/urine-color/symptoms-causes/syc-20367333.

42. *ST* I, 13, 6, co. "When anything is predicated of many things univocally, it is found in each of them according to its proper nature; as animal is found in each species of animal. But when anything is predicated of many things analogically, it is found in only one of them according to its proper nature, and from this one the rest are denominated. So healthiness is predicated of animal, of urine, and of medicine, not that health is found anywhere else except in the animal [*non quod sanitas sit nisi in animali tantum*]; but from the health of the animal, medicine is called healthy, in so far as it is the cause of health, and urine is called healthy, in so far as it indicates health. And

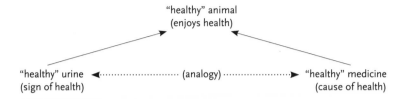

Figure 3-1. Analogy of Many to One

Since health belongs properly to the animal, we can call the animal the "prime analogate."[43]

The second way that names may be used analogously is "according as one thing is proportionate to another."[44] Here the analogy arises not among many things related in some way to one thing, but simply because of the relationship of one thing to another. Aquinas gives the example of "health" as applied to just two things: medicine and animal. "Health," which belongs properly to the animal, may also be said of medicine as the cause of the animal's health, as shown in figure 3-2. The organism is again the prime analogate, but now we posit an analogy between the health of the organism and medicine as the cause of its health.[45]

---

although health is neither in medicine nor in urine, yet in either there is something whereby the one causes, and the other indicates health" (*ST* I, 16, 6, co.). (I have modified the translation of the Benziger edition slightly. See St. Thomas Aquinas, *Summa Theologiae*, trans. Thomas Gornall, SJ [London: Eyre and Spottiswoode, 1964], 4:91).

43. "In names predicated of many in an analogical sense, all are predicated because they have reference to some one thing; and this one thing must be placed in the definition of them all" (*ST* I, 13, 6, co.). "In predications of this sort that to which a term is primarily and intrinsically applied is fittingly called the 'prime analogate;' the items to which it is then referred are termed 'secondary analogates'" (James F. Anderson, *Reflections on the Analogy of Being* [The Hague: Martinus Nijhoff, 1967], 15).

44. *ST* I, 13, 5, co.

45. Etienne Gilson explains this well: "Analogy or proportion, as conceived by St. Thomas, is to be found in two principal cases. First, several things are in relation to one other thing, although their relations to this other are different. There is said to be analogy among the names of these things because they are all in relation to the same thing. So we can speak of a healthy medicine and a healthy urine. The urine is healthy because it is a sign of health; a medicine is healthy because it is the cause of health. There is, then, analogy between all things that are healthy, in no matter what sense they are so, because whatever is healthy is so in relation to the state of healthiness in a living being. In the second case it is no longer a question of analogy or proportion binding together several things because they are all in relation to another thing, but of the analogy binding one thing

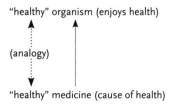

Figure 3-2. Analogy of One Thing to Another

Only in this second way does Aquinas allow that "some things are said of God and creatures analogically, and not in a purely equivocal nor in a purely univocal sense."[46] The reason is that when we apply names to God to speak of the divine essence or substance, God must always be the prime analogate. Whatever perfection we name must belong primarily to God and secondarily to the creature. So God is supreme goodness, while goodness belongs to the creature insofar as it reflects or participates in the divine goodness that is its cause: "The words, *God is good*, or *wise* signify ... that these exist in him in a more excellent way. Hence as regards what the name signifies, these names are applied primarily to God rather than to creatures, because these perfections flow from God to creatures."[47]

This means that in speaking of God, we may not think of analogy as a relationship of *many* things to *one*, placing God among the *many* in relationship to *one* that is something other than God—as if, for instance, divine goodness and creaturely goodness were analogous in virtue of some absolute goodness that transcends both, as suggested in figure 3-3. To ensure that we do not make God just one of many analogates, Aquinas specifies that, when speaking of God, we should use analogy in the

---

to another because of the relationship uniting them. For example, we speak of a healthy medicine and a healthy person because this medicine causes the health of this person. It is no longer here the analogy of the sign and of the cause of one and the same thing (urine and medicament), but rather the analogy of the cause and its effect. Certainly, when we say that a medicine is healthy, we are not pretending that it is in good health; the term 'healthy' is not therefore purely univocal in the remedy and in the sick person. But the remedy is nevertheless healthy, since it causes health. Thus the term 'healthy' is not purely equivocal in the remedy and the sick person" (Gilson, *Christian Philosophy*, 106.)

46. *ST* I, 13, 5, co.
47. *ST* I, 13, 6, co.

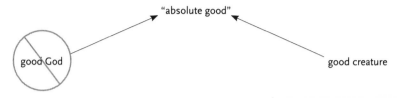

Figure 3-3. God and the Analogy of Many to One

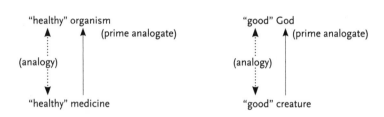

Figure 3-4. God and the Analogy of One to Another

second way, not "as many things are proportionate to one" but "according as one thing is proportionate to another."[48] As healthy medicine refers to the healthy organism as the prime analogate, so the goodness of the creature refers to divine goodness as the prime analogate. As health belongs primarily to the animal and in a secondary sense to medicine, so goodness (and every other perfection) always belongs primarily to God and in a secondary sense to creatures, as shown in figure 3-4.[49]

The foundation of all such analogous language is God's causality. We take words like "good" and "wise" that we know in their creaturely

48. *ST* I, 13, 5, co. "When we turn now to the analogical predication of God, we need to keep in mind that, according to Thomas's mature doctrine, such analogical predication occurs exclusively on the basis of this latter analogy of *unius ad alterum*" (Hütter, "Attending," 236).

49. Aquinas's example can be a bit confusing since the lines of causality seem reversed: medicine is the cause of health in the animal, while God is the cause of goodness in the creature. It would have been easier if Aquinas had again used the example of urine: the healthy animal is the cause of healthy urine, while the good God is the cause of the good creature. Still, Aquinas's example works (of course) if we remember that the point of the example is that, as "health" is applied in a secondary sense to medicine and primarily to the animal, so "goodness" is applied in a secondary sense to the creature and in a primary sense to God.

context and then apply them to God. Since God is the cause of the creature, the creature is (in some way) like God. Since the word describes the creature, and the creature is like God, the word can also (in some way) describe God: "Whatever is said of God and creatures is said according to the relation of a creature to God as its principle and cause, wherein all perfections of things pre-exist excellently."[50] Although there can be no numerical or quantitative proportion or likeness between God and creatures (as if God were simply bigger and better), there is a kind of proportion or likeness in that God is the cause of the creature.[51] Analogy is based on this proportion and provides "a mean between pure equivocation and simple univocation. For in analogies the idea is not, as it is in univocals, one and the same, yet it is not totally diverse as in equivocals; but a term which is thus used in a multiple sense signifies various proportions to some one thing."[52]

Analogy is essential when we try to speak of God, but it is easily misunderstood. For instance, in Aquinas's examples of "healthy" applied to an animal, medicine, and urine, only the animal is properly healthy. Neither medicine nor urine can be said to enjoy good health. So it might seem that, when "good" is applied to God and creatures, only God and not creatures can properly be called good. Aquinas explains, however, that even though everything is called good in view of divine goodness, every creature—everything that has being—still has its own goodness and can properly be called good:

It is absolutely true that there is first something which is essentially being and essentially good, which we call God.... Hence from the first being, essentially such, and good, everything can be called good and a being, inasmuch as it participates in it by way of a certain assimilation which is far removed and defective.... Everything is therefore called good from the divine goodness, as from the first exemplary, effective and final principle of all goodness. Nevertheless, everything is called good by reason of the similitude of the divine goodness belonging to it, which is formally its own goodness, whereby it is denominated good. And so of all things there is one goodness, and yet many goodnesses.[53]

50. *ST* I, 13, 5, co.
51. See *ST* I, 12, 1, ad 4.
52. *ST* I, 13, 5, co.
53. "Et sic est bonitas una omnium; et etiam multae bonitates" (*ST* I, 6, 4, co.). As William Wallace explains: "In attribution, which is sometimes referred to as two- or three-term analogy,

The Relation between God and Creatures

The topic of God's relationship to creatures comes up in Aquinas's discussion of how we should understand scriptural language that seems to imply change or temporality in God. The psalms proclaim, "Lord, you have become our refuge."[54] More broadly, God seems to "become" creator, savior, and deliverer only when he creates, saves and delivers us. Aquinas asserts that "God was not *Lord* until he had a creature subject to himself."[55] Such language is needed to describe God's relationship to creatures, but how can it be reconciled with the doctrine of God's immutability and eternity?

To parse this out, Aquinas considers the nature of "relation." Just as we employ the analogy of creaturely goodness to speak of divine goodness, so we must use the analogy of creaturely relation to speak of relation in God.[56] Among creatures, every relation involves two terms, in each of

---

a perfection is predicated of each analogate, but one analogate is primary with respect to the other(s), and the perfection of the primary is attributed to the others by virtue of some relationship to the primary, usually that of causality. If the perfection is predicated properly and instrinsically of only the primary analogate and not of the other(s), the analogy is called *extrinsic attribution*; an example would be 'healthy' as said of man and then attributed to other subjects because of some causal relationship to health in man, e.g., healthy food, healthy exercise, etc. If the perfection is attributed properly and intrinsically of all analogates, on the other hand, even though one is primary, the analogy is called *intrinsic attribution*; an example would be 'is' or being as attributed to substance and accident, for here the being that is primary in substance is predicated properly of accident as dependent upon substantial being" (William A. Wallace, *The Elements of Philosophy: A Compendium for Philosophers and Theologians* [New York: Alba House, 1977], 90). Wallace goes on to explain the merits of the analogy of intrinsic attribution: "In contrast to the formal or static analogy of proportions, the analogy of intrinsic attribution is dynamic in that it is based explicitly on causality and dependency. To extend the example of existence of substance and accidents to that of subsistent being, *esse* belongs properly to *ipsum esse subsistens* alone, but it is predicated of other beings because they receive their *esse* in dependence on subsistent being itself. Such analogy is called intrinsic attribution because each being really does have *esse* intrinsically, even though it is from another.... Despite this 'inner' or intrinsic aspect, however, whenever analogy of attribution is used it also emphasizes the 'otherness' of the characteristic participated. Accidents are beings by participation in the *esse* of substance, and all beings are such by participation in the *esse* of subsistent being. In this way the analogy of proper proportionality can be seen to be related to, and to presuppose, the analogy of intrinsic attribution in the order of being. The use of both allows subsistent being to be transcendent or 'other,' when compared to other beings, and at the same time it allows *esse* to be participated and thus to be immanent or 'within' other beings" (Ibid., 126).

54. Ps 89:1, as quoted in *ST* I, 13, 7, ad 2.

55. *ST* I, 13, 7, ad 6.

56. On the nature of the relationship between God and creation in Thomas Aquinas, see Michael J. Dodds, OP, "Ultimacy and Intimacy: Aquinas on the Relation between God and the

which the relation may be real or merely logical (of idea only). This gives rise to three distinct types of relationship: (1) of idea only in both terms, (2) real in both terms, and (3) of idea only in one term and real in the other.[57] If the relation is of idea only in both terms, then the relation is purely conceptual and exists only in the mind and not in the thing. The relationship of identity is of this sort. A thing that is actually one is considered as two and so said to be "identical" with itself.[58] This relationship exists only in one's head. The second possibility is that the relation is real in each term. Such "real relations" are found among things that belong to the same order of being. The third possibility is that the relation is real in one term and of idea only in the other. This third type is often called a "mixed relation."[59] Such relations are found among things that belong, in some sense, to different orders of being.

Since creatures all belong to the created order of being, we can find real relations among them. These may be based either on the property of quantity or on the action of one creature on another. In the first way, one thing may, for example, have the relation of being larger or smaller than another. In the second way, creaturely action may ground a relationship, as the act of generating a child may establish the relation of parenthood.[60] All such creaturely relations involve a note of mutual dependency. The existence of the relationship in one term depends in some way on the other term. One thing cannot have the property of being "larger" except with respect to something that is "smaller," and vice versa. One cannot have the relationship of parenthood except with respect to a child that one has generated. Aquinas considers all such relationships to be real. They are not just in our minds but are actual aspects of the world.[61] They are

---

World," in *Ordo Sapientiae et Amoris: Hommage au Professeur Jean-Pierre Torrell, OP*, ed. Carlos-Josaphat Pinto de Oliveira (Fribourg: Editions Universitaires, 1993), 211–27.

57. See *ST* I, 13, 7, co.

58. See *ST* I, 13, 7, co.

59. See A. Krempel, *La doctrine de la relation chez saint Thomas* (Paris: Librairie Philosophique J. Vrin, 1952), 458.

60. "Now there are other relations which are realities as regards both extremes, as when for instance a habitude exists between two things according to some reality that belongs to both; as is clear of all relations consequent upon quantity; as great and small, double and half, and the like; for quantity exists in both extremes: and the same applies to relations consequent upon action and passion, as motive power and the movable thing, father and son, and the like" (*ST* I, 13, 7, co.). Cf. *De pot.* 7, 9, co.

61. "Some have said that relation is not a reality, but only an idea. But this is plainly seen to

found in creatures that belong to the same creaturely order and so may have mutual dependencies.

A "mixed relation" (real in one term and of idea only in the other) may be found among things that belong, in some sense, to different orders of being. Even within the creaturely realm of things, there are some distinctions in being that may give rise to mixed relations. As an example, we might think of the very diminutive Alice in her encounter with the mushroom in Lewis Carroll's *Alice's Adventures in Wonderland*. She's told that one side of the mushroom will make her grow taller, while the other will make her grow shorter. She's faced with a philosophical dilemma: "Alice remained looking thoughtfully at the mushroom for a minute, trying to make out which were the two sides of it; and, as it was perfectly round, she found this a very difficult question." Then "the wise little Alice" seems to have an intuition about mixed relations. Although the mushroom doesn't really have a left side and a right side and can't really be related to Alice in terms of left and right, Alice really does have a left side and a right side, and so she really can break off one chunk from the side she sees as left and another from the side she sees as right in relation to herself: "At last she stretched her arms round it as far as they would go, and broke off a bit of the edge with each hand."[62] The relationship of left and right is real in Alice, but of idea only in the mushroom. If Alice were to walk around the mushroom, it might be first on her left and then on her right, without any change in the mushroom, but only in Alice. This is because the relation of left and right is real in Alice, but of idea only in the mushroom. So there is a "mixed relation" between Alice and the mushroom. Since a mixed relationship is real in one term, it is not merely imaginary, even though it is of idea only in the other term. It's the kind of relationship that is attained between beings that belong to different orders of being—even if the difference is something as trivial as having a right side and a left side or not.[63]

---

be false from the very fact that things themselves have a mutual natural order and habitude" (*ST* I, 13, 7, co.).

62. Lewis Carroll, *Alice's Adventures in Wonderland* (Chicago: Volume One Publishing, 1998), 68–69.

63. Since Aquinas isn't into mushrooms, he uses the example of a column: "For instance, 'on the right' is not applied to a column, unless it stands as regards an animal on the right side; which relation is not really in the column, but in the animal" (*ST* I, 13, 7, co.).

Another creaturely example is the relation between a knower and the thing known. My knowledge of a tree is dependent on the tree, but the tree does not depend on my knowledge. So the noetic relationship between the tree and me is real in me, but of idea only in the tree. Here again, we have different orders of being, since my knowledge is immaterial while the tree is material:

Sometimes a relation in one extreme may be a reality, while in the other extreme it is an idea only; and this happens whenever two extremes are not of one order; as sense and science [i.e., sense knowledge and intellectual knowledge] refer respectively to sensible things and to intellectual things; which, inasmuch as they are realities existing in nature, are outside the order of sensible and intellectual existence. Therefore in science and in sense a real relation exists, because they are ordered either to the knowledge or to the sensible perception of things; whereas the things looked at in themselves are outside this order, and hence in them there is no real relation to science and sense, but only in idea, inasmuch as the intellect apprehends them as terms of the relations of science and sense.[64]

Having discovered three creaturely types of relationship (of idea only in both terms, real in both terms, or of idea only in one term and real in the other), we need to decide which should be applied analogously to the relation between God and creatures. We can easily see that this relation cannot be of idea only in both terms, since the creature's dependence on God is real and not of idea only. Whether we should call it "real" or "mixed" requires a bit more thought.

Since God is the source of creatures, God neither depends on creatures nor belongs to the same order of being. Therefore, it would be inappropriate to attribute to God the real relations of mutual dependency that are characteristic of beings belonging to the same order. Since creatures really depend on God and are ordered to God as parts of his creation, they are really related to God. Since God does not depend on creatures

64. *ST* I, 13, 7, co. "Some things are relative to each other on an equal basis, as master and servant, father and son, great and small; and he [Aristotle] says that these are relative as contraries; and they are relative of themselves because each of these things taken in its quiddity is said to be relative to something else. But other things are not relative on an equal basis, but one of them is said to be relative, not because it itself is referred to something else, but because something else is referred to it, as happens, for example, in the case of knowledge and the knowable object. For what is knowable is called such relatively, not because it is referred to knowledge, but because knowledge is referred to it" (*In meta*. X, lect. 8, nos. 2087–88).

and is not part of the order of creation, God has no corresponding relation to creatures: "As the creature proceeds from God in diversity of nature, God is outside the order of the whole creation, nor does any relation to the creature arise from his nature; for he does not produce the creature by necessity of his nature, but by his intellect and will."[65] This means that the relation between God and creatures cannot be understood as a real relation involving mutual dependency, but must be seen as a mixed relation—real in one term and of idea only in the other.

Here we come to Aquinas's often-misunderstood teaching on the relationship between God and creation: "Since therefore God is outside the whole order of creation, and all creatures are ordered to him, and not conversely, it is manifest that creatures are really related to God himself; whereas in God there is no real relation to creatures, but a relation only in idea, inasmuch as creatures are referred to him."[66] The assertion that God has no real relation to creatures is sometimes taken to imply that God must be detached, uncaring, indifferent, and unloving. It is not surprising, then, that many theologians reject the idea that God has no real relation to creatures. William Lane Craig, for example, calls the assertion an "absurdity," and David Tracy thinks it jeopardizes Christianity's "most fundamental religious affirmation."[67] William Norris Clarke simply declares it "no longer fruitful or relevant for us today."[68] Properly understood, however, it affirms both God's transcendence and his intimate involvement in creation.

We have said that relations between creatures may be based on quantity or action. God's relation to creation cannot be based on quantity since God is not a material being. It must rather be understood in terms of God's action. But God's action is fundamentally different from that of creatures. While a creature's action is an incidental aspect of its being, God's action is one with God's being.[69] When one creature acts on an-

<hr>

65. *ST* I, 28, 1, ad 3.

66. *ST* I, 13, 7, co. "Therefore there is no real relation in God to the creature; whereas in creatures there is a real relation to God; because creatures are contained under the divine order, and their very nature entails dependence on God" (*ST* I, 28, 1, ad 3).

67. William Lane Craig, *God, Time, and Eternity* (Dordrecht: Kluwer, 2001), 61, 78; David Tracy, *Blessed Rage for Order: The New Pluralism in Theology* (New York: Seabury, 1975), 177.

68. Clarke, "What Is Most," 25.

69. "God does not act through a mediating action which is understood as proceeding from God and terminating in the creature. But his action is his substance, and whatever is in it is

other, it is incidentally present to the other. When God acts on or in a creature, God is substantially present.[70] Since God's most fundamental action is to give being, and since being is most intimate to the creature, in God's action his very substance is most intimately present to the creature.[71]

A real relation of mutual dependence may arise from the incidental action of one creature on another. Such a relation, however, is simply too tangential to express the intimacy and immediacy of divine presence that arises through God's substantial action in the creature. Real relations of mutual dependence arise between creatures that are never more than "beside" one another. They cannot capture the closeness of divine presence that arises from the action of God, who is never simply *beside* but is most deeply *within* the creature. To predicate such a relation of God would be to reduce God to the level of one creature existing beside another. In ef-

---

altogether outside the genus of created being through which the creature is referred to God" (*De pot.* 7, 9, ad 4). "God does not work by an intermediary action to be regarded as issuing from God and terminating in the creature: but his action is his substance and is wholly outside the genus of created being whereby the creature is related to him. Nor again does any good accrue to the creator from the production of the creature: wherefore his action is supremely liberal.... It is also evident that he is not moved to act and that without any change in himself he makes all changeable things. It follows then that there is no real relation in him to creatures, although creatures are really related to him, as effects to their cause" (*De pot.* 7, 10, co.).

70. "The natural mover or agent moves and acts by an intermediary movement or action that is between the mover and the thing moved, between the agent and the patient: wherefore at least in this intermediary, agent and patient, mover and thing moved must come together. Wherefore the agent as such is not outside the genus of the patient as such: and consequently each has a real relation to the other, especially seeing that this intermediary action is a perfection proper to the agent so that the term of that action is a perfection of the agent. This does not apply to God" (*De pot.* 7, 10, ad 1). "There are two kinds of contact; corporeal contact, when two bodies touch each other; and virtual contact, as the cause of sadness is said to touch the one made sad. According to the first kind of contact, God, as being incorporeal, neither touches, nor is touched; but according to virtual contact he touches creatures by moving them; but he is not touched, because the natural power of no creature can reach up to him. Thus did Dionysius understand the words, 'There is no contact with God'; that is, so that God Himself be touched" (*ST* I, 105, 2, ad 1). "Human persons then, unlike divine persons, change in every new relation. The relations they establish are through changes in their natures, through and in which they relate to others. Thus human persons are never related to one another as they are in themselves, but always by some changeable mediating action of their nature. This is easily seen in human love. A person grows in love and tries to express it, but he soon realizes that no expression of his love captures and makes real the totality of his love. This is because the person cannot relate himself as he is, with all his love, to the other person, but must use mediating and changeable actions" (Weinandy, *Does God Change,* 184).

71. "It must be said that God is in all things and innermostly" (*ST* I, 8, 1, co.).

fect, the notion of "real relation" is simply too remote to express the intimacy of God's presence. [72]

Aquinas therefore predicates a mixed relation between God and creatures. A mixed relation does not imply the mutual dependency of real relations found among creatures that are merely alongside each other. Its reality in the creature is the result of God's creative act in calling the creature into existence.[73] Aquinas can therefore affirm that *there is* a relation between the creator and the creature, precisely the mixed relation that pertains to beings that belong to different orders: "If by proportion is meant a definite excess, then there is no proportion in God to the creature. But if proportion stands for relation alone, then there is relation between the creator and the creature: in the latter really, but not in the former."[74]

This teaching preserves at once the reality of the relatedness of God and creatures, the transcendence and immanence of God, and the dependence of creatures.[75] It also allows us to see how language that implies relation to creatures can be said of God temporally without implying any change in God.

Since therefore God is outside the whole order of creation, and all creatures are ordered to him, and not conversely, it is manifest that creatures are really related to God himself; whereas in God there is no real relation to creatures, but a rela-

72. "The Creator, because of his transcendence as Creator, is 'more' and 'more intensely' *in* the world than creatures themselves are capable of being since he is more immanent in individual created things, and so more immanent in the universe, than creatures themselves" (Raphael Schulte, "Wie ist Gottes Wirken in Welt und Geschichte theologisch zu verstehen?" [How is God's action in the world and in history to be understood theologically?] in *Vorsehung und Handeln Gottes*, ed. Theodor Schneider and Lothar Ullrich [Leipzig: St. Benno Verlag, 1988], 141). "God is operative at the heart of all creaturely activity but without being acted upon by creatures in return in such wise as to gain something previously lacking to him. This is the basis of Aquinas' generally misunderstood teaching that the creature is really related to God, whereas God's relation to the creature is a relation of reason only.... It is not meant to imply that God does not actually create, know, love, redeem the world, and the like. The resulting relationship is not a mere extrinsic denomination on the part of human knowers. It is designated a relation of reason to convey that the fundament for it is something intrinsically intelligible within God, namely an actual exercise of causality on God's part vis a vis the creature" (Hill, "Implicate World," 87). See also Matthew R. McWhorter, "Aquinas on God's Relation to the World," *New Blackfriars* 94, no. 1049 (2013): 3–19.

73. See *ST* I, 45, 3.

74. *De pot.* 7, 10, ad 9.

75. "To predicate real relations of God to us ... would be to deprive him of his divinity, to make him intrinsically dependent upon us" (Krempel, *La doctrine*, 460).

tion only in idea, inasmuch as creatures are referred to him. Thus there is nothing to prevent these names which import relation to the creature from being predicated of God temporally, not by reason of any change in him, but by reason of the change of the creature; as a column is on the right of an animal, without change in itself, but by change in the animal.[76]

Names such as "Lord" and "Creator" that are said of God temporally are true predications. They are not just pious fictions founded on mere logical relationships (relations of idea only in both terms) that exist only in our heads. Rather, they express the true sort of relationship that attains between God and creatures, the mixed relation proper to beings belonging to different orders: "Since God is related to the creature for the reason that the creature is related to him: and since the relation of subjection is real in the creature, it follows that God is Lord not in idea only, but in reality; for he is called Lord according to the manner in which the creature is subject to him."[77]

The Divine Name

Among the names we apply to God is the word "God" itself. Although we know God only from his operations and effects, we truly name the divine nature when we call him "God" since that name implies God's universal providence, and "all who speak of God intend to name God as exercising providence over all." Although the name is taken from the operation of divine providence, it is "imposed to signify the divine nature."[78]

Beyond our naming, God has also named himself: "It is written that when Moses asked, 'If they should say to me, What is his name? what shall I say to them?' The Lord answered him, 'Thus shalt thou say to them, HE WHO IS hath sent me to you' (Ex 3:13–14)."[79] Aquinas discusses this name in many places and suggests various reasons for its appropriateness.[80] In the *Summa*, he singles out three. First, it signifies "being itself" and so is appropriate for God since he alone is subsistent being itself (*ipsum esse subsistens*). Secondly, it shows God's boundlessness

76. *ST* I, 13, 7, co.
77. *ST* I, 13, 7, ad 5.
78. *ST* I, 13, 8, co.
79. *ST* I, 13, 11, sed contra.
80. See Dodds, *Unchanging God*, 120n264.

as "the infinite ocean of substance" who is determined to no mode of being. Thirdly, the present tense of the name makes it most appropriate for God "whose existence knows not past or future."[81] The only name that might be more appropriate would be "the Tetragrammaton," which Aquinas views as a proper name or personal name that signifies "the substance of God itself, incommunicable and, if one may so speak, singular."[82]

81. *ST* I, 13, 11, co.
82. *ST* I, 13, 11, ad 1.

CHAPTER 4

DIVINE KNOWLEDGE AND LIFE

Having considered whether God exists and "the manner of his existence, or, rather, what is *not* the manner of his existence," Aquinas now turns to "whatever concerns his operations—namely, his knowledge, will, and power."[1] Knowledge and will may be seen as immanent motions, while power has the character of transient motion since it is "the principle of the divine operation as proceeding to the exterior effect." Aquinas also includes a discussion of divine life since "to understand is a kind of life."[2]

God's Knowledge

Since we've discovered how we know and speak of God,[3] Aquinas now allows us to put our learning to work in the discussion of divine knowledge. He begins as always with a creaturely analogy. Creaturely knowledge is in proportion to the immateriality of the creature. Plants are inca-

1. *ST* I, 2, prologue.
2. *ST* I, 14, prologue.
3. *ST* I, 12–13.

pable of knowledge since they are wholly material; animals are capable of sense knowledge, which requires a kind of immateriality. For example, the plant can possess the accidental form or quality of redness only in a physical way, by turning red (like an apple). The animal can sense the redness of the apple and so possess that form without itself turning red. Sensation therefore involves some sort of immateriality. Humans manifest a still greater degree of immateriality. They can know not only particular accidental attributes of things through sensation (like animals) but also the substantial actuality of those things—knowing not just how things appear to the senses, but what they *are*. Through abstraction, they can form universal concepts of particular things (like the idea of "dog" that applies to all particular dogs).[4] Since Aquinas has already shown that God, as pure actuality, "is in the highest degree of immateriality," he can now argue that, given the proportion between immateriality and knowledge, God "occupies the highest place in knowledge."[5] So, without pretending to know the nature of divine knowledge, he is able to show that knowledge is proper to God, that God understands and comprehends himself, and that his intellect is one with his substance.[6]

Aquinas also argues that God knows not only himself but other things as well. Since God is the first efficient cause (as established in the Second Way), in knowing himself, God must also know his causality or power. But to know that perfectly he must know all things to which his power extends. Therefore, "God must necessarily know things other than himself."[7]

In discussing God's knowledge, Aquinas never forgets that it is not like ours. While our knowledge is a quality in us, God's is identical with his substance. Though our knowledge is multiplied according to the various things we know, God's knowledge is one.[8] Our knowledge is derived

4. "It is clear that the immateriality of a thing is the reason why it is cognitive; and according to the mode of immateriality is the mode of knowledge. Hence ... plants do not know, because they are wholly material. But sense is cognitive because it can receive images free from matter, and the intellect is still further cognitive, because it is more separated from matter and unmixed" (*ST* I, 14, 1, co.).

5. *ST* I, 14, 1, co. See *ST* I, 2, 3; *ST* I, 3, 4; *ST* I, 7, 1.

6. *ST* I, 14, 2–4.

7. *ST* I, 14, 5, co. See also Brian J. Shanley, OP, "Eternal Knowledge of the Temporal in Aquinas," *American Catholic Philosophical Quarterly* 71, no. 2 (1997): 197–224.

8. *ST* I, 14, 1, ad 1 and ad 2; *ST* I, 14, 2, ad 2.

from things and depends on them. For instance, you can't really know what haggis is until you've tried it. God's knowledge, on the contrary, is the cause of things. Aquinas therefore compares God's knowledge to that of an artist. As a statue springs from an artist's imagination, so all of creation comes forth from the mind and will of God.[9] For this reason, God is recognized as the exemplar cause of all things. In knowing himself, he knows all things. He sees things "not in themselves, but in himself; inasmuch as his essence contains the similitude of things other than himself."[10]

Knowledge of Contingent Things

The question of whether God's knowledge imposes necessity on creatures has become a major conundrum in contemporary theology. Aquinas is aware of the issue: "From a necessary cause proceeds a necessary effect. But the knowledge of God is the cause of things known. Since therefore that knowledge is necessary, what he knows must also be necessary."[11] If we add the time factor, the problem becomes more nettlesome: if God infallibly knows that something will happen, that thing cannot not happen, and therefore cannot be contingent. A number of contemporary theologians, convinced by such arguments, contend that if God's knowledge is necessary, it must rob the world of contingency and freedom. Paul Helm sees divine foreknowledge as "logically incompatible with human (indeterministic) freedom."[12] Charles Hartshorne argues: "It simply cannot be that everything in God is necessary, including his knowledge that this world exists, unless the world is in the same sense necessary and there is no contingency whatever."[13]

Aquinas recognizes that the problem might be solved by simply denying that God's knowledge extends to contingent things.[14] Although he

9. *ST* I, 14, 8, co.

10. *ST* I, 14, 5, co. See *ST* I, 4, 3; *ST* I, 6, 4.

11. *ST* I, 14, 13, obj. 1.

12. Paul Helm, *Eternal God: A Study of God without Time* (New York: Oxford University Press, 1988), 98. See also Stephen M. Cahn, "Does God Know the Future?" in *Questions about God: Today's Philosophers Ponder the Divine*, ed. Steven M. Cahn and David Shatz (Oxford: Oxford University Press, 2002), 149.

13. Charles Hartshorne, *The Divine Relativity: A Social Conception of God* (New Haven, Conn.: Yale University Press, 1948), 14.

14. "The knowledge of God is not of contingent things" (*ST* I, 14, 13, obj. 1).

does not endorse this solution, many contemporary theologians do. So Arthur Peacocke argues that God can create a world of freedom and contingency only by imposing limits on his knowledge and power.

Considerations . . . on the role of "chance" in creation impel us also to recognize, more emphatically than ever before, the constraints which we must regard God as imposing upon himself in creation and to suggest that *God has a "self-limited" omnipotence and omniscience.* For, in order to achieve his purposes, he has allowed his inherent omnipotence and omniscience to be modified, restricted and curtailed by the very open-endedness that he has bestowed upon creation.[15]

Aquinas solves the dilemma not by limiting God's knowledge but by remembering his eternity. Since God is eternal, he knows contingent events both in their causes before they happen and in their actual occurrence. As present in its causes, a contingent event is not yet determined to one outcome, and so "is not subject to any certain knowledge."[16] In the moment of its occurrence, however, the contingent event has a note of necessity. Aquinas calls this the "necessity of supposition": supposing that something is happening, it cannot also not be happening while it happens. As it happens, the contingent thing is determined to one outcome and can therefore "be infallibly the object of certain knowledge."[17] For example, I can be certain that Socrates is (freely) sitting while he sits. The certitude of my knowledge does not deprive his act of its freedom.

From eternity, God knows contingent things both in their causes and in their actual occurrence. As my certain knowledge of Socrates's free act in the moment of its happening does not deprive it of its freedom, so God's certain knowledge from eternity of all contingent events in the moment of their happening does not deprive them of their contingency: "Hence it is manifest that contingent things are infallibly known by God

15. Arthur Peacocke, *Theology for a Scientific Age: Being and Becoming—Natural, Divine, and Human* (Minneapolis: Fortress Press, 1993), 121. Clark Pinnock agrees that the creation of the world "involved a self-limitation on God's part" (Clark H. Pinnock, *Most Moved Mover: A Theology of God's Openness* [Grand Rapids, Mich.: Baker Books, 2001], 56). See also Gloria L. Schaab, "A Procreative Paradigm of the Creative Suffering of the Triune God: Implications of Arthur Peacocke's Evolutionary Theology," *Theological Studies* 67, no. 3 (2006): 544, 553, 555; Terrence E. Fretheim, *The Suffering God: An Old Testament Perspective* (Philadelphia: Fortress Press, 1984), 36–37. For other ways that contemporary theology has limited God's knowledge, see Dodds, *Unlocking*, 114–18.
16. *ST* I, 14, 13, co.
17. *ST* I, 14, 13, co.

inasmuch as they are subject to the divine sight in their presentiality; yet they are future contingent things in relation to their own causes."[18]

Knowledge of Changeable Things

Aquinas makes short work of the question of whether God's knowledge is changeable: Since God's knowledge is his substance, and since his substance is unchanging, his knowledge must be also unchanging.[19] We will spend a bit more time on this question, however, since it has become a controversial issue in contemporary theology.

As so often happens, the source of the trouble is our tendency to think that God is like us. If our knowledge did not change, it would soon cease to be true since our knowledge is derived from things that are constantly changing.[20] A number of contemporary theologians consider God's knowledge to be like ours and therefore changeable. Richard E. Creel argues, for instance, that God's knowledge of "what is happening is determined by what is happening.... It cannot be an illusion that change is occurring in this world, and change cannot be known adequately except by an awareness that undergoes a corresponding change caused by the thing of which one is aware. This is a metaphysical principle to which there can be no exception."[21] William L. Craig contends that as the world "is in constant flux, so also must God's knowledge of what is happening be in constant flux."[22] Paul Helm thinks that the exercise of creaturely choices

18. *ST* I, 14, 13. See also *De malo* 16, 7, ad 15. On how God's knowledge is compatible with creaturely contingency, see Peter Laughlin, "Divine Necessity and Created Contingence in Aquinas," *The Heythrop Journal* 50, no. 4 (2009): 649–57; Eleonore Stump and Norman Kretzmann, "God's Knowledge and Its Causal Efficacy," in *The Rationality of Belief and the Plurality of Faith: Essays in Honor of William P. Alston*, ed. Thomas D. Senor (Ithaca, N.Y.: Cornell University Press, 1995), 94–124; David B. Burrell, CSC, "Divine Practical Knowing: How an Eternal God Acts in Time," in *Divine Action: Studies Inspired by the Philosophical Theology of Austin Farrer*, ed. Brian Hebblethwaite and Edward Henderson (Edinburgh: T and T Clark, 1990), 93–102; Charles E. Gutenson, "Does God Change?" in *God under Fire: Modern Scholarship Reinvents God*, ed. Douglas S. Huffman and Eric L. Johnson (Grand Rapids, Mich.: Zondervan, 2002), 231–52; Harm J. M. J. Goris, *Free Creatures of an Eternal God: Thomas Aquinas on God's Infallible Foreknowledge and Irresistible Will* (Leuven: Peeters, 1996).

19. *ST* I, 14, 15, co. "If, however, God's understanding is his being, his understanding must be simple, eternal and unchangeable...." (*SCG* I, c.45.7).

20. *ST* I, 16, 8, co.

21. Richard E. Creel, *Divine Impassibility: An Essay in Philosophical Theology* (Cambridge: Cambridge University Press, 1986), 205.

22. Craig, *Time and Eternity*, 97, 241. See also Craig, *God, Time*, 283–84.

"will change God by increasing his knowledge."[23] William Hasker agrees: "When I do something wrong, God comes to be in a state of knowing that I am doing something wrong, and this is a change in God."[24] Grace Jantzen argues that thinking itself implies change, so an immutable God "could not think or perceive or have any conscious processes, because these would involve changes in God."[25]

Such dilemmas can be overcome if we remember that God is not like us.[26] While our knowledge is derived from and dependent on the things we know, God's knowledge creates the things God knows.[27] Unlike our limited knowledge, God's is complete and perfect, encompassing all things that have, will, or could possibly exist.[28]

Although we cannot comprehend God's knowledge, we can argue that changes in creatures do not change it. We begin with the principle that the thing known is in the knower "according to the mode of the knower."[29] This principle is analogously true of God's knowledge.[30] Since God is subsistent and unchanging *esse*, and his knowledge is one with his being, it is "in" him according to his immutable and eternal mode of being.[31] Since God is eternal, he knows all things past, present, and future, in a single intuition. Therefore, his knowledge does not change when creatures change.[32] He knows contingent events eternally both in their causes (as contingent) and in their actual occurrence (as determined or necessary by supposition).[33] His knowledge of them is therefore unchanging.[34]

The eternal mode of divine knowing, of course, escapes our powers of thought. Although we can describe it "only after the manner of our own knowledge," we must be careful not to attribute the limitations of

23. Helm, *Eternal God*, 92.
24. William Hasker, "Does God Change?" in *Questions about God: Today's Philosophers Ponder the Divine,* ed. Steven M. Cahn and David Shatz (Oxford: Oxford University Press, 2002), 143.
25. Jantzen, *God's World*, 55.
26. *ST* I, 4, 3, ad 4.
27. *ST* I, 14, 8, co.; *De pot.* 7, 10, ad 5.
28. *ST* I, 14, 5–6 and 9–14; *De ver.* 2, 13, co.
29. *ST* I, 14, 1, ad 3.
30. *De ver.* 2, 13, ad 3.
31. *SCG* I, c.45.7.
32. *De ver.* 2, 5, ad 11.
33. *SCG* I, c.67.3; *De ver.* 2, 12, ad 2.
34. *De ver.* 12, 3, co.

our knowledge to God. By following that discipline, however, we can truly affirm that God's knowledge of contingent things implies no change in God.[35]

God's Life

To discuss divine life, Thomas first considers creaturely life, following his general principle that God is known through creatures.[36] The question of what life is continues to baffle both philosophers and scientists.[37] Like Aquinas, however, they tend to associate life with movement. While biology may single out the phenomenon of metabolism,[38] Aquinas frames his understanding in terms of the larger idea of self-motion: "We say that an animal begins to live when it begins to move of itself: and as long as such movement appears in it, so long as it is considered to be alive."[39] Yet Aquinas takes the term "motion" itself in a very broad sense, to include both immanent and transient motion: "It is clear that those things are properly called living that move themselves by some kind of movement, whether it be movement properly so called, as the act of an imperfect being, i.e., of a thing in potentiality, is called movement; or movement in a more general sense, as when said of the act of a perfect thing, as understanding and feeling are called movement."[40] Aquinas is careful to point

---

35. *De ver.* 2, 12, co. On God's eternal knowledge of contingent events, see Thomas D. Sullivan, "Omniscience, Immutability and the Divine Mode of Knowing," *Faith and Philosophy* 8, no. 1 (1991): 21–35; Christopher Hughes, *On a Complex Theory of a Simple God: An Investigation in Aquinas' Philosophical Theology* (Ithaca, N.Y.: Cornell University Press, 1989), 120–27; William J. Hill, OP, "Does God Know the Future? Aquinas and Some Moderns," *Theological Studies* 36, no. 1 (1975): 3–18.

36. See Michael J. Dodds, OP, "The God of Life, the Science of Life, and the Problem of Language," in *God: Reason and Reality*, ed. Anselm Ramelow, OP (Munich: Philosophia Verlag, 2013), 197–233.

37. "I have observed and am resigned to the fact that it is practically impossible to bring physicists, chemists, and biologists to an agreement on what life is" (Pier Luigi Luisi, *The Emergence of Life: From Chemical Origins to Synthetic Biology* [New York: Cambridge University Press, 2010], 18).

38. "Metabolism is an inescapable characteristic of all living things, from the minimally alive to the maximally alive. A reasonable answer to the question 'What is life?', then, seems to be: an embodied metabolism" (Edward Regis, *What Is Life? Investigating the Nature of Life in the Age of Synthetic Biology* [New York: Farrar, Straus and Giroux, 2008], 166).

39. *ST* I, 18, 1, co. Aquinas builds on Aristotle's definition: "By life we mean self-nutrition and growth (with its correlative decay)" (*On the Soul* II, 1, [412a 14–15]).

40. *ST* I, 18, 1, co. On the distinction between immanent and transient motion, see appendix 1.

out, however, that although motion is a sign of life, life is not simply a way of moving, but a mode of being.[41]

Having established the nature of life in creatures, Aquinas then asks whether life can be attributed to God. Scripture provides the answer: "My heart and my flesh have rejoiced in the living God."[42] If life implies self-motion, then God must have life in the most perfect degree since it has been shown that knowing (understood as immanent motion) belongs to God and that God is in no way moved by another. As the Fourth Way showed that God has being and goodness in the most perfect way, so now it is demonstrated that God "must have life in the most perfect degree."[43]

41. *ST* I, 18, 2.
42. Ps 83:8, as quoted in *ST* I, 18, 3, sed contra.
43. *ST* I, 18, 3, co. and ad 1.

CHAPTER 5

DIVINE WILL

Aquinas sees the reality of the divine will as a revealed truth: "The Apostle says 'That you may prove what is the will of God.'"[1] His task is to help his students understand this truth. For that, he uses the analogy of the relationship between creaturely knowledge and will. He first considers the will as such, then things such as love that belong "strictly" or "absolutely" to the will, and finally things such as providence which belong to the intellect in relation to the will.[2]

The analogous principle is that "will follows upon intellect." As sense knowledge is followed by an inclination called "sense appetite," so intellectual knowledge is followed by will. Since we attribute intellect to God, we must also analogously attribute will: "And so there must be will in God, since there is intellect in him." Yet God's will is not like ours. Our will is a power in us, while God's will "is his own existence."[3] Although our will is drawn to an end beyond ourselves, God has no end apart from himself but is rather himself the end of all things.[4]

1. *ST* I, 19, 1, sed contra, quoting Rom 12:2.
2. "The first consideration is about the divine will itself; the second about what belongs strictly to his will; the third about what belongs to the intellect in relation to his will" (*ST* I, 19, prologue).
3. *ST* I, 19, 1, co.
4. *ST* I, 19, 1, ad 1.

By our will, we not only desire the good that we lack but also delight in the good we possess. In the second way, our will is analogously like God's: "In this respect will is said to be in God, as having always good which is its object." Still, God does not so much *possess* goodness: he simply *is* goodness "which is not distinct from his essence."[5] Although our act of willing itself is immanent motion, our will also involves a kind of transient motion (the actuation of a potency) when it is aroused by a perceived good. God's will, on the contrary, is simply immanent motion since it involves no potency but is rather identical with his essence and goodness. It "is not moved by another than itself, but by itself alone, in the same sense as understanding and willing are said to be motion."[6]

As positing God's knowledge of things other than himself gave rise to certain questions,[7] so does the assertion that God wills things other than himself. To resolve such issues, Aquinas again employs a creaturely analogy. If it is appropriate for creatures to share their goodness with others, it is all the more appropriate for God to do so.

Every agent, in so far as it is perfect and in act, produces its like. It pertains, therefore, to the nature of the will to communicate as far as possible to others the good possessed.... If natural things, in so far as they are perfect, communicate their good to others, much more does it appertain to the divine will to communicate by likeness its own good to others as much as possible.[8]

Note that this argument does not tell us *why* God shares his goodness with creatures, much less imply that God is bound to do so. It merely allows us to understand that this sharing of divine goodness is fitting or appropriate while maintaining that God "wills things apart from himself only for the sake of the end, which is his own goodness."[9]

The Freedom of God's Will

Since God wills other things in willing his own goodness and since he wills his own goodness necessarily, it might seem that he must also will

5. *ST* I, 19, 1, ad 2.
6. *ST* I, 19, 1, ad 3. On the distinction between immanent and transient motion, see appendix 1.
7. *ST* I, 14, 5, and chapter 4 of this book.
8. *ST* I, 19, 2, co.
9. *ST* I, 19, 2, ad 2 and ad 3.

other things necessarily. Aquinas addresses this dilemma by distinguishing between *absolute necessity* and the *necessity of supposition*.[10] We say that something is absolutely necessary when the predicate is contained in the subject. So it is absolutely necessary that a human being is an animal, since the predicate (animality) is contained in the definition of subject (rational animal). It is not absolutely necessary, however, that "Socrates sits" since *sitting* is not part of the definition of Socrates. His act of sitting may, however, be necessary *by supposition* in the sense that *supposing* he is sitting, he cannot *not* be sitting while he sits.

God wills his own goodness by absolute necessity as his proper object, but he wills other things only insofar as they are "ordered to his goodness as their end."[11] Things ordered to an end, however, are not willed necessarily unless they are required for the attainment or possession of that end. In this way, a ship is necessary for a cruise, since you can't go on a cruise unless you have a ship. But a Porsche is not necessary for a drive. since a Ford will do just as well (*faute de mieux*).

Although God's goodness is the end of all things, God does not require such things in order to will (or possess) his own goodness: "Since the goodness of God is perfect, and can exist without other things inasmuch as no perfection can accrue to him from them, it follows that his willing things apart from himself is not absolutely necessary."[12] We can say, however, that God's will is necessary by supposition since, given that God is willing something, it would be contradictory to say that he is also not willing it.

In this way, without pretending to know the nature of the divine will, Aquinas can affirm that God wills creation freely. The focus throughout his discussion is on the creature (that we know), not on the divine will (that we don't know). We know (from the Fourth Way) that all creaturely goodness is from God and that creatures cannot therefore add to God's goodness. It follows that the fullness of divine goodness does not require the goodness of creatures. We can conclude that God's willing the goodness of creatures is not necessary but free. We cannot, of course, under-

10. We have already seen this distinction in our discussion of God's knowledge of contingent things in chapter 4 of this book.

11. *ST* I, 19, 3, co.

12. *ST* I, 19, 3, co.; *ST* I, 19, 10.

stand *how* in one act God both *necessarily* wills his own goodness and *free-ly* wills the goodness of creatures, but we can affirm *that* these assertions are true—a truth established by our knowledge of creatures.[13]

God's will is the cause of things, but is itself uncaused. God does not act by the necessity of nature (as in the Neoplatonic scheme of the emanation of all things from a first principle), but by the freedom of love.[14] While our human willing of the means is in some way caused by our willing the end (as we will a ship for the sake of a cruise), this cannot be the case with God since God wills both means and end in one act and since "a thing cannot be its own cause."[15]

Generally, we think of the "means" as those things that are ordered to the "end." In creation, creatures are, in a sense, the "means" since they are ordered to the "end" which is divine goodness (although they are not "means" as if they were required for divine goodness, or as if God could not possess his goodness without them). Still, they are ordered to divine goodness and that ordering is what gives rise to the order that we find in the universe. The world is not a chaos of random things, but a cosmos in which one thing is ordered to another. God wills that order, in willing that one thing be ordered to another and that all things be ordered to divine goodness. In Genesis, for instance, God wills that the green plants be ordered to the animals as their food.[16] But his willing food for the animals is not the cause of his willing the green plants. In Aquinas's succinct formulation: "He wills this to be as a means to that; but does not will this on account of that."[17]

The Fulfillment of God's Will

Because God is the first cause, his will must always be fulfilled: "Since the will of God is the universal cause of all things, it is impossible that the divine will should not produce its effect."[18] Even the sinner who acts contrary to God's will cannot escape or violate its universal sway: "The sinner,

---

13. See Dodds, *Unchanging God*, 178–80.
14. *ST* I, 19, 4.
15. *ST* I, 19, 5, co.
16. See Gn 1:30.
17. "Vult ergo hoc esse propter hoc, sed non propter hoc vult hoc" (*ST* I, 19, 5, co.).
18. *ST* I, 19, 6, co.

who by sin falls away from the divine will as much as lies in him, yet falls back into the order of that will, when by its justice he is punished."[19] Yet the very punishment of the sinner seems to raise another question about the universal efficacy of God's will: "It seems that the will of God is not always fulfilled. For the Apostle says (1 Tm 2:4): 'God will have all men to be saved, and to come to the knowledge of the truth.' But this does not happen. Therefore the will of God is not always fulfilled."[20] Aquinas addresses this objection by referring to St. John Damascene's distinction between antecedent and consequent will. For instance, a human judge who wills in a general way that all men live (antecedently) may also will that a certain murderer be executed (consequently, in view of all the particular circumstances). So without introducing any distinction into the divine will itself, we may say that God wills antecedently that all men be saved, but consequently that the sinner be condemned.[21]

God's Unchanging Will and the Contingency of Creatures

To discuss whether God's will is changeable, Aquinas again uses a human analogue. We change our will either because of some change in our physical disposition (as we might decide to stand when we get tired of sitting) or because of a change in our knowledge (as we might decide to quit smoking after reading medical reports). Since Aquinas has already shown that God (unlike us) is unchanging in being and knowledge, he concludes that God is also unchanging in will.[22] Aquinas is aware that some scriptural passages affirm God's unchanging will, while others speak of God as repenting or changing his will. To solve this dilemma, he accepts the first sort literally and the second metaphorically.[23]

19. *ST* I, 19, 6, co.
20. *ST* I, 19, 6, obj. 1. On the question of whether all are saved, see the section on "Predestination" in chapter 7 of this book.
21. "This distinction must not be taken as applying to the divine will itself, in which there is nothing antecedent nor consequent, but to the things willed" (*ST* I, 19, 6, ad 1).
22. *ST* I, 19, 7, co. See *ST* I, 9, 1; *ST* I, 14, 15.
23. See *ST* I, 19, 7, ad 1 and ad 2. On the difference between Aquinas and contemporary theologians (who do the opposite of Aquinas by accepting passages about God's unchanging will metaphorically and those about his changing will literally), see Dodds, *Unchanging God*, 105–11.

Since God's will is necessary and unchanging, it might seem that whatever God wills must happen necessarily.[24] This would, of course, eliminate human freedom as well as all contingency in the natural world. Faced with this consequence, some contemporary theologians have simply asserted that God's will is contingent and changeable. So Walter Kaiser argues that God "can change in his actions toward us as much as any other living person can change."[25]

The dilemma between God's unchanging will and the contingency of creatures arises, however, only when God's transcendence is forgotten and God's causality is viewed as univocal with that of creatures. Created causes can be broadly classified as necessary or contingent. Necessary causes cannot *not* produce their effects. The laws of nature, for instance, are popularly taken as necessary causes. So in *Star Trek*, Scotty must constantly remind the captain that he "cannot defy the laws of nature" since they necessarily produce certain effects.[26] Contingent causes, on the other hand, may or may not produce their effects. These include human free will and chance.[27] Their effects are always uncertain—they may or may not happen. If God's will were classified univocally in the same way as creaturely causes, it would be either necessary (and so eliminate all contingency, including chance and human freedom) or contingent (and so produce only uncertain results, jeopardizing God's providential plan of salvation).

Aquinas answers these dilemmas by affirming the transcendence of God's will, as utterly beyond the creaturely categories of necessity and contingency. As such, God's will is the source of both necessary and contingent causality in creatures, while not itself belonging to either category.

24. *ST* I, 19, 8.

25. Walter C. Kaiser, Jr., *Malachi: God's Unchanging Love* (Grand Rapids, Mich.: Baker Book House, 1984), 93. Robert Chisholm maintains that "the human response to his [God's] announcement determines what he will do" (Robert B. Chisholm, "Does God 'Change His Mind?'" *Bibliotheca Sacra* 152 [October–December 1995]: 399). A. van de Beek believes that scriptural references to God's repentance imply "constant change in God's plans, feelings, and actions" (A. van de Beek, *Why? On Suffering, Guilt and God* [Grand Rapids, Mich.: Eerdmans, 1990], 273).

26. On the real nature of scientific laws as descriptive rather than prescriptive, see "Nature" in appendix 1.

27. On the causality of chance, see "Causality" in appendix 1.

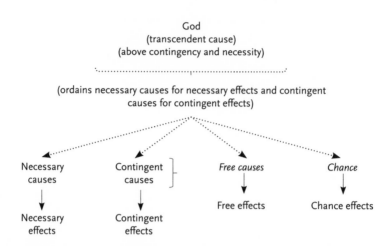

Figure 5-1. The Primary Causality of God and the Secondary Causality of Creatures

Note: God, as the source of all actuality, is involved in every production of actuality or being. In exercising his causal influence, God wills not only the things that are actualized but also the way in which they are actualized.

Here, the dotted bracket suggests the transcendent realm of divine causality, as the dotted arrows indicate the transcendent influence of divine causality. The solid arrows indicate how the different categories of natural causes produce the different types of natural effects. The bracket beside "contingent causes" is meant to indicate that "free causes" and "chance" are subsets of contingent causes.

When a cause is efficacious to act, the effect follows upon the cause not only as to the thing done, but also as to the manner of being done or of being.... Since then the divine will is perfectly efficacious, it follows not only that things are done which God wills to be done, but also that they are done in the way that he wills.... Therefore to some effects he has attached necessary causes, that cannot fail; but to others defectible and contingent causes, from which arise contingent effects.[28]

Aquinas explains this in more detail in his commentary on Aristotle's work, *On Interpretation.*

There is a difference to be noted on the part of the divine will, for the divine will must be understood as existing outside of the order of beings, as a cause produc-

28. *ST* I, 19, 8, co.

ing the whole of being and all its differences. Now the possible and the necessary are differences of being, and therefore necessity and contingency in things and the distinction of each according to the nature of their proximate causes originate from the divine will itself, for he disposes necessary causes for the effects that he wills to be necessary, and he ordains causes acting contingently (i.e., able to fail) for the effects that he wills to be contingent. And according to the condition of these causes, effects are called either necessary or contingent, although all depend on the divine will as on a first cause, which transcends the order of necessity and contingency. This, however, cannot be said of the human will, nor of any other cause, for every other cause already falls under the order of necessity or contingency; hence, either the cause itself must be able to fail or, if not, its effect is not contingent, but necessary. The divine will, on the other hand, is unfailing; yet not all its effects are necessary, but some are contingent.[29]

God's causality transcends the whole order of created causality and all of its modes or categories. It does not interfere with creaturely causality but is rather its source, whether the creature's mode of causality be necessary, contingent, free, or chance, as shown in figure 5-1.[30]

29. *In peri herm.* I, lect. 14, no. 22. Cf. *In meta.* VI, lect. 1, no. 1222.
30. This diagram also appears, with further explanation, in Dodds, *Unlocking*, 208.

CHAPTER 6

DIVINE LOVE, JUSTICE, AND COMPASSION

The discussion of God's love, justice, and compassion follows logically on the discussion of the divine will. Human emotion is used as a model for ordering the discussion: "In the appetitive part of the soul there are found in ourselves both the passions of the soul, as joy, love, and the like; and the habits of the moral virtues, as justice, fortitude, and the like. Hence we shall first consider the love of God, and secondly his justice and mercy."[1]

Love

When Aquinas asks "whether there is love in God," he finds the answer in the sublime words of St. John: "God is love."[2] To show why it is appropriate to attribute love to God, he employs a human analogy. Since our will is ordered "essentially and especially" toward the good, and since love regards the good universally, "love is naturally the first act of the will and

1. *ST* I, 20, prologue.
2. 1 Jn 4:16. See *ST* I, 20, 1, sed contra.

appetite."[3] Since we have seen that there is will in God, and since love is the first act of the will, "we must attribute love to him." It is important to notice the modesty of Aquinas's claim. He doesn't say that we have now discovered the proper reason why there is *necessarily* love in God, only that we have shown a cogent reason why it is necessary *for us* to "attribute" or "posit" love in God (*necesse est in eo ponere amorem*).[4]

While the analogy of human love is helpful, Aquinas is careful to show the difference between human love and divine love. To the extent that love and other passions, such as anger and sorrow, imply imperfection or limitation in us, they are not attributed to God or are applied only metaphorically. To the extent that passions such as "love and joy and delight" imply no imperfection, however, they are attributed properly to God in an eminent way.[5]

God's love for creation is not a mere metaphor. God truly loves all things: "To every existing thing, God wills some good. Hence, since to love anything is nothing else than to will good to that thing, it is manifest that God loves everything that exists."[6] His love "is a binding force [*vis concretiva*], inasmuch as God wills good to others."[7] Unlike our love, however, which is awakened by the good we find in others, God's love "infuses and creates goodness."[8] Aquinas follows Pseudo-Dionysius in describing this overflow of divine love and goodness as a kind of ecstasy.

A lover is placed outside himself, and made to pass into the object of his love, inasmuch as he wills good to the beloved; and works for that good by his providence even as he works for his own. Hence Dionysius says: "On behalf of the truth we must make bold to say even this, that he himself, the cause of all things, by his abounding love and goodness, is placed outside himself by his providence for all existing things."[9]

3. *ST* I, 20, 1, co. On the structure of the emotions in Aquinas's psychology, see *ST* I, 81, 2; *ST* I-II, 23, 1–3. See also Nicholas E. Lombardo, OP, *The Logic of Desire: Aquinas on Emotion* (Washington, D.C.: The Catholic University of America Press, 2011); Diana Fritz Cates, *Aquinas on the Emotions: A Religious-Ethical Inquiry* (Washington, D.C.: Georgetown University Press, 2009).

4. *ST* I, 20, 1, co.

5. *ST* I, 20, 1, ad 1 and ad 2; *ST* I, 19, 11, co.

6. *ST* I, 20, 2, co.

7. *ST* I, 20, 1, ad 3.

8. *ST* I, 20, 2, co.

9. *ST* I, 20, 2, ad 1. "And we must dare to affirm (for 'tis the truth) that the Creator of the Universe Himself, in His Beautiful and Good Yearning towards the Universe, is through the excessive

God's love for human creation is genuine friendship since he wishes to share with us nothing less than the good which is himself.

Every love of God is followed at some time by a good caused in the creature, but not co-eternal with the eternal love. And according to the difference of this good, the love of God for the creature is looked at differently. For one is common, whereby he loves "all things that are" (Wis 11:25), and thereby gives things their natural being. But the second is a special love, whereby he draws the rational creature above the condition of its nature to a participation of the divine good. And according to this love, he is said to love someone simply, since it is by this love that God simply wishes the eternal good, which is himself, for the creature.[10]

God's love for us begins in this life but finds its fulfillment in the next.

Charity signifies not only the love of God, but also a certain friendship with him; which implies, besides love, a mutual return of love, together with a certain mutual communion.... That this belongs to charity is evident from 1 Jn 4:16: "He who abides in love abides in God, and God abides in him," and from 1 Cor 1:9, where it is written: "God is faithful, by whom you are called into the fellowship of his Son." Now this fellowship of man with God, which consists in a certain familiar colloquy with him, is begun here, in this life, by grace, but will be perfected in the future life, by glory.[11]

Justice

Finding justice attributed to God in scripture, Aquinas explains how we should understand this attribution. The "commutative justice" characteristic of equals in their social interactions cannot apply to the relation between God and creatures. There is a way, however, in which the "distributive justice" that marks the dealings between ruler and subjects may be said of God. God is never a debtor but always the most liberal giver, and

---

yearning of His Goodness, transported outside of Himself in His providential activities towards all things that have being, and is touched by the sweet spell of Goodness, Love and Yearning, and so drawn from His transcendent throne above all things, to dwell within the heart of all things, through a super-essential and ecstatic power whereby He yet stays within Himself" (Dionysius the Areopagite, *The Divine Names*, chap. 4, no. 13, in *The Divine Names and The Mystical Theology*, trans. C. E. Rolt [London: SPCK, 1979], 106).

10. *ST* I-II, 110, 1, co.

11. *ST* I-II, 65, 5, co. On divine friendship, see Dodds, *Unchanging God*, 213–17.

yet there is a sense in which "God pays what is due."[12] First, God renders
to himself what is due to him: "It is due to God that there should be fulfilled in creatures what his will and wisdom require, and what manifests
his goodness." Secondly, although whatever a creature possesses, including its very existence and nature, is a gratuitous gift of God, still we may
say that God "exercises justice when he gives to each thing what is due to
it by its nature and condition." Yet God is never in debt to others "since
he is not directed to other things, but rather other things to him."[13]

Compassion

Divine compassion has become a major issue in contemporary theology.[14] Since we know about God from creatures, what we know of divine compassion must be based on our knowledge of human compassion,
especially the compassion of Jesus, who was moved with pity for the
crowds, wept over the city of Jerusalem, and joined in weeping with Mary
and others at the death of his friend Lazarus.[15] For humans, compassionate sadness proceeds from love and is a sign of love. Not to be moved at
the plight of another bespeaks the vice of indifference or apathy.[16]

Since we attribute love to God, it is appropriate that we follow scripture in affirming divine compassion: "He is a merciful and gracious God."[17]

12. *ST* I, 21, 1, ad 3.

13. *ST* I, 21, 1, ad 3.

14. See James F. Keating and Thomas Joseph White, OP, eds., *Divine Impassibility and the
Mystery of Human Suffering* (Grand Rapids, Mich.: Eerdmans, 2009); Thomas G. Weinandy,
OFM Cap., *Does God Suffer?* (Notre Dame, Ind.: University of Notre Dame Press, 2000); Michael
J. Dodds, OP, "Thomas Aquinas, Human Suffering, and the Unchanging God of Love," *Theological
Studies* 52, no. 2 (1991): 330–44; Dodds, *Unchanging God*; Herbert McCabe, OP, "The Involve-
ment of God," *New Blackfriars* 66, no. 785 (1985): 464–76; Rob Lister, *God Is Impassible and Im-
passioned: Toward a Theology of Divine Emotion* (Wheaton, Ill.: Crossway, 2012); Gavrilyuk, *Suffering.*

15. Mt 9:36; Lk 19:41; Jn 11:33–36. For Aquinas on the human virtue of mercy, see *ST* II-II, 30.

16. Aquinas calls lack of compassion a kind of obduracy: "Two characteristics pertain to avarice, one of which is to be excessive in retaining, and in furtherance of this, obduracy [*obduratio*] in
regard to mercy or inhumanity arises from avarice, namely, because the avaricious man hardens his
heart so that he will not out of compassion come to the aid of anyone at the expense of his posses-
sions" (*De malo* 13, 3, co.). "It [covetousness] exceeds in retaining, and in this respect covetousness
gives rise to insensibility to mercy [*obduratio contra misericordiam*] because, to wit, a man's heart is
not softened by mercy to assist the needy with his riches" (*ST* II-II, 118, 8, co.).

17. Ps 110:4, as quoted in *ST* I, 21, 3, sed contra.

Our compassion itself is to be a reflection of God's: "Be merciful as your Father is merciful."[18] We must remember, however, that for compassion, as for all divine attributes, "although it may be admitted that creatures are in some way like God, it must nowise be admitted that God is like creatures."[19] Here we find the crux of the current controversy: which aspects of human compassion should be attributed to God and which should not?

For Aquinas, compassion involves two fundamental aspects: "being affected with the sorrow of another as though it were one's own" and "endeavoring to dispel the misery of the other."[20] Since he has shown that sorrow may be attributed to God only metaphorically,[21] he argues that "to sorrow over the misery of others does not belong to God, but it does most properly belong to him to dispel that misery, whatever be the defect we call by that name."[22]

To some contemporary theologians, however, it seems that God cannot be genuinely loving unless he really suffers at the distress of his people. For Jürgen Moltmann, "a God who cannot suffer cannot love either."[23] To John Macquarrie, "a God of love is inevitably vulnerable, for there is no love that does not suffer."[24] William Placher argues that in Mark's gospel, "we encounter a God defined by perfect love and perfect freedom. Love means a willingness to take risks, to care for the other in a way that causes the other's fate to affect one's own, to give to the other at real cost to oneself, to chance rejection."[25] According to S. Paul Schilling, "if God cannot feel anguish, he cannot love."[26] Elizabeth Johnson argues that "suffering

18. Lk 6:36.
19. *ST* I, 4, 3, ad 4.
20. *ST* I, 21, 3, co.
21. *ST* I, 20, 1, ad 2.
22. *ST* I, 21, 3, co.
23. Jürgen Moltmann, *The Trinity and the Kingdom*, trans. by M. Kehl (New York: Harper and Row, 1981), 38; Jürgen Moltmann, *The Crucified God* (New York: Harper and Row, 1974), 222, 230. For a critique of Moltmann's argument that divine love is incompatible with immutability, see Henry Jansen, "Moltmann's View of God's (Im)mutability: The God of the Philosophers and the God of the Bible," *Neue Zeitschrift für systematische Theologie und Religionsphilosophie* 36, no. 3 (1994): 293; and Henri Blocher, "Divine Immutability," in *The Power and Weakness of God: Impassibility and Orthodoxy*, ed. Nigel M. de S. Cameron (Edinburgh: Rutherford House Books, 1990), 9–10.
24. John Macquarrie, *The Humility of God* (Philadelphia: Westminster, 1978), 69.
25. William C. Placher, *Narratives of a Vulnerable God: Christ, Theology, and Scripture* (Louisville, Ky.: Westminster John Knox Press, 1994), 16.
26. S. Paul Schilling, *God and Human Anguish* (Nashville, Tenn.: Abingdon, 1977), 252–53.

can be conceived of ontologically as an expression of divine being insofar as it is an *act* freely engaged as a consequence of care for others."[27]

In denying suffering in God, Aquinas does not render God indifferent. Although God's compassion is expressed in the action of dispelling our misery, it springs from divine affection: "It is commonly said that in him [God] there is not compassion according to passion, but according to effect. Nevertheless, this effect proceeds from the affection [*affectu*] of the will, which is not a passion, but a simple act of the will."[28] This simple act of will is one with the divine being: the act by which God loves himself and all things.[29] In it, we find our union with God: "God does not have mercy [*miseretur*] except on account of love, insofar as he loves us as something of himself."[30]

A suffering God can never be devoid of self-interest since he must always be concerned in some way with the relief of *his own* suffering.[31] This is quite different from the agapeic love of the impassible God: "It does not belong to the First Agent, who is agent only, to act for the acquisition of some end; God intends only to communicate his perfection, which is his goodness; while every creature intends to acquire its own perfection."[32] The concern of the impassible God is not for himself but for the creature: "In dispelling our affliction through his favors, God does not ordain this to his advantage but to ours."[33] The compassion of impassible God is utterly gratuitous, concerned only with welfare of his people.[34]

---

27. Elizabeth A. Johnson, *She Who Is: The Mystery of God in a Feminist Theological Discourse* (New York: Crossroad, 1992), 265.

28. "communiter dicitur, quod non est in eo misericordia secundum passionem, sed secundum effectum; qui tamen effectus ex affectu voluntatis procedit; qui non est passio, sed simplex voluntatis actus" (*Sent.* IV, 46, 2, 1, qc. 1, co.).

29. "By the same love, however, God loves both himself and others on account of his goodness...." (*SCG* IV, c.23.11).

30. "Deus non miseretur nisi propter amorem, inquantum amat nos tamquam aliquid sui" (*ST* II-II, 30, 2, ad l).

31. "The creation of the world and human beings for freedom and fellowship is always bound up with the process of God's deliverance from the sufferings of his love.... The deliverance or redemption of the world is bound up with the self-deliverance of God from his sufferings. In this sense, not only does God suffer with and for the world; liberated men and women suffer with God and for him" (Moltmann, *Trinity*, 60).

32. *ST* I, 44, 4, co.

33. *Sent.* IV, 46, 2, 1, qc. 1, co. Cf. *SCG* I, c.93.7

34. See William J. Hill, OP, "Two Gods of Love: Aquinas and Whitehead," *Listening* 14, no. 3 (1979): 249–65.

In this, the compassion of the impassible God manifests greater intimacy than the suffering of the passible God.[35] A suffering God must always be in some sense removed from his people as he "reacts" to their distress with *his own* divine suffering that is distinct from *theirs*. In contrast, the impassible God is simply one with his people in *their* suffering.

But he [God] is related in this way in overcoming the miseries of others, as a man is related in overcoming their miseries. For as a man, in driving away the misery of anyone considers the good of the one whose misery he drives away, so God in dispelling our afflictions through his favors, does not ordain this to his advantage, but ours; hence insofar as our misery is in some way his, in the view of the one who drives it away, so God is said to be merciful and to have mercy.[36]

We might say that, as the suffering of Jesus is the very suffering of God since Jesus *is* God in the mystery of the Incarnation,[37] so the suffering of God's people is the very suffering of Christ through his union of love with them in the mystery of his Mystical Body.[38] As Aquinas explains, the sufferings of the members of Christ's Body are truly the sufferings of Christ: "'I make up those things which are lacking from the suffering of Christ' [Col 1:24] that is, [from the suffering] of the whole Church whose head is Christ.... For this was lacking, that as Christ suffered in his own body, so he would suffer in Paul, his member, and similarly in others."[39] All of these statements point to a God who suffers *as we do*, a God who suffers in the *humanity* of Christ and the *humanity* of his followers—the God who identifies himself with them and so makes their suffering his own. So Jesus does not say, "You were hungry and I grieved for you," but "*I* was hungry.... *I* was thirsty."[40] As Aquinas comments, "'Hence whatever

35. See Dodds, "Thomas Aquinas"; Dodds, *Unchanging God*, 213–32.

36. "Sed ipse [Deus] hoc modo se habet in repellendo miserias aliorum, sicut se habet homo in repellendo miseriam suam. Sicut homo enim in repellendo miseriam alicujus considerat hominis utilitatem cujus repellit miseriam; ita et Deus per sua beneficia repellens nostram miseriam, non ordinat hoc ad suam utilitatem, sed ad nostram; unde inquantum nostra miseria est quasi sua secundum reputationem quamdam ipsius qui eam repellit, sic dicitur misericors, et misereri" (*Sent.* IV, 46, 2, 1, qc. 1, co.).

37. See *ST III*, 16, 4, co.

38. "As a natural body is one, though made up of various members, so the whole Church, which is the Mystical Body of Christ, is reckoned as one person with its head, who is Christ" (*ST* III, 49, 1, co.).

39. *Super ad col.* 1, lect. 6 [line 55 c.].

40. Mt 25:35.

you do to one of these least of my brothers, you do to me' [Mt 25:40], ... because the head and the members are one body."[41] Divine compassion involves no distinct suffering in God, not because God is distant from us but because of his utter intimacy. As Gerald Vann observes: "Thus the very immutability of God is not a denial of his involvement in the sorrows of these present times, but a triumphant vindication of it."[42]

41. *Super ev. matt.* 25, lect. 3.
42. Gerald Vann, OP, *The Pain of Christ and the Sorrow of God* (New York: Alba House, 2000), 84.

CHAPTER 7

DIVINE PROVIDENCE

Once Aquinas has considered what belongs strictly or absolutely to the will, he moves on to things "which have a relation to both intellect and will." Here we find the consideration of providence "in respect to all created things," and predestination "in respect especially of man as regards his eternal salvation." [1] Here we will also consider the problem of theodicy—the question of evil and suffering. Aquinas deals with this question in several places, but it seems appropriate to consider it as part of the discussion of divine providence since evil would seem the most serious challenge to God's providential plan.

Providence and Governance

Aquinas alludes to divine providence in the Fifth Way, which "is taken from the governance of the world." He argues that the behavior of beings without intelligence, insofar as it involves acting for an end, cannot be

---

1. "Having considered all that relates to the will absolutely, we must now proceed to those things which have relation to both the intellect and the will, namely providence, in respect to all created things; predestination and reprobation and all that is connected with these acts in respect especially of man as regards his eternal salvation" (*ST* I, 22, prologue).

attributed to mere chance, but must be "directed by some being endowed with knowledge and intelligence." He concludes that "some intelligent being exists by whom all natural things are directed to their end; and this being we call God."[2] Providence is simply God's "plan of the order of things towards their end." It involves both the plan (which is, "properly speaking, providence") and the execution of the plan ("which is termed government").[3]

Aquinas argues that all things are subject to God's providence and governance. He is aware that some early philosophers, such as Democritus and Epicurus, completely denied the existence of providence by attributing the origin of all things to necessity or chance.[4] Some contemporary thinkers also argue that God's causality does not extend to chance events lest it deprive them of their contingent character.[5] We have already seen that God's transcendent causality does not deprive secondary causes (including chance) of their proper causality, but is rather its source.[6] Because God is the first agent (as we know from the Second Way), his causality "extends to all being," so that "all things that exist in whatsoever manner are necessarily directed by God toward some end."[7]

God has immediate providence over all things since everything is included in the divine plan.[8] Here again, we find God intimately involved in creation. Yet the proper causality of creatures is not excluded, since the execution of the plan (governance) is achieved through creaturely intermediaries. The "abundance of God's goodness" is manifest in that "the dignity of causality is imparted even to creatures."[9]

God's providential plan cannot be thwarted or hindered by creatures

---

2. *ST* I, 2, 3, co.

3. *ST* I, 22, 1, co. and ad 2; *ST* I, 22, 3, co.

4. *ST* I, 22, 2, co. and ad 3.

5. "God chose a world in which chance has a role to play, thereby ... accepting limitation of his power to control" (John C. Polkinghorne, *Science and Creation: The Search for Understanding* [Boston: Shambhala, 1989], 63).

6. See the section on "God's Unchanging Will and the Contingency of Creatures" in chapter 5 of this book.

7. *ST* I, 22, 2, co.

8. "God has immediate providence over everything, because he has in his intellect the types of everything, even the smallest" (*ST* I, 22, 3, co.).

9. *ST* I, 22, 3, co. See also Corey L. Barnes, "Natural Final Causality and Providence in Aquinas," *New Blackfriars* 95, no. 1057 (2014): 349–61.

since their very causality is part of it. Yet God's plan does not impose necessity on creaturely events. The assertions in the previous two sentences would involve a flat contradiction if we thought of God's causality as univocal with that of creatures. But we have seen that God transcends all categories of creaturely causality including necessity and contingency. God can cause not only what happens but also the mode of its happening—whether it be necessary, contingent, free, or chance: "It pertains to divine providence to produce every grade of being. And thus it has prepared for some things necessary causes, so that they happen of necessity; for others contingent causes, that they may happen by contingency, according to the nature of their proximate causes."[10]

Predestination

As a theologian, Aquinas is committed to exploring the meaning of predestination as revealed in Scripture.[11] He follows the scriptural account in seeing predestination as a work of divine love, a divine prerogative not dependent on human merit.[12] The discussion brings two realities into sharp focus: the primary causality of God and the fact of human freedom. The relationship between these two realities is a mystery, and, in accor-

10. *ST* I, 22, 4, co. "The order of divine providence is unchangeable and certain, so far as all things foreseen happen as they have been foreseen, whether from necessity or from contingency" (*ST* I, 22, 4, ad 2). See also Bernard McGinn, "The Development of the Thought of Thomas Aquinas on the Reconciliation of Divine Providence and Contingent Action," *Thomist* 39, no. 4 (1975): 741–52; Michał Paluch, OP, "Recovering a Doctrine of Providence," *Nova et Vetera* (English ed.) 12, no. 4 (2014): 1159–72.

11. For instance, Romans 8:30, as quoted in *ST* I, 23, 1, sed contra: "Whom he predestined, them he also called." On Aquinas's doctrine of predestination, see Michał Paluch, *La profondeur de l'amour divin: Evolution de la doctrine de la prédestination dans l'oeuvre de Thomas d'Aquin* (Paris: J. Vrin, 2004); Matthew Levering, "Aquinas on Romans 8: Predestination in Context," in *Reading Romans with St. Thomas Aquinas*, ed. Matthew Levering and Michael Dauphinais (Washington, D.C.: The Catholic University of America Press, 2012), 196–215.

12. According to scripture: "In love, he destined us for adoption to himself" (Eph 1:4–5). In Aquinas: "Predestination presupposes election . . . and election presupposes love" (*ST* I, 23, 4, co.). According to scripture: "For by grace you have been saved through faith, and this is not from you; it is the gift of God" (Eph 2:8). And also: "He has mercy on whom he wills, and he hardens whom he wills" (Rom 9:18). In Aquinas: "In another way, the effect of predestination may be considered in general. Thus it is impossible that the whole effect of predestination in general should have any cause coming from us; because whatsoever is in man disposing him towards salvation, is all included under the effect of predestination" (*ST* I, 23, 5, co.).

dance with his theological method, Aquinas allows it to remain so. He is well-equipped to discuss this mystery through the principles he established earlier in his discussions of divine causality, providence, and the relationship between God and contingent things.[13]

Predestination is simply God's "plan of the direction of a rational creature toward the end of eternal life."[14] Just as an arrow requires the direction of the archer in order to reach the target (since such intentional action is beyond its nature), so we require divine direction since the attainment of eternal life is beyond our natural capacity. Predestination is founded on divine love, since to love is simply to will some good to someone and God gratuitously wills the good of eternal salvation to the elect.[15] As no cause can be assigned to the divine will,[16] the merits of the elect cannot be viewed as the cause of their predestination. Rather, our merits, as consequences of our good acts, are part of predestination since "that which flows from free will is also of predestination."[17] As the certainty of the divine will does not impose necessity on contingent things, so the infallibility of predestination does not violate human free will: "The order of predestination is certain; yet free-will is not destroyed; so that the effect of predestination occurs contingently. Moreover all that has been said about the divine knowledge and will must also be taken into consideration; since they do not destroy contingency in things, although they themselves are most certain and infallible."[18] Creaturely actions are not the cause of predestination, but as secondary causes, they may contribute to its achievement.[19]

13. *ST* I, 2, 3; *ST* I, 14, 13; *ST* I, 19, 6–9; *ST* I, 22, 4. As Aquinas notes elsewhere: "It is possible to show that predestination and election impose no necessity, by the same reasoning whereby we showed above that divine providence does not take away contingency from things" (*SCG* III, c.163.2).

14. *ST* I, 23, 1, co.

15. *ST* I, 23, 4.

16. *ST* I, 19, 5.

17. "Now there is no distinction between what flows from free will, and what is of predestination; as there is no distinction between what flows from a secondary cause and from a first cause. For the providence of God produces effects through the operation of secondary causes.... Wherefore, that which flows from free will is also of predestination" (*ST* I, 23, 5).

18. *ST* I, 23, 6, co. On divine knowledge and will in relation to contingent things, see *ST* I, 14, 13; Q. 19, 4.

19. "In predestination two things are to be considered—namely, the divine ordination; and its effect. As regards the former, in no possible way can predestination be furthered by the prayers of

Since God's providence does not deprive humans of free will, it is possible for them to sin and so fail to attain eternal life. To discuss this possibility, Aquinas makes a distinction between divine will and divine permission. God "in no way wills the evil of sin."[20] He "neither wills evil to be done, nor wills it not to be done, but wills to permit evil to be done; and this is good."[21] In fact, "this is part of the infinite goodness of God, that he should permit evil to exist, and out of it produce good."[22] Sin and reprobation are a matter of divine permission: "As men are ordained to eternal life through the providence of God, it likewise is part of that providence to permit some to fall away from that end; this is called reprobation."[23]

Aquinas considers reprobation not just a possibility but a fact: "God does reprobate some."[24] He sees reprobation as probably more common than salvation.

Since their eternal happiness, consisting in the vision of God, exceeds the common state of nature, and especially in so far as this is deprived of grace through the corruption of original sin, those who are saved are in the minority. In this especially, however, appears the mercy of God, that he has chosen some for that salvation, from which very many in accordance with the common course and tendency of nature fall short.[25]

---

the saints. For it is not due to their prayers that anyone is predestined by God. As regards the latter, predestination is said to be helped by the prayers of the saints, and by other good works; because providence, of which predestination is a part, does not do away with secondary causes but so provides effects, that the order of secondary causes falls also under providence. So, as natural effects are provided by God in such a way that natural causes are directed to bring about those natural effects, without which those effects would not happen; so the salvation of a person is predestined by God in such a way, that whatever helps that person towards salvation falls under the order of predestination; whether it be one's own prayers or those of another; or other good works, and such like, without which one would not attain to salvation. Whence, the predestined must strive after good works and prayer; because through these means predestination is most certainly fulfilled" (*ST* I, 23, 8, co.).

20. *ST* I, 19, 9, co. Likewise, God's knowledge "is not the cause of evil; but is the cause of the good whereby evil is known" (*ST* I, 14, 10, ad 2).

21. *ST* I, 19, 9, ad 3.

22. *ST* I, 2, 3, ad 1.

23. *ST* I, 23, 3, co.

24. *ST* I, 23, 3, co. "He wills this good to some in preference to others; since he reprobates some" (*ST* I, 23, 4, co.).

25. *ST* I, 23, 7, ad 3.

Yet Aquinas does not speculate about exact numbers.[26] The Church is also silent on this question even as it doctrinally affirms the existence of hell and the possibility of eternal damnation.[27] A number of contemporary theologians have speculated on the possibility of an empty hell.[28] Thomas Gilby, OP, suggests that the difference in opinion between Aquinas and such theologians on the likelihood of damnation may be attributed to their different historical contexts.[29]

26. "It is, however, better to say that to God alone is known the number for whom is reserved eternal happiness" (*ST* I, 23, 7, co.).

27. The *Catechism of the Catholic Church* references scripture and doctrinal pronouncements in its statement: "The teaching of the Church affirms the existence of hell and its eternity" (*Catechism*, nos. 1034–35).

28. As John Paul II notes, writing as a theologian and not invoking papal authority: "The problem of hell has always disturbed great thinkers in the Church, beginning with Origen and continuing in our time with Mikhail Bulgakov and Hans Urs von Balthasar.... This is a mystery, truly inscrutable, which embraces the holiness of God and the conscience of man. The silence of the Church is, therefore, the only appropriate position of Christian faith. Even when Jesus says of Judas, the traitor, 'It would be better for that man if he had never been born' (Mt 26:24), his words do not allude for certain to eternal damnation" (Pope John Paul II, *Crossing the Threshold of Hope*, ed. Vittorio Messori [Toronto: Alfred A. Knopf, Inc., 1994], 185–86). Richard Schenk critiques von Balthasar and argues for the theological importance of affirming the possibility of damnation. See Richard Schenk, OP, "The Epoché of Factical Damnation? On the Costs of Bracketing Out the Likelihood of Final Loss," in *Soundings in the History of a Hope: New Studies on Thomas Aquinas*, 131–61 (Ave Maria, Fla.: Sapientia Press, 2016). Edward Schillebeeckx also finds the possibility of eternal loss to be theologically significant. He rejects the idea of an assured universal salvation (*apokatastasis*) as "too superficial" and as suggesting "too cheap a view of mercy and forgiveness." As he explains: "In their situated freedom human beings are in fact in a position to do both good and evil. In this sense both heaven and hell are human possibilities. Whether there are in fact people who definitively choose evil I do not know; that is a quite different question. No man or woman can discover that; a judgment on that belongs only to God" (Edward Schillebeeckx, OP, *Church: The Human Story of God*, trans. John Bowden [New York: Crossroad, 1993], 136). For a brief account of the history of the concept of hell and its theological significance, see Martin Henry, "Does Hell Still Have a Future?" *The Heythrop Journal* 66, no. 1 (2015): 120–35. The best analogy I've found for understanding how free choice might lead to damnation and how that choice is made, is C. S. Lewis, *The Great Divorce* (New York: Macmillan, 1976).

29. "A thorny question for theologians, nevertheless the high mystery of human predestination in Christ (Ephesians I, 3–14; 3, 11) by the freedom of God's love and favor, is set forth as a message of encouragement in the New Testament. So, too, should it be taken in this Question [*ST* I, 23], despite the severity of the insistence that we can claim no rights in the matter, and the expression of a common theological mood which regards heaven as rare.... The reading seems somewhat imperturbable about the human predicament, but accords with the mood of the time.... In truth, however, questions as to the actual numbers and proportions of the saved are unanswerable, and settled neither by Scripture nor the Fathers nor by teaching authority.... On the data we have, a general optimism and a general pessimism alike are baseless; ecclesiastical authority has rarely intervened, and then only to snub extravagances.... The present article [*ST* I, 23, 7] speaks for its period, not for a constant tradition" (Thomas Gilby, OP, "Notes," in *Summa Theologiae*,

Predestination is something God wills, while reprobation, like sin, is something God permits: "As predestination includes the will to confer grace and glory, so also reprobation includes the will to permit a person to fall into sin, and to impose the punishment of damnation on account of that sin."[30] Reprobation therefore "differs in its causality from predestination." Predestination is the cause both of the present grace and of the future reward to which it leads. Reprobation is not the cause of present sin, though it is the cause of present abandonment by God and of future eternal punishment.[31] It is not God, but the sinner, who is responsible for his sin: "Although anyone reprobated by God cannot acquire grace, nevertheless that he falls into this or that particular sin comes from the use of his free will. Hence it is rightly imputed to him as guilt."[32]

Fundamentally, Aquinas sees predestination as a manifestation of divine goodness: "Predestination has in this way, in regard to its effect, the goodness of God for its reason; towards which the whole effect of predestination is directed as to an end; and from which it proceeds, as from its first moving principle."[33] As the elect manifest God's mercy, the reprobate show his justice: "Let us then consider the whole of the human race, as we consider the whole universe. God wills to manifest his goodness in men; in respect to those whom he predestines, by means of his mercy, as sparing them; and in respect of others, whom he reprobates, by means of his justice, in punishing them. This is the reason why God elects some and rejects others."[34] God's unequal treatment cannot be called unjust: "Neither on this account can there be said to be injustice in God, if he prepares unequal lots for not unequal things. This would be altogether contrary to the notion of justice, if the effect of predestination were granted as a debt,

by St. Thomas Aquinas, ed. Thomas Gilby, OP [London: Eyre and Spottiswoode, 1967], 5:106–7, note a; 5:136–37, note k).

30. *ST* I, 23, 3, co.

31. "Reprobation differs in its causality from predestination. This latter is the cause both of what is expected in the future life by the predestined—namely, glory—and of what is received in this life—namely, grace. Reprobation, however, is not the cause of what is in the present—namely, sin; but it is the cause of abandonment by God. It is the cause, however, of what is assigned in the future—namely, eternal punishment. But guilt proceeds from the free-will of the person who is reprobated and deserted by grace" (*ST* I, 23, 3, ad 2).

32. *ST* I, 23, 3, ad 3.

33. *ST* I, 23, 5, co.

34. *ST* I, 23, 5, ad 3.

and not gratuitously. In things which are given gratuitously, a person can give more or less, just as he pleases (provided he deprives nobody of his due), without any infringement of justice. This is what the master of the house said: 'Take what is thine, and go thy way. Is it not lawful for me to do what I will?' (Mt 20:14–15)."[35]

Aquinas's account, however well-reasoned, may still leave us uneasy. It might all appear to depend on the willfulness of the divine will: "Yet why he chooses some for glory, and reprobates others, has no reason except the divine will."[36] This could seem troubling unless we remember that we're talking about the *divine* will, which is one with God's being, wisdom, goodness, love, and mercy. God's will could never be "willful" if that word is defined as "obstinate, governed by will without regard to reason," but God's will could be supremely "willful" if the word means "intentional" since God's will and wisdom are one: "it is impossible for God to will anything but what his wisdom approves."[37] One with the divine will, God's goodness "is the reason of his willing all other things."[38] Identical with the divine will, God's mercy informs all his works:

In every work of God, viewed at its primary source, there appears mercy. In all that follows, the power of mercy remains, and works indeed with even greater force; as the influence of the first cause is more intense than that of second causes. For this reason does God out of abundance of his goodness bestow upon creatures what is due to them more bountifully than is proportionate to their deserts: since less would suffice for preserving the order of justice than what the divine goodness confers; because between creatures and God's goodness there can be no proportion.[39]

35. *ST* I, 23, 5, ad 3.
36. *ST* I, 23, 5, ad 3.
37. *ST* I, 21, 1, ad 2. "The reason for the permission of sin (and thus reprobation) is the wisdom of divine government that conforms to the nature of things as it is thought by divine wisdom. Human nature being fallible in its freedom, God allows it to sometimes fail" (Serge-Thomas Bonino, OP, "Contemporary Thomism through the Prism of the Theology of Predestination," in *Thomism and Predestination: Principles and Disputations*, ed. Steven A. Long, Roger W. Nutt, and Thomas Joseph White, OP [Ave Maria, Fla.: Sapientia Press, 2017], 47). On the two meanings of "willful," see *Webster's Seventh New Collegiate Dictionary* (Springfield, Mass.: G. and C. Merriam Company, 1970), 1021.
38. *ST* I, 19, 4, ad 3. "God is said to have equally care of all, not because by his care he deals out equal good to all, but because he administers all things with a like wisdom and goodness" (*ST* I, 20, 3, ad 1). "God can do nothing that is not in accord with his wisdom and goodness" (*ST* I, 21, 4, co.).
39. *ST* I, 21, 4, co. "While we do not know the radius of the grace of salvation, we have

Given the mystery of God, the lack of a complete explanation is what we should expect in the discussion of predestination. This lack should therefore lead to trust rather than suspicion; we might rather be suspicious of too much explanation.[40] Compared to the accounts of some of his later followers, for instance, Aquinas's account of predestination, divine causality, and human freedom is notably sparse.[41] He is content to confess the transcendence of divine causality—which can therefore account for both the actuality of the effect accomplished through the secondary cause and for the mode of that effect, whether necessary or free—but in a way that ever exceeds our comprehension.[42] By his wise silence, Aquinas preserves

---

been told in Sacred Scripture that 'where sin has abounded there grace yet more abounds' (Rom 5:4). God does not owe it to the defectible creature to preserve it from all defect. But his love and mercy are the irradiant source of every good—including every volitional good—and his grace abounds.... [I]t is crucial to perceive, and to rest in the perception, that God has revealed himself as Omnipotent Mercy, whose redemptive Incarnation is infinitely efficacious. It is this that is the very formal motive of hope—and not despair—namely, that God in his efficacious grace truly and infinitely suffices for the salvation of our fallible and defectible freedom" (Steven A. Long, "St. Thomas Aquinas, Divine Causality, and the Mystery of Predestination," in *Thomism and Predestination: Principles and Disputations*, ed. Steven A. Long, Roger W. Nutt, and Thomas Joseph White, OP [Ave Maria, Fla.: Sapientia Press, 2017], 76). "We shall try to interpret a few passages of St. Paul, principally on the subject of predestination. These questions about grace are extremely mysterious and profound. If, in discussing them, we forget that God is a God of love, if we speak about them without steeping them in the atmosphere of divine goodness that knocks at men's hearts, we may well say what would seem theologically—or rather, verbally, literally—exact, but what would in fact be a deformation, misleading and false" (Charles Journet, *The Meaning of Grace*, trans. A. V. Littledale [New York: P. J. Kenedy and Sons, 1960], 35).

40. "Rather than take up the post-Reformation scholastic challenge to fill in the gaps and so provide an exhaustive account of the mechanics of divine causation, I shall argue instead that Aquinas's refusal to say more than he does is not a weakness in his position but rather a strength.... To go any further than Aquinas does in trying to explain divine creative causation, as the Bañiezians do, is inevitably to lose sight of its transcendence. And to do that is to betray the central premise of Aquinas's resolution of the apparent conflict between divine causation and human freedom.... Aquinas's silence about exactly how it all works is not an oversight or a failure of nerve, but rather an acknowledgement of the limitations of human thought in the face of divine transcendence. Any attempt to say much more than Aquinas said compromises the transcendence of divine creative causation that is essential for divine causation and human freedom to be held together" (Brian J. Shanley, OP, "Divine Causation and Human Freedom in Aquinas," *American Catholic Philosophical Quarterly* 72, no. 1 [1998]: 101, 116).

41. From the vast literature on these issues, the reader might profitably consult: Steven A. Long, Roger W. Nutt, and Thomas Joseph White, OP, eds., *Thomism and Predestination: Principles and Disputations* (Ave Maria, Fla.: Sapientia Press, 2017); Robert Joseph Matava, *Divine Causality and Human Free Choice: Domingo Bañez, Physical Premotion and the Controversy de Auxiliis Revisited* (Leiden: Brill, 2016); John H. Wright, SJ, "Divine Knowledge and Human Freedom: The God Who Dialogues," *Theological Studies* 38, no. 1 (1977): 450–77; Shanley, "Divine Causation."

42. "Behind the failures of both Bañez and Molina (and their respective adherents) to ar-

the mystery of predestination.[43] As Michał Paluch remarks: "We do not know how the mystery of predestination will be accomplished in history. But because ... the Incarnation of Christ has surpassed every expectation even among the angels themselves, one may hope that the final realization of his plan of love will again surpass all that man dare and can conceive."[44] For Aquinas, the mystery of predestination is one with the mystery of the cross—a mystery of love: "The cross is braced by its depth which lies concealed beneath the ground. It is not seen because the depth of divine love

---

ticulate a satisfactory account of the causal relationship between God and human action, is a diminished sense of the transcendence of the Creator. It is not enough to read the traditional Bañezianism-Molinism struggle simply as divergent attempts to fill the gaps in Aquinas's account in the altered climate of the Post-Reformation problematic; for what counts as a gap to be filled in depends upon still deeper assumptions. It is rather that Bañez and Molina are separated from Aquinas by a fundamental change in background understanding. They are much more confident that mundane causal categories can be used to explain the relationship between God and human freedom and they seem consequently to assume that there is an inherent antagonism between God and the human will which must be resolved in favor of one of the contending parties; both of these assumptions are foreign to Aquinas because both compromise divine transcendence" (Shanley, "Divine Causation," 120–21). On the loss of transcendence in discussions of divine causality and free will among Thomists after Aquinas, see Placher, *Domestication*, 71–87.

43. "Such is, in my opinion, ... the genius of Thomism in an area where the theologian knows that his science has reached its limits. He doesn't want to sacrifice any of the problem's data, metaphysical or theological: neither the universal determining causality of pure Act, nor grace's primacy, nor God's innocence and his saving will. The theologian surrenders neither to the absurdity of a contradiction between the Word of God and right reason, nor to the apologetic cop out of a created freedom conceived as first cause. He contents himself (but that's a lot) to lay out the mystery in its rightful place, that is, to turn one's gaze toward the superintelligible essence of a God in whom power, wisdom, and goodness kiss" (Bonino, "Contemporary Thomism," 50). "Aquinas and some of his subsequent interpreters in the Thomistic tradition provide us with a refined account of the doctrine [of] predestination, one that rightly underscores both the omnipotence and innocence of God, the primacy of grace and the reality of human freedom, the eternity of divine foreknowledge and the real distinction between what God wills and what God merely permits or tolerates. The Thomist account is able to hold these features in healthy tension in such a way as to present us with a mystery that is both luminous and obscure, intelligible and numinous. The balance and depth of this account preserve the truths of the New Testament and of the Augustinian heritage of Western theology in consonance with the sound principles of realistic metaphysics and of ordinary human experience" (Thomas Joseph White, OP, "Catholic Predestination: The Omnipotence and Innocence of Divine Love," in *Thomism and Predestination: Principles and Disputations*, ed. Steven A. Long, Roger W. Nutt, and Thomas Joseph White, OP [Ave Maria, Fla.: Sapientia Press, 2017], 100–101).

44. "Nous ne savons pas comment le mystère de la prédestination s'accomplira dans l'histoire. Mais puisque selon notre Docteur l'incarnation du Christ a dépassé chez les anges eux-mêmes toute attente, il est permis d'espérer que la réalisation finale de son dessein d'amour dépassera à nouveau tout ce que l'homme ose et peut concevoir" (Paluch, *La profondeur*, 317).

which sustains us is not visible insofar as the plan of predestination ... is beyond our intelligence."[45]

God and Evil

The question of God and evil arises in many contexts in Aquinas's writings. We found it in the early questions of the *Summa Theologica* when the presence of evil seemed to negate the very existence of God.[46] It arose again in his discussions of God's knowledge, will, and providence.[47] It also occurs in his discussions of the distinction between good and evil and the causes of sin.[48] It may be helpful, therefore, to take a moment to bring his various arguments together.

The question of God and evil was a dilemma for philosophers long before the time of Aquinas. We find its classic formulation in Epicurus:

God ... either wishes to take away evils, and is unable; or he is able, and is unwilling; or he is neither willing nor able, or he is both willing and able. If he is willing and is unable, he is feeble, which is not in accordance with the character of God; if he is able and unwilling, he is envious, which is equally at variance with God; if he is neither willing nor able, he is both envious and feeble, and therefore not God; if he is both willing and able, which alone is suitable to God, from what source then are evils? or why does he not remove them?[49]

It was some centuries after Aquinas that the philosopher Gottfried Wilhelm Leibniz coined the word *theodicy* (from the Greek *theos* [god] and *dikē* [justice]) to name the effort to justify the presence of evil in a world created by a good and omnipotent God.[50]

---

45. *Super ad eph.* III, lect. 5 (§180). A question on "The Book of Life" (*ST* I, 24) follows Aquinas's discussion of predestination. We will not review it here, since Aquinas sees the Book of Life fundamentally as a metaphor for predestination, which we have already discussed. See *ST* I, 24, 1, co. and ad 1.

46. *ST* I, 2, 3, obj. 1.

47. *ST* I, 14, 10; *ST* I, 19, 9; *ST* I, 22, 2, ad 2.

48. *ST* I, 48, 2, ad 3; *ST* I, 48, 5; *ST* I, 49, 2; *ST* I-II, 79, 1–2.

49. The argument of Epicurus is found in Lactantius, *A Treatise on the Anger of God*, chap. 13, in *The Ante-Nicene Fathers: Translations of the Writings of the Fathers down to A.D. 325*, ed. Alexander Roberts and James Donaldson (Grand Rapids, Mich.: Eerdmans, 1994), 7:271.

50. See Gottfried Wilhelm Leibniz, *Theodicy: Essays on the Goodness of God, the Freedom of Man, and the Origin of Evil* (New Haven, Conn.: Yale University Press, 1952), originally published in 1710 as *Essais de Théodicée sur la bonté de Dieu, la liberté de l'homme et l'origine du mal.*

The question of evil would seem especially acute in Aquinas's theology, which emphasizes the primary causality and infinite goodness of God: if God is the first cause of all things, how is God not the cause of evil?[51] But if God is the cause of evil, how can God be called good? Although seemingly acute in Aquinas's theology, the question of evil is by no means unique to it. It must arise in any theology that proclaims creation as the work of an omniscient, omnipotent, and loving creator. Only an omnipotent being can create something from nothing, and only a God of unbounded goodness would do so for no other motive than love.[52] Yet the reality of evil in the created world is evident. To address the question of evil authentically, therefore, it seems theology must deny neither the power and goodness of God nor the reality of evil. This will not lead to a "solution" to the problem of evil but only point to a mystery. Yet perhaps that is the purpose of theology, as Charles Journet says: "The aim of the theologian dealing with a mystery is to do away with phrases which diminish the mystery."[53]

Not all contemporary theologians follow this path. Some try to solve the problem of evil by limiting God's influence in the world. John Polkinghorne maintains that God freely limits himself: "It has been an important emphasis in much recent theological thought about creation

---

51. For more extensive treatments of the question of theodicy in Aquinas, see Eleonore Stump, *Wandering in Darkness: Narrative and the Problem of Suffering* (Oxford: Oxford University Press, 2013); Eleonore Stump, *Aquinas* (New York: Routledge, 2003), 461–70; Brian Davies, OP, *The Reality of God and the Problem of Evil* (New York: Continuum, 2006); David B. Burrell, CSC, *Deconstructing Theodicy: Why Job Has Nothing to Say to the Puzzle of Suffering* (Grand Rapids, Mich.: Baker Academic, 2008).

52. "Although to create a finite effect does not show an infinite power, yet to create it from nothing does show an infinite power" (*ST* I, 45, 5, ad 3). On God's goodness in the act of creating, see *ST* I, 19, 2, ad 2; *ST* I, 19, 3; *ST* I, 20, 2.

53. Charles Journet, *The Meaning of Evil*, trans. Michael Barry (New York: P. J. Kenedy and Sons, 1963), 14. "St. Thomas's account of evil ... does not seek to explain the evil in the world. When we speak of God we do not clear up a puzzle; we draw attention to a mystery" (McCabe, *God and Evil*, 128). After examining various approaches to the question of God and human suffering, Edward Schillebeeckx remarks: "I think at this point it would be good to resort to Thomas Aquinas. True, in reality he is seldom understood and little studied.... However, he does seem to me one of the few people who can give us some reasonably satisfactory viewpoints which at the same time leave all the darkness in its incomprehensibility.... On the one hand is the incomprehensible depth of the mystery of God, and on the other hand the negative depth of what finitude and freedom can involve" (Edward Schillebeeckx, OP, *Christ: The Experience of Jesus as Lord*, trans. John Bowden [New York: Crossroad, 1983], 728–29).

to acknowledge that by bringing the world into existence God has self-limited divine power by allowing the other truly to be itself.... Not all that happens is in accordance with God's will because God has stood back, making metaphysical room for creaturely action."[54] It seems, however, that divine self-limitation does little to resolve the problem of evil but only raises new questions. For instance, is the good of human freedom sufficient to warrant all the evils that follow upon God's act of self-limitation?[55] And if the limitation was freely imposed, why does God not remove it and come to the aid of his suffering creatures?[56]

Other theologians see God's limitation not as a free act but as an intrinsic aspect of his being. This position gets God off the hook since he can't be responsible for things beyond his control. Here we might think of process theology, which sees limitation as intrinsic to the divine nature: "Process thought is distinctive in holding that limitations of divine knowledge and power arise from metaphysical necessity rather than from voluntary self-limitation."[57] Other theologians limit God's influence to certain realms of creation. Nancey Murphy, for instance, restricts God's causality to the sphere of quantum indeterminacy and finds this to be an advantage in dealing with theodicy: "Those of us who argue for the locus of divine action at the quantum level have been accused of allowing too little scope for special divine acts. This criticism, though, becomes a strength when confronting the problem of evil."[58] Francisco Ayala argues

54. John C. Polkinghorne, *Belief in God in an Age of Science* (New Haven, Conn.: Yale University Press, 1998), 13. See also John C. Polkinghorne, *Science and Providence: God's Interaction with the World* (Boston: New Science Library, 1989), 59–68.

55. "It is far from clear, however, that the autonomy and integrity of the natural order is, in itself, a *great enough good* to justify all the misery and loss that results from events running their course untouched" (Thomas F. Tracy, "The Lawfulness of Nature and the Problem of Evil," in *Physics and Cosmology: Scientific Perspectives on the Problem of Natural Evil*, ed. Nancey Murphy, Robert John Russell, and William Stoeger [Vatican City and Berkeley, Calif.: Vatican Observatory and Center for Theology and the Natural Sciences, 2007], 163).

56. On this question, see Wesley J. Wildman, "Incongruous Goodness, Perilous Beauty, Disconcerting Truth: Ultimate Reality and Suffering in Nature," in *Physics and Cosmology: Scientific Perspectives on the Problem of Natural Evil*, ed. Nancey Murphy, Robert John Russell, and William Stoeger (Vatican City and Berkeley, Calif.: Vatican Observatory and Center for Theology and the Natural Sciences, 2007), 289–90.

57. Ian G. Barbour, "God's Power: A Process View," in *The Work of Love: Creation as Kenosis*, ed. John Polkinghorne (Grand Rapids, Mich.: Eerdmans, 2001), 12.

58. Nancey Murphy, "Science and the Problem of Evil: Suffering as a By-product of a Finely Tuned Cosmos," in *Physics and Cosmology: Scientific Perspectives on the Problem of Natural Evil*,

that withdrawing God's influence from the contingencies of nature is an advantage when facing questions of theodicy: "Theologians in the past struggled with the issue of dysfunction because they thought it had to be attributed to God's design. Science, much to the relief of many theologians, provides an explanation that convincingly attributes defects, deformities and dysfunctions to natural causes."[59]

Some theologians try to mitigate the problem of suffering in creation by attributing suffering to God. Whitehead, for instance, describes God as "the fellow sufferer who understands."[60] The image of divine suffering certainly bespeaks divine compassion, but has little power to address the problem of *creaturely* suffering. And as we noted in our discussion of divine compassion, the suffering God is inevitably concerned with *his own* suffering. In Paul Fiddes's theology, for instance, God "fulfills his own being *through* suffering, since he can only become more truly himself through suffering with the world."[61]

Aquinas would have no use for such "solutions" to the problem of evil. Since God is the creator, all things require his providential care.[62] To Aquinas, it would be senseless to say that God sustains all things in being if one did not also say that God is providentially involved in all that they do and in all that happens to them: "Suppose someone says that God takes care of these singulars to the extent of preserving them in being, but not in regard to anything else; this is utterly impossible. In fact, all other events that occur in connection with singulars are related to their preservation or corruption. So, if God takes care of singulars as far as their preservation is concerned, he takes care of every contingent event connected with them."[63] God's providential influence pervades all creation: "If these contingent events are traced back further to the highest, divine cause, it

ed. Nancey Murphy, Robert John Russell, and William Stoeger (Vatican City and Berkeley, Calif.: Vatican Observatory and Center for Theology and the Natural Sciences, 2007), 141.

59. Francisco J. Ayala, "Intelligent Design: The Original Version," *Theology and Science* 1, no. 1 (2003): 29.

60. Whitehead, *Process and Reality*, 351.

61. Paul S. Fiddes, *The Creative Suffering of God* (Oxford: Clarendon Press, 1988), 108–9.

62. "God is the cause not indeed only of some particular kind of being, but of the whole universal being.... Wherefore, as there can be nothing which is not created by God, so there can be nothing which is not subject to his government" (*ST* I, 103, 5, co.).

63. *SCG* III, c.75.7.

will be impossible to find anything that lies outside its sphere of influence, since its causality extends to all things insofar as they are beings."[64]

God is the universal cause of being, but evil as such (as Aquinas explains in union with Augustine) is not being or actuality, but rather the lack of being: the privation of an actuality that should be present (for example, the lack of sight in a being that should be capable of seeing).[65] This makes Aquinas's theology fundamentally optimistic since it means that goodness must always have ontological precedence over evil. [66] In fact, the very presence of evil in the world may be used as an argument for the existence of God.

Now, with these considerations we dispose of the error of those who, because they noticed that evils occur in the world, said that there is no God. Thus, Boethius introduces a certain philosopher who asks: "If God exists, whence comes evil?" But it could be argued to the contrary: "If evil exists, God exists." For, there would be no evil if the order of good were taken away, since its privation is evil. But this order would not exist if there were no God.[67]

The doctrine of evil as privation applies to both natural and moral evils. Natural evil is part of the structure of creation, since creation includes beings that are capable of failure (such as the flower that blossoms today and withers tomorrow). The failure or corruption of such a being is a "natural evil [*malum naturae*]."[68] If there were no such contingent beings, however, there could be no creaturely causality, since causality im-

---

64. *In meta.* VI, lect. 3, no. 1215.

65. "Evil is the absence of the good which is natural and due to a thing" (*ST* I, 49, 1, co.). In the context of this ontology, Aquinas explains that God can know evil. Evil is not directly knowable, since only what has being and actuality is knowable: "Evil is not of itself knowable, forasmuch as the very nature of evil means the privation of good; therefore evil can neither be defined nor known except by good" (*ST* I, 14, 10, ad 4). Evil is known through the good of which it is the privation. God knows that good since he is its source. His knowledge "is not the cause of evil; but is the cause of the good whereby evil is known" (*ST* I, 14, 10, ad 2). God knows his effects (which are good) by knowing his essence, "and in knowing them, he knows the opposite evils" (*ST* I, 14, 10, ad 3). Since a thing is knowable insofar as it exists, and since the essence of evil is the privation of good, "by the very fact that God knows good things, he knows evil things also; as by light is known darkness" (*ST* I, 14, 10, co.).

66. "There is nothing wholly evil in the world, for evil is ever founded on good.... Therefore something is said to be evil through escaping from the order of some particular good. If it wholly escaped from the order of divine government, it would wholly cease to exist" (*ST* I, 103, 7, ad 1).

67. *SCG* III, c.71.10.

68. *Sent.* I, 39, 2, 2, co.

plies change, and change always involves the corruption of one thing and the generation of another.[69] The world would be less perfect if it did not contain contingent creatures.[70] God intends the good of the universe and so preserves the nature of each creature, including a creature's capacity to fail.[71]

Moral evil presents a greater challenge for theology than natural evil. It consists in the lack of some due perfection in the free action of some agent (human or angelic). This is the evil of sin or, in Aquinas's terminology, the "evil of fault [*malum culpae*]."[72] Aquinas is careful to point out that God is in no way the cause of this evil: "God wills no good more than he wills his own goodness.... Hence he in no way wills the evil of sin, which is the privation of right order towards the divine good."[73] Since moral evil essentially involves not actuality but privation, God's action, as the first cause of all actuality, is not required or involved as such in its production. Rather, a human being (or angel) is the "first cause" of that lack or negation of being.[74] Aquinas carefully parses the act of sin, argu-

---

69. "If the inclination to generate its like were taken away from fire (from which inclination there results this particular evil which is the burning up of combustible things), there would also be taken away this particular good which is the generation of fire and the preservation of the same according to its species.... In the order of nature, there would not be the generation of one thing unless there were the corruption of another. So, if evil were totally excluded from the whole of things by divine providence, a multitude of good things would have to be sacrificed.... Therefore evil should not be totally excluded from things by divine providence" (*SCG* III, c.71.5–6).

70. "Since God, then, provides universally for all being, it belongs to his providence to permit certain defects in particular effects, that the perfect good of the universe may not be hindered, for if all evil were prevented, much good would be absent from the universe. A lion would cease to live, if there were no slaying of animals; and there would be no patience of martyrs if there were no tyrannical persecution" (*ST* I, 22, 2, ad 2). "The death of the fly is the life of the spider" (*Sent.* I, 39, 2, 2, co.).

71. "Any prudent man will endure a small evil in order that a great good will not be prevented. Any particular good, moreover, is trifling in comparison with the good of universal nature. Again, evil cannot be kept from certain things without taking away their nature, which is such that it may or may not fail; and while this nature may harm something in particular, it nevertheless gives some added beauty to the universe. Consequently, since God is most prudent, his providence does not prevent evil, but allows each thing to act as its nature requires it to act" (*De ver.* 5, 4, ad 4).

72. "We may speak of the evil of fault [*malum culpae*], which is found in that which is not determined [by nature] to one action, as all things that act from free will" (*Sent.* II, 1, 1, 1, ad 3).

73. *ST* I, 19, 9, co.

74. "The first cause of the defect of grace is on our part; but the first cause of the bestowal of grace is on God's" (*ST* I-II, 112, 3, ad 2). "Nothing other than the will is the direct cause of human sin" (*De malo* 3, 3, co.). "Here we have finitude, as it were, as 'the first cause.' As soon as there are *creatures*, there is the *possibility* (not the necessity) of a negative and original *initiative of finitude*, if

---

ing that, to the extent that it is an act and has actuality, it must—like all actuality—have its source in God. Precisely to the extent that it is an act, however, it is not evil since evil consists in privation. To the extent that it is privation or evil or sin, it has its source in the creature.[75]

On the relationship between sin and the divine will, Aquinas argues that God neither wills such evil to be (since then God would be the cause of sin) nor wills it not to be (since then it could not be), but wills to permit it to be.[76] This permission of evil is not contrary to divine goodness.[77] God wills to allow creatures to use their freedom in accordance with their nature, and this includes at least the possibility of moral evil. Such evil is contrary to God's will and certainly contrary to the divine law, but it is not contrary to divine providence in the sense of being able to frustrate God's providential plan for all things. If a particular action departs from God's providence in one way, it remains under it in another.[78]

There is a special place for human beings in God's providential plan:

I can put it that way.... For Thomas, it is a senseless philosophical undertaking to look for a particular cause, a ground or motive for evil and suffering in God; these do not necessarily follow from our finitude, but they do draw their fundamental possibility from there" (Schillebeeckx, *Christ*, 728–29). "Creatures are indeed capable of an utterly initiatory role, but it will not be one of acting but of failing to act, of 'refusing' to enter into the process initiated by actively willing 'the good'" (David B. Burrell, CSC, *Freedom and Creation in Three Traditions* [Notre Dame, Ind.: University of Notre Dame Press, 1993], 90–91).

75. "The effect of the deficient secondary cause is reduced to the first non-deficient cause as regards what it has of being and perfection, but not as regards what it has of defect; just as whatever there is of motion in the act of limping is caused by the motive power, whereas what there is of obliqueness in it does not come from the motive power, but from the curvature of the leg. And, likewise, whatever there is of being and action in a bad action, is reduced to God as the cause; whereas whatever defect is in it is not caused by God, but by the deficient secondary cause" (*ST* I, 49, 2, ad 2).

76. See *ST* I, 19, 9, ad 3. While language about the "permission of evil" keeps us from two errors (making God the cause of evil and positing evil as beyond the reach of divine providence), it is not so much a "solution" to the problem of evil as a way of preserving its mystery: "In so far as this distinction [between the good that God wills and the evil that God permits] means anything, the expression 'divine tolerance of evil' simply means (and this is a tautology) that on the one hand evil is actually evil, has no ground of existence and therefore also no justification for existence, and that on the other hand God still remains God, i.e., author of the good and fighter against evil. Therefore the expression 'God's permissive will' has no theoretical meaning as an *explanation*: it simply describes the dead end of human thinking when it is confronted with the incomprehensible history of human suffering" (Schillebeeckx, *Christ*, 699).

77. "To do evil is in no way proper to those who are good. To do evil for the sake of a good is blameworthy in a man, and cannot be attributed to God. On the other hand, to direct evil to a good is not opposed to one's goodness. Hence permitting evil in order to draw some good from it can be attributed to God" (*De ver.* 5, 4, ad 10).

78. See *ST* I, 19, 6, co.

"There is one orderly plan in accord with which rational creatures are subjected to divine providence, and another by means of which the rest of creatures are ordered."[79] Humans are not simply cogs in the larger wheels of creation. To explain human destiny merely in terms of the workings of the larger universe would be utterly inadequate.[80] Every human person has a transcendent value as an individual, not merely as a member of a species.[81] God guides humans in their actions in a special way, since their actions, unlike those of other material living things, do not proceed simply from their nature but from free will.[82] They share in a special way in God's loving care.[83]

79. *SCG* III, c.111.1.

80. "A different order of providence is required for human affairs than is required for brutes. Consequently, if the ordering of human affairs were only that proper to brutes, human affairs would seem to be entirely without providence. Yet, that order is sufficient for the providence of brutes" (*De ver.* 5, 6, ad 3). Jacques Maritain notes the special significance of human suffering: "The suffering of a man is the suffering of a person, of a whole. Here he is considered no longer as part of the universe, but insofar as he is a person he is considered as a whole, a universe to himself; to suffer that pain as part of the universe in the perspective of nature or of the world taken as God's work of art, does not do away with the fact that as far as the person is concerned it is an utter anomaly" (Jacques Maritain, *Saint Thomas and the Problem of Evil* [Milwaukee, Wisc.: Marquette University Press, 1942], 12). Eleonore Stump finds a special way of personalizing the permission of evil in Aquinas: "God would allow a human person to suffer only if through that suffering alone God can provide an outweighing benefit that goes primarily to the sufferer. This is a claim Aquinas himself explicitly asserts. So, for example he says ... 'But whatever happens with regard to the noblest parts [of the universe] is ordered only to the good of those parts themselves, because care is taken of them for their own sake, and for their sake care is taken of other things.... But among the best parts of the world are God's saints.... He takes care of them in such a way that he doesn't allow any evil for them which he doesn't turn into their good' [St. Thomas Aquinas, *In Rom.* 8, 6]" (Stump, *Wandering*, 384–85).

81. "Each thing is ordered to its action by God according to the way in which it is subordinated to divine providence. Now a rational creature exists under divine providence as being governed and provided for in himself, and not simply for the sake of his species, as is the case with other corruptible creatures. For the individual that is governed only for the sake of the species is not governed for its own sake, but the rational creature is governed for his own sake.... And so only rational creatures receive direction from God in their acts, not only for the species but for the individual" (*SCG* III, c.113.1).

82. "Divine providence extends to all singular things, even to the least. In the case of those beings, then, whose actions take place apart from the inclination appropriate to their species, it is necessary for them to be regulated in their acts by divine providence, over and above the direction which pertains to the species. But many actions are evident, in the case of the rational creature, for which the inclination of the species is not enough. The mark of this is that such actions are not alike in all, but differ in various cases. Therefore, the rational creature must be directed by God in his acts, not only specifically but also individually.... The governing of the acts of a rational creature, insofar as they are personal acts, pertains to divine providence" (*SCG* III, c.113.3, no. 5).

83. "The governance of providence stems from the divine love whereby God loves the things

An especially difficult question is the relationship between God's providential care and the suffering of the innocent. Aquinas is aware of the problem, as he notes in the prologue to his *Commentary on the Book of Job*:

Now in this book the author proceeds to demonstrate his proposition from the supposition that natural things are governed by divine providence. Now what especially seems to impugn God's providence where human affairs are concerned is the affliction of just men, for although it seems at first sight unreasonable and contrary to providence that good things should sometimes happen to bad men, it can be excused in one way or another as the result of divine mercy. But that just men should be afflicted without cause seems to undermine totally the foundation of providence. Therefore, there are proposed for the intended discussion as a kind of theme the many grave afflictions of a certain man, perfect in every virtue, named Job.[84]

As Jesus himself point out, there is no one-to-one correspondence between suffering and individual guilt.[85] There is, however, a relationship between sin and suffering. Aquinas teaches that all evil found in human beings is either sin or punishment for sin.[86] This includes punishment for original sin: "Death and all consequent bodily defects are punishments of original sin."[87] Yet original sin does not solve the question of innocent suffering. For all share equally in Adam's sin, yet all do not suffer equally, and the just often seem to suffer more than the unjust.

Aquinas believes that God can bring good out of the suffering of the

---

created by him. In fact, love consists especially in this, 'that the lover wills the good for his loved one.' So the more that God loves things, the more do they fall under his providence.... It may then be gathered from this, that he loves intellectual substances best. Therefore, their acts of will and choice fall under his providence" (*SCG* III, c.90.6). Cf. *ST* I-II, 91, 2, co.

84. *Super iob*, Prologue. See Roger W. Nutt, "Providence, Wisdom, and the Justice of Job's Afflictions: Considerations from Aquinas' *Literal Exposition on Job*," *The Heythrop Journal* 56, no. 1 (2015): 44–66.

85. In reference to the Galileans persecuted by Pilate and the people killed by a falling tower at Siloam, Jesus says: "Do you think that they were more guilty than everyone else? By no means!" (Lk 13:1–5). And when his disciples see the man born blind and ask Jesus, "Who sinned, this man or his parents, that he was born blind?" Jesus answers, "Neither he nor his parents sinned; it is so that the works of God might be made visible through him" (Jn 9:1–3).

86. "Every evil found in voluntary things is to be looked upon as penalty [*poena*] or fault [*culpa*]" (*ST* I, 48, 5, co.).

87. *ST* I, 85, 5, co. See also *De malo* 5, 1–5.

just. This does not mean that evil as such is ever a "means" to good.[88] Yet God can bring good out of evil.

For evil is twofold: the evil of fault and the evil of punishment. Now God does not cause the evil of fault, but permits it; yet he would not permit it unless he intended some good from it. So Augustine says in his *Enchiridion*: "God is so good that he would never permit any evil to occur, unless he was so powerful as to draw some good from every evil." Therefore, he allows certain sins to be committed because he intends some good; in this way, he allows the rage of tyrants so that martyrs may be crowned. Much more, therefore, should it be said that the evil of punishment, which he causes … is never applied except for the good he intends. And among these goods the best is that the works of God be manifested, and from them that God be known. Therefore, it is not unfitting if he sends afflictions or allows sins to be committed in order that some good come from them…. Sometimes afflictions are sent as a correction, as we read: "Your discipline will teach me" [Ps 17:36]. And sometimes a person is afflicted not to correct past wrongs, but to preserve him from future ones, as we read of Paul: "And to keep me from being too elated by the abundance of revelations, a thorn was given me in the flesh, a messenger of Satan, to harass me, to keep me from being too elated" (2 Cor 12:7). Again, sometimes it is done to encourage virtue: "Virtue is made perfect in infirmity" [2 Cor 12:9].[89]

---

88. "Some have said that although God does not will evil, yet he wills that evil should be or be done, because, although evil is not a good, yet it is good that evil should be or be done. This they said because things evil in themselves are ordered to some good end; and this order they thought was expressed in the words 'that evil should be or be done.' This, however, is not correct; since evil is not of itself ordered to good, but accidentally. For it is beside the intention of the sinner, that any good should follow from his sin; as it was beside the intention of tyrants that the patience of the martyrs should shine forth from all their persecutions. It cannot therefore be said that such an ordering to good is implied in the statement that it is a good thing that evil should be or be done, since nothing is judged of by that which appertains to it accidentally, but by that which belongs to it essentially" (*ST* I, 19, 9, ad 1). "Evil has no formal cause, rather is it a privation of form; likewise, neither has it a final cause, but rather is it a privation of order to the proper end" (*ST* I, 49, 1, co.). Evil is not itself ordered to good, but through God's providential power, it can be so ordered: "We are led to have patience in adversity. Although every created thing comes from God and accordingly is good in its own nature, nevertheless if in some way they harm us and bring us pain, we must believe that this suffering is from God. This argument does not apply to sinful guilt, because no evil stems from God. And therefore, if all pain which a human being might suffer comes from God, he ought to endure it patiently, both because it comes from God and because the suffering is ordered to the good. Thus, sufferings purge sins, humble the outlaw, and spur the good to the love of God" (St. Thomas Aquinas, *Collationes credo in Deum*, in *The Sermon-Conferences of St. Thomas Aquinas on the Apostles' Creed*, trans. and ed. Nicholas Ayo, CSC [Notre Dame, Ind.: University of Notre Dame Press, 1988], 41–43).

89. *Super ev. ioann.*, chap. 9, lect. 1, no. 1301.

Aquinas finds divine justice and mercy even in the afflictions of the just: "Justice and mercy appear in the punishment of the just in this world, since by afflictions lesser faults are cleansed in them, and they are the more raised up from earthly affections to God."[90] Ultimately, however, the good to be attained through suffering goes beyond our present life: "It is right that we should first of all be conformed to Christ's sufferings, before attaining to the immortality and impassibility of glory, which was begun in him and by him acquired for us. So it is fitting that our bodies should remain, for a time, subject to suffering, in order that we may merit the impassibility of glory, in conformity with Christ."[91]

90. *ST* I, 21, 4, ad 3.

91. *ST* I-II, 85, 5, ad 2. "Now the created rational nature alone is immediately subordinate to God, since other creatures do not attain to the universal, but only to something particular, while they partake of the Divine goodness either in 'being' only, as inanimate things, or also in 'living,' and in 'knowing singulars,' as plants and animals; whereas the rational nature, inasmuch as it apprehends the universal notion of good and being, is immediately related to the universal principle of being. Consequently the perfection of the rational creature consists not only in what belongs to it in respect of its nature, but also in that which it acquires through a supernatural participation of Divine goodness. Hence ... man's ultimate happiness consists in a supernatural vision of God: to which vision man cannot attain unless he be taught by God.... Now man acquires a share of this learning, not indeed all at once, but by little and little, according to the mode of his nature.... Hence in order that a man arrive at the perfect vision of heavenly happiness, he must first of all believe God, as a disciple believes the master who is teaching him" (*ST* II-II, 2, 3, co.).

CHAPTER 8

DIVINE POWER

After completing his discussion of God's intellect and will using the analogy of immanent motion, Aquinas turns to transient motion to discuss "the power of God, the principle of the divine operation as proceeding to the exterior effect."[1] In considering divine power, we first have to clear up some possible confusions regarding the word "power" itself in both medieval and contemporary contexts. The medieval Latin word *potentia* can mean both "power" and "potency." We generally understand the word "power" in an active sense as the ability *to act* or *to do* something. The word "potency," however, can have a passive sense as the capacity *to be acted upon* or *to be done unto*—as water has the potency to be heated. As Aquinas explains, "Active power [*potentia activa*] is the principle of acting upon something else; whereas passive power [*potentia passiva*] is the principle of being acted upon by something else." Since God is pure act, the passive sense of "power" or "potency" must be denied of him, while the active sense of the words must be affirmed "in the highest degree."[2]

---

1. "Having considered what belongs to the divine substance, we have now to treat of God's operation. And since one kind of operation is immanent, and another kind of operation proceeds to the exterior effect, we treat first of knowledge and of will (for understanding abides in the intelligent agent, and will is in the one who wills); and afterwards of the power of God, the principle of the divine operation as proceeding to the exterior effect" (*ST* I, 14, prologue).

2. *ST* I, 25, 1, co.

In contemporary usage, the word "power" is fraught with possible negative connotations. We can see this in the adage: "Power tends to corrupt and absolute power corrupts absolutely." Edward Schillebeeckx explains the problem: "The word 'power' has been seriously infected by human beings. Human power can certainly also be liberating and productive, but it is often destructive and enslaving, imprisoning and manipulative. Precisely because we usually experience relationships of power in this sense, modern men and women are wary about using the term 'omnipotent' for God; it conjures up too much the dictatorial power which enslaves men and women."[3] In attributing power to God, we need to deny its possibly negative connotations. For this, we can employ the way of negation along with the way of eminence, remembering that God's surpassing power is one with his unbounded goodness and love.[4]

We use the word "omnipotence" to describe God's power, but it also requires some clarification. As Aquinas notes, "it seems difficult to explain in what his omnipotence precisely consists: for there may be doubt as to the precise meaning of the word 'all' when we say that God can do all things."[5] This gives rise to that favorite philosophical pastime of trying to find something God can't do. For instance, if God can do "all" things, can he make a rock so heavy that he can't lift it? If he can't make such a rock, then he's not omnipotent when it comes to making stuff. If he can, then he's not omnipotent as regards lifting stuff.

To parse the term "all-powerful," Aquinas first considers the word "power." It refers to things that are possible, and things may be possible either in relation to some power or absolutely. Taking "possible" in the first sense, there are two alternatives. First, we might think of God's power in relation to that of creatures and say that God can do all things that are possible to creatures. But this does not make God all-powerful, since the power of creatures is always limited. Second, we could think of what is possible in relation to divine power and say that God can do everything possible to divine power. But this evidently becomes a vicious circle and

3. Schillebeeckx, *Church*, 85.
4. "Since the divine essence, through which God acts, is infinite, it follows that his power likewise is infinite" (*ST* I, 25, 2).
5. *ST* I, 25, 3, co.

doesn't get us any closer to understanding the nature of divine omnipotence.[6] So rather than consider what's possible in relation to some power, we might consider what's possible absolutely.

A thing is possible absolutely if it is not self-contradictory. So we can say that God is omnipotent since he can do all things that are not self-contradictory. This does not mean that God is limited by the principle of non-contradiction—only that when we propose self-contradictions (such as square circles) as challenges to God's power, we are really just uttering nonsense syllables and not actually saying anything: "Whatsoever has or can have the nature of being is numbered among the absolutely possible things, in respect of which God is omnipotent. Now, nothing is opposed to the idea of being except non-being. Therefore, that which implies being and non-being at the same time is repugnant to the idea of an absolutely possible thing, within the scope of the divine omnipotence."[7] The notion of a rock too heavy for an omnipotent being to lift involves just such a self-contradiction (implying that the being both is and is not omnipotent). Regarding such self-contradictions, "it is better to say that such things cannot be done, than that God cannot do them."[8]

For the same reason, God cannot make the past not to have been. This also involves a self-contradiction. As it is nonsense to assert that a thing both is and is not, it is also nonsense to say that a thing both was and was not.[9] Sin is also something God cannot do, but this is not because sin involves any self-contradiction. It is rather because sin itself is not a manifestation of power but of weakness, involving a privation or lack of being—a "falling short" in one's action.[10]

Another puzzler is whether God can do anything other than what he does. Aquinas finds a couple of mistakes that philosophers made regarding this question. Some thought God acted from the necessity of his nature and so could not do otherwise. Aquinas has already shown, however, that God's actions proceed from his will and that God does not will nec-

---

6. *ST* I, 25, 3, co.
7. *ST* I, 25, 3, co.
8. *ST* I, 25, 3, co.
9. *ST* I, 25, 4.
10. *ST* I, 25, 3, ad 2.

essarily but freely.[11] Others argued that God's wisdom and justice would restrict him to just one course of action. Aquinas responds that the present order of creation "is not so adequate to the divine wisdom that the divine wisdom should be restricted to this present order of things."[12] Order is determined by relation to an end. If the order of things is so proportionate to the end towards which they are directed that the end is unattainable without them, then the agent is restricted to that order. That may sound complicated, but we can illustrate it in a simple example: "if you want to make an omelet, you've got to break a few eggs." Since all things are ordered to divine goodness and since there is no proportion between God's goodness and the things that are ordered to it, God is not restricted to any particular ordering of things. God can therefore do things other than those which he does.

A final question is whether God can do better than what he has done. It might seem that, since God is infinite goodness, he should at least aspire to the Cub Scout motto of "Do your best." But if God is already doing his best, he can't do better. And if God was doing his best in creating this world, then it would seem that this must be "the best of all possible worlds."[13] If not—if God could have done better, but didn't—then God begins to look like something of a slouch in his act of creating.

Aquinas addresses such questions by analyzing the term "better." When we talk about God doing something "better," we may be referring either to the goodness of creatures (the things created) or the goodness of God (the divine mode of creating). As regards the goodness of creatures, we might consider the goodness of the individual creature or the goodness of one creature compared to another. With respect to the individual creature, we might consider either its essence or what is accidentally added to its essence. Regarding its essence, God can't make any individual thing better than it is because if he did, it would no longer be that thing.

11. *ST* I, 19, 3; *ST* I, 19, 10; *ST* I, 25, 5, co.

12. *ST* I, 25, 5, co.

13. Leibniz coined the phrase, "the best of all possible worlds" in 1710 in his *Essais de Théodicée sur la bonté de Dieu, la liberté de l'homme et l'origine du mal.* "God has chosen the best of all possible worlds.... It is thus one must think of the creation of the best of all possible universes, all the more since God not only decrees to create a universe, but decrees also to create the best of all" (Leibniz, *Theodicy*, nos. 168, 196, pp. 228, 249).

Just as the number "4" would no longer be "4" if some quantity were added to it, so the essence of any creature would no longer be that essence, but a higher mode of being, if some essential goodness were added to it. Regarding what is accidentally added to essence, God could make anything better than it is. As to the goodness of one creature in comparison to another, God can always make some new creature better than each of the things he has made. If we consider the goodness of God in his divine mode of creating, however, God cannot do anything better than he does since he does each thing from his infinite wisdom and goodness.[14]

Regarding the goodness of the whole universe, Aquinas offers what we might consider an ecological argument. The harmony and interrelation of all the parts of the present universe are such that it cannot be better, since "if any one thing were bettered, the proportion of order would be destroyed." Still, God could make a different universe altogether which could be better than this one: "Yet God could make other things, or add something to the present creation; and then there would be another and a better universe."[15] He cautions us, however, against thinking that "more is better." Equating "better" with quantity would lead not to a "best" world, but only to incoherence.

No agent intends material plurality as the end forasmuch as material multitude has no certain limit, but of itself tends to infinity, and the infinite is opposed to the notion of end. Now when it is said that many worlds are better than one, this has reference to a material multitude [*multitudinem materialem*]. But the best in this sense is not the intention of the divine agent; forasmuch as for the same reason it might be said that if he had made two worlds, it would be better if he had made three; and so on to infinity.[16]

Although Thomas doesn't directly address the question of whether this is the best of all possible worlds, his notion of divine transcendence would seem to rule out the very idea of a best possible world. No degree of creaturely goodness could ever be deemed "best" or in some way "closest" to divine goodness—any more than some point on an infinitely divisible number line could be called "closest" to zero, as shown in figure 8-1. Here,

14. *ST* I, 25, 6, co.
15. *ST* I, 25, 6, ad 3.
16. *ST* I, 47, 3, ad 2.

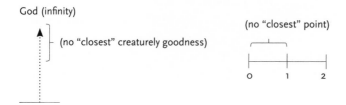

God (infinity)

(no "closest" creaturely goodness)

(no "closest" point)

0   1   2

Figure 8-1. No "Best of All Possible Worlds"

we must remember that God created a world that, from among infinite possibilities, participates in his unbounded goodness in a way that is not *best* (which is impossible), but *very good*: "God looked at everything he had made, and he found it very good."[17]

17. Gn 1:31.

CHAPTER 9

DIVINE BEATITUDE

Aquinas's discussion of divine happiness (*beatitudo*) serves as a sort of capstone to his discussion of the one divine essence: "After considering all that pertains to the unity of the divine essence, we come to treat of the divine beatitude."[1] Following his pattern of finding a human analogue to speak of God's attributes, he looks to human happiness, using elements of Aristotle's definition: "Nothing else is understood to be meant by the term beatitude than the perfect good of an intellectual nature; which is capable of knowing that it has a sufficiency of the good which it possesses, to which it is competent that good or ill may befall, and which can control its own actions."[2] Aquinas doesn't explicitly employ the way of negation to deny aspects of the definition that don't apply to God (such as faring well or ill), but simply uses the way of eminence to single out aspects of the definition that apply to God in a surpassing way: "Two of these [*utrumque*] belong in a most excellent manner to God, namely, to be perfect, and to possess intelligence."[3] Since Aquinas has already established God's

1. *ST* I, 26, prologue.

2. *ST* I, 26, 1, co. See also *ST* I, 20, 2, ad 3; *Nicomach.* I, 7–10 (1097a 15 – 1101a 20).

3. *ST* I, 26, 1, co. I have modified the translation of the Benziger edition ("All of these belong ... to God"), since not all of the aspects of happiness in Aristotle's definition can be attributed to God. Aquinas's word *utrumque* does not mean "all," but "two of which." The Gilby translation is

perfection and knowledge, he can now affirm God's happiness: "Whence beatitude belongs to God in the highest degree."[4]

Continuing the analogy, Aquinas explains that "beatitude must be assigned to God in respect to his intellect" since beatitude is defined as "the perfect good of an intellectual nature" and since "the beatitude of every intellectual nature consists in understanding."[5] This allows for a sort of parallel between human and divine beatitude: God is called blessed in respect of his intellect, and humans enjoy beatitude through their intellectual union with him: "Beatitude must be assigned to God in respect of his intellect; as also the blessed, who are called blessed [*beati*] by reason of the assimilation to his beatitude."[6] The parallel does not imply that God's happiness is like ours since our knowing is distinct from our being, while "in God, to be and to understand are one and the same thing; differing only in the manner of our understanding them."[7] Our beatitude consists in knowing God, who is the common object of all the blessed. But because the act of knowing is a created thing and distinct in each person, one individual may share in the vision of God more perfectly than another.[8] In God's own beatitude, however, the divine act of knowing is one with the divine being and alike "uncreated."[9]

As all perfection and goodness are a participation in God's perfection and goodness, so all happiness is a participation in God's happiness. Aquinas therefore argues that all happiness is included in God's happiness: "Whatever is desirable in whatsoever beatitude, whether true or false, pre-exists wholly and in a more eminent degree in the divine beatitude."[10] False or inauthentic happiness, to the extent that it falls short of the nature of true happiness, is not in God; yet with regard to "whatever semblance it has, however slight, of beatitude, the whole of it pre-exists in

---

more accurate: "Two of these notes most nobly apply to God, namely to be perfect and to be intelligent" (St. Thomas Aquinas, *Summa Theologiae* I, 26, 1, co., trans. Thomas Gilby, OP [London: Eyre and Spottiswoode, 1967], 5:179).

4. *ST* I, 26, 1, co. On God's perfection and knowledge, see *ST* I, 4 and 14.

5. *ST* I, 26, 2, co.

6. *ST* I, 26, 2, co.

7. *ST* I, 26, 2, co.

8. *ST* I, 26, 3, co.; *ST* I, 12, 6.

9. *ST* I, 26, 3, co.

10. *ST* I, 26, 4, co.

the divine beatitude."[11] Because our joy is in some way a participation in God's own happiness, we can say God rejoices in the joys of his creatures: "Each thing takes joy in its like as in something agreeable.... Now, every good is a likeness of the divine good.... It remains, then, that God takes joy in every good."[12] The consideration of divine beatitude concludes the discussion of the one divine essence: "We have now spoken enough concerning what pertains to the unity of the divine essence."[13]

It is puzzling that divine beatitude, so integral to Aquinas's theology, has become so problematic in contemporary thought. Josef Pieper pointed this out back in 1958: "The religious sense of our time allows small place, if any, to the thought that perfect happiness is one of the 'attributes' of God. In St. Thomas's *Summa Theologica*, on the other hand, we read that it would be to miss the reality of God not to think of him as the perfectly happy Being."[14] To the contemporary mind, as Pieper continues, the idea of God's infinite and eternal happiness "gives rise to a disturbing implication. If God's happiness does not rest upon anything's happening, it cannot be diminished or intensified by any events whatsoever in the realm of Creation and in the historical world of man. That is, in truth, a notion of frightful import."[15]

The source of the disturbance, however, is the tendency, ever more prevalent in contemporary theology, to think of God and creatures univocally—implicitly to view God as a being like any other. Certainly a human whose "happiness index" underwent no change at the distress of others would rightly be faulted for apathy and indifference. Imbue such a person with unlimited power and you do have "a notion of frightful import." Small wonder then that many contemporary theologians temper God's happiness with a certain measure of sadness and suffering. So, Gloria Schaab says, "I join my voice with those who say that understandings

11. *ST* I, 26, 4, ad 1.

12. *SCG* I, c.90.6–7. "Love, therefore, and joy and delight are passions insofar as they denote acts of the sensitive appetite; not, however, as they denote acts of the intellective appetite. It is in this latter sense that they are in God" (*ST* I, 20, 1, ad 1; I have corrected the Benziger translation).

13. *ST* I, 26, 4, ad 2. The chapters on God's happiness occupy a similar place in the structure of the *Summa contra Gentiles*. See *SCG* I, chaps. 100–102.

14. Josef Pieper, *Happiness and Contemplation*, trans. Richard and Clara Winston (London: Faber and Faber, 1958), 29.

15. Ibid., 30.

of God as immutable, impassible, and unlimited in power are no longer viable in a cosmos beset by suffering and death."[16] Ronald Goetz notes: "The age-old dogma that God is impassible and immutable, incapable of suffering, is for many no longer tenable. The ancient theopaschite heresy that God suffers has, in fact, become the new orthodoxy."[17]

To correct our tendency to think that God is like us (and so reduce God to the level of creatures), we need a good dose of the "way of negation." We have to remember that God is not like us in his being or goodness or happiness.[18] If God's happiness is one with his being, as Aquinas teaches,[19] then to diminish God's happiness is to diminish his being

If we find divine *happiness* an uncomfortable concept, we must find the notion of divine *unhappiness* still less tolerable. An unhappy God must ultimately be a God of hopelessness. After all, what do we hope for, if not for happiness?[20] As John Piper says: "It is good news that God is gloriously happy. No one would want to spend eternity with an unhappy God. If God is unhappy then the goal of the gospel is not a happy goal, and that means it would be no gospel at all. But, in fact, Jesus invites us to spend eternity with a happy God when he says, 'Enter into the joy of your master' (Matthew 25:23)."[21] And as Josef Pieper argues, "If God were not happy, or if his happiness depended upon what happened in the human realm and not upon himself alone, if his happiness were not beyond any conceivable possibility of disturbance; if there were not, in the Source

16. Gloria L. Schaab, "The Creative Suffering of the Triune God: An Evolutionary Panentheistic Paradigm," *Theology and Science* 5, no. 3 (2007): 290. For Aquinas's theology of God's compassion and impassibility, see chapter 6 of this book.

17. Ronald Goetz, "The Suffering God: The Rise of a New Orthodoxy," *Christian Century* 103, no. 13 (April 16, 1986): 385.

18. "Some things, however, are both agent and patient at the same time: these are imperfect agents, and to these it belongs to intend, even while acting, the acquisition of something. But it does not belong to the First Agent, who is agent only, to act for the acquisition of some end; he intends only to communicate his perfection, which is his goodness; while every creature intends to acquire its own perfection, which is the likeness of the divine perfection and goodness" (*ST* I, 44, 4, co.). "The happiness of God does not consist in the action by which he made creatures, but in the action by which he enjoys himself, not needing creatures [Ad primum ergo dicendum, quod felicitas Dei non consistit in operatione qua creaturas condidit, sed in operatione qua seipso perfruitur, creaturis non egens]" (*Sent.* II, 15, 3, 3, ad 1). See Pieper, *Happiness*, 30.

19. "God is his blessedness" (*SCG* I, c.101.1).

20. "The proper and principal object of hope is eternal happiness" (*ST* II-II, 17, 2, co.).

21. John Piper, *The Pleasures of God: Meditations on God's Delight in Being God* (Sisters, Ore.: Multnomah Publishers, 2000), 26.

of reality, this infinitely, inviolably sound Being—we should not be able even to conceive the idea of a possible healing of the empirical wounds of Creation."[22]

We have imbibed a hermeneutic of suspicion, and our suspicions are aroused the moment we hear of divine happiness: how can God be happy when creation is suffering? We must trust divine wisdom, one with divine goodness and happiness. As God's love is not aroused by our goodness but is rather the source of all good, neither is it shaken by a lack of goodness (evil) in creation, but brings good even out of evil.[23] This is our hope, ever grounded in the abiding love and goodness and happiness of God.

22. Pieper, *Happiness*, 30.
23. *ST* I, 2, 3, ad 1.

CHAPTER 10

CREATION AND DIVINE ACTION

Aquinas discusses creation as the third part of his treatise on God: "In treating of God there will be a threefold division: For we shall consider (1) Whatever concerns the Divine Essence; (2) Whatever concerns the distinctions of Person; (3) Whatever concerns the procession of creatures from him."[1] His discussion of the procession of creatures is again in three parts: "This consideration will be threefold: (1) of the production of creatures; (2) of the distinction between them; (3) of their preservation and government."[2] To give an overview of this vast material, we will consider first the nature of the divine act of creation and then the character of God's action in the created world.

1. *ST* I, 2, prologue.
2. *ST* I, 44, prologue.

Creation

Divine Causality

Aquinas begins his account of creation with a review of the nature of God as the efficient, formal exemplar, and final cause of all things. Since God is self-subsisting being (*ipsum esse per se subsistens*), he is the efficient cause of being in all other things, which are "beings by participation."[3] God is also the exemplar cause: "We must say that in the divine wisdom are the types of all things, which types we have called ideas—i.e., exemplar forms existing in the divine mind."[4] God is likewise the final cause of all things, the ultimate Good which is implicitly intended in the action of every creature: "All things desire God as their end, when they desire some good thing, whether this desire be intellectual or sensible, or natural, i.e., without knowledge; because nothing is good and desirable except forasmuch as it participates in the likeness of God."[5] As we will see, this rich account of divine causality disappeared with the advent of modern science when causality itself was reduced to a mechanistic understanding of efficient causality, leading to a crisis in the discussion of divine action.

The Act of Creation

It should come as no surprise that the act of creation—the production of something from nothing—is very mysterious. If you've ever tried to think of nothing, you've probably failed and ended up thinking of something—such as empty space, or darkness, or even the very word n-o-t-h-i-n-g. To get a handle on the act of creation, therefore, we cannot start with nothing and must settle for something. We begin with change, in which something turns into something else, and then use this as an analogy for creation. We might think of an artist who turns a block of marble into a statue. She begins with marble that lacks the intended shape. That "lack" or privation of the form of the statue is a kind of non-being. Analogously,

---

3. *ST* I, 44, 1, co.
4. *ST* I, 44, 3, co. See also *ST* I, 15, 1.
5. *ST* I, 44, 4, ad 3. God is not a material cause, but is the cause of primary matter, the fundamental principle of potency which comes to be in the creation of substances composed of primary matter and substantial form: "It is necessary to say that also primary matter is created by the universal cause of things" (*ST* I, 44, 2 co.).

as the production of the statue is from the *not-being*, which is *not-statue*, "so creation, which is the emanation of all being, is from the *not-being* which is *nothing*."[6] If God had produced creatures from some pre-existing stuff, God would not be the cause of that stuff, and so would not be the cause of all being. But that would contradict what we've already established: "Now it has been shown that nothing can be, unless it is from God, who is the universal cause of all being. Hence it is necessary to say that God brings things into being from nothing."[7]

We use the analogy of change or motion to get some inkling of the act of creation, but even as we do so, we have to remember that creation is not change. Change involves both "action" on the part of the agent (e.g., the sculptor) and "passion" on the part of the object acted upon (e.g., the marble).[8] While the change is happening, the same activity of sculpting is "action" with respect to the sculptor and "passion" with respect to the marble. So Aquinas says with Aristotle that "action and passion coincide as to the substance of motion, and differ only according to diverse relations."[9] Since creation is not motion, we have to remove or deny motion in this analogy, which leaves us only with the relationships of action and passion: "It must follow that when motion is withdrawn, only diverse relations remain in the Creator and in the creature."[10] Those are the relations of action and passion: "God by creation produces things without movement. Now when movement is removed from action and passion, only relation remains."[11] The relation of passion belongs to the creature: "Hence creation in the creature is only a certain relation to the Creator as to the principle of its being; even as in passion, which implies movement, is implied a relation to the principle of motion."[12] The relation of action belongs to God, but even as we assign this relation to God, we must remember that any attribute we assign to God is simply the divine essence,[13] and that any relation we posit between God and creatures

6. *ST* I, 45, 1, co.
7. *ST* I, 45, 2, co.
8. On the meaning of "action" and "passion" in this context, see "Motion" in appendix 1.
9. *ST* I, 45, 2, ad 2. See *Physics* III, chap. 5 (202b 20).
10. *ST* I, 45, 2, ad 2.
11. *ST* I, 45, 3, co.
12. *ST* I, 45, 3, co.
13. *ST* I, 27, 3, ad 2.

must be a mixed relation, real in the creature but of idea only in God: "Creation signified actively means the divine action, which is God's essence, with a relation to the creature. But in God relation to the creature is not a real relation but only a relation of reason; whereas the relation of the creature to God is a real relation."[14] Although we use the analogy of change or motion, we must remember that creation does not imply a change, but only the instantiation of the creature with a relationship of dependence on the Creator.[15]

Creation is the common act of the three divine persons, but also the action of each: "The divine persons, according to the nature of their procession, have a causality respecting the creation of things.... God the Father made the creature through his Word, which is his Son; and through his Love, which is the Holy Spirit."[16] We can therefore speak of "traces" of the Trinity in creation.[17]

Regarding the question of whether the world had a beginning, Aquinas does not think it is possible to show by rational argument that the world always existed.[18] Neither can reason prove that the world had a beginning. Attempts to show this by reason can be a disservice to faith: "Hence that the world began to exist is an object of faith, but not of demonstration or science. And it is useful to consider this, lest anyone, presuming to demonstrate what is of faith, should bring forward reasons that are not cogent, so as to give occasion to unbelievers to laugh, thinking that on such grounds we believe things that are of faith."[19]

In discussing whether reason can show that the world had a beginning, it is important to say a brief word on the relation between the scientific notion of the Big Bang and the theological doctrine of creation. Contemporary science uses the term Big Bang to designate the initial ex-

14. *ST* I, 45, 3, ad 1. On the nature of "mixed" relations, see the section on "The Relation between God and Creatures" in chapter 3 of this book. On the importance of the distinction between a real relation and a relation of reason with respect to the act of creation, see W. Matthews Grant, "Aquinas, Divine Simplicity, and Divine Freedom," *Proceedings of the American Catholic Philosophical Association* 77 (2003): 129–44.

15. See William E. Carroll, "Creation and Science in the Middle Ages," *New Blackfriars* 88, no. 1018 (2007): 678–89.

16. *ST* I, 45, 6, co. See Emery, *Trinitarian Theology*, 338–59.

17. *ST* I, 45, 7. See Levering, *Engaging*, 8–12.

18. *ST* I, 46, 1. See also *De aeternitate*.

19. *ST* I, 46, 2, co.

pansion of the universe from a point of seemingly infinite density, known as the "initial singularity." The beginning of that expansion is dated at about 13.8 billion years ago. Science also recognizes the possibility that the presently expanding universe may at some time begin to contract, leading to what has been called a Big Crunch, a moment at which the universe will again be reduced to a point of seemingly infinite density. It is also possible that the universe may have undergone a series of Big Bang expansions followed by Big Crunch contractions, giving rise to an endless succession of universes. There is, therefore, no compelling reason to identify the Big Bang, as known to science, with the moment of creation as professed by faith, when God called the world into existence out of nothingness. To distinguish the two, the Big Bang is sometimes called the "scientific beginning" of the universe (the beginning insofar as science can trace the history of the universe), while the moment of creation is called the "ontological beginning" (the absolute beginning of created reality).[20]

Divine Action

Divine Action and Governance

Aquinas considers God's action in the world under the heading of divine government. We have already seen that he defines government as the execution of God's providential plan.[21] He considers first the nature of divine government in general and then its particular effects.[22] The effects of government include God's role in ongoing creaturely existence and change.[23]

---

20. On the distinction between the ontological beginning and the scientific beginning of the universe, see William E. Carroll, *Creation and Science: Has Science Eliminated God?* (London: Catholic Truth Society, 2011), 35–38; William R. Stoeger, SJ, "The Origin of the Universe in Science and Religion," in *Cosmos, Bios, Theos: Scientists Reflect on Science, God and the Origins of the Universe, Life, and Homo Sapiens*, ed. Henry Margenau and Roy Abraham Varghese (LaSalle, Ill.: Open Court, 1992), 254–69; William R. Stoeger, SJ, "The Big Bang, Quantum Cosmology, and *creatio ex nihilo*," in *Creation and the God of Abraham*, ed. David B. Burrell, Carlo Coglioti, Janet Soskice, and William R. Stoeger (New York: Cambridge University Press, 2010), 152–75. For an argument in favor of identifying the scientific beginning with the ontological beginning of the universe, see Spitzer, *New Proofs*, 13–46. On the notions of Big Bang and Big Crunch, see Dodds, *Unlocking*, 71–72, 74.

21. *ST* I, 22, 1, ad 2.

22. *ST* I, 103, prologue.

23. *ST* I, 104, prologue; *ST* I, 105, prologue.

He looks both at "the change of creatures by God" and at "the change of one creature by another."[24] The first part of the *Summa Theologica* concludes with his account of the dynamic interactions and relations among creatures as secondary causes under the primary causality of God. Although the medieval world is often accused of proposing a static universe, this rich account of the intricate interactions between the divine, angelic, human, and purely material realms of being can make our contemporary mechanistic worldview look rather shallow and monotonous.

There's a contemporary ring to Aquinas's question of "whether the world is governed by anyone" in that he starts by noting that "certain ancient philosophers denied the government of the world, saying that all things happened by chance."[25] Those "ancients" are still with us in many contemporary narratives that attribute our present universe simply to chance.[26] Aquinas responds to such accounts philosophically by noting that observable patterns in nature cannot be the result of mere chance. Theologically, he argues that "it belongs to the divine goodness, as it brought things into existence, to lead things to their end, and this is to govern."[27]

All things are subject to God's government since God is their cause and "the same thing gives existence as gives perfection, and this belongs to government."[28] Nothing can happen outside the order of God's government, and nothing can resist it since "God is the first universal cause, not of one genus only, but of all being in general."[29] Yet God shares his government with creatures, acting through them to lead all things to ful-

---

24. *ST* I, 105, prologue.

25. *ST* I, 103, 1, co.

26. "Pure chance, absolutely free but blind, at the very root of the stupendous edifice of evolution: this central concept of modern biology is no longer one among other possible or even conceivable hypotheses. It is today the *sole* conceivable hypothesis, the only one compatible with observed and tested fact. And nothing warrants the supposition—or the hope—that on this score our position is likely ever to be revised.... [M]an knows at last that he is alone in the universe's unfeeling immensity, out of which he emerged only by chance" (Jacques Monod, *Chance and Necessity: An Essay on the Natural Philosophy of Modern Biology* [New York: Alfred A. Knopf, 1972], 112–13, 180).

27. *ST* I, 103, 1, co. On the nature of chance in Aristotle and Aquinas, see "Causality" in appendix 1.

28. *ST* I, 103, 5, co

29. *ST* I, 103, 7, co.; *ST* I, 103, 8.

fillment: "Now it is a greater perfection for a thing to be good in itself and also the cause of goodness in others, than only to be good in itself. Therefore God so governs things that he makes some of them to be causes of others in government."[30] Through his government, God holds creatures in existence, again acting through them to achieve his purpose.[31]

Divine Action and Empirical Science

An important topic in contemporary theology is whether it is still possible to speak of God's action in the world in view of all that empirical science now explains. To some it seems that introducing God as an additional cause of worldly events is superfluous, since science will (eventually) be able to explain them all.[32] Theologians have sometimes played into this argument by introducing a divine cause for some phenomenon of nature that science has not yet explained—some "gap" in the scientific account. Often enough, the divine cause must then be withdrawn when science discovers a natural explanation. The "god" who's introduced in this way has become known as the "god of the gaps," a god who's constantly retreating before the advance of science.[33]

To understand the proper place of the divine cause in relation to the scientific account of nature, we first need to consider the idea of causali-

30. *ST* I, 103, 6, co. "Now, these two theses—that things are dependent for their existence on God but are distinct from God—when conjoined with the principle *agere sequitur esse* [action follows being], yield a conception of divine causality known as the *doctrine of divine concurrence*. This 'concurrentist' position is perhaps most easily understood by comparison with two rival views known as *occasionalism* and *mere conservationism*. Occasionalism holds that nothing in the created world has any causal efficacy at all, and that only God ever really causes anything to happen.... Mere conservationism, meanwhile, holds that although God keeps things in existence, they have their causal efficacy independently of him.... Concurrentism rejects these two views and takes a middle-ground position between them. Against occasionalism, it maintains that ... created things have genuine causal power. Against mere conservationism, it maintains that created things nevertheless cannot exercise this causal power independently of God" (Feser, *Five Proofs*, 234–35).

31. *ST* I, 104, 1–2. Regarding how creatures can be instrumental causes of being, not in the act of creation but in the governance of the universe, see John F. Wippel, "Thomas Aquinas on Creatures as Causes of Esse," *International Philosophical Quarterly* 40, no. 2 [2000]: 213; Gregory T. Doolan, "The Causality of the Divine Ideas in Relation to Natural Agents in Thomas Aquinas," *International Philosophical Quarterly* 44, no. 3 (2004): 398–402

32. This argument is reminiscent of one that Aquinas himself raised against the existence of God. See *ST* I, 2, 3, obj. 2.

33. See Thomas F. Tracy, "Particular Providence and the God of the Gaps," *CTNS Bulletin* 15, no. 1 (1995): 1–18.

ty itself. The notion of causality employed by Aristotle and Aquinas was greatly reduced in the wake of modern science, with severe consequences for our understanding of divine causality. The idea of causality has expanded once again with the advent of contemporary science, presenting new opportunities to speak of divine action. We will briefly review that history.

Causality and Modern Science

Following Aristotle, Aquinas affirmed four kinds of causes: material, formal, efficient, and final.[34] That understanding of causality was constricted with the coming of modern science. In accord with its mathematical method, modern science rightly tended to ignore aspects of reality that were not measurable. With its success, however, a conviction arose that what was not measurable was not real: things that couldn't be measured simply didn't exist. So the method of science became an ideology—a metaphysics with no legitimate foundation in philosophy or science. The result was not science but scientism.[35]

To the scientistic mentality, causes that could not be measured could not be real. So formal and final causes became unreal. The material cause was no longer conceived as pure potentiality but as the fundamental, measurable "stuff" of the universe (the atoms). As Mario Bunge explains: "The Aristotelian teaching of causes lasted in the official Western culture until the Renaissance. When modern science was born, formal and final causes were left aside as standing beyond the reach of experiment; and material causes were taken for granted in connection with all natural happenings.... Hence, of the four Aristotelian causes only the efficient cause was regarded as worthy of scientific research."[36]

Efficient causality itself was reduced to the force that moves the at-

34. For a brief account of the four causes, see appendix 1.
35. "Scientism is fundamentally the transformation of the methodology of empirical science into a metaphysics, a move from the quantitative investigation of nature to the assumption that being is always quantitative. While the former is a legitimate methodology, the latter is mere ideology" (Dodds, *Unlocking*, 51n27). See also Susan Haack, *Defending Science Within Reason: Between Scientism and Cynicism* (Amherst, N.Y.: Prometheus Books, 2003).
36. Mario Bunge, *Causality*, 32. See also Wallace, *Causality*, 2:246; Stewart Umphrey, *The Aristotelian Tradition of Natural Kinds and Its Demise* (Washington, D.C.: The Catholic University of America Press, 2018).

oms.[37] David Hume argued that since causation is not directly observable, it must be merely a habit of our thinking as we get used to seeing one thing constantly conjoined to another.[38] Causality became a property of thought rather than things. No longer an *ontological* reality in the world, it became an *epistemological* property of our thinking. It shifted from the ontological category of *dependence* to the epistemological category of *predictability*. The world was considered a deterministic realm, governed by inexorable laws that allowed no room for outside causes. It was best studied by a reductionistic method that explained all phenomena in terms of their most fundamental components.

Causality and Contemporary Science

New ways of understanding causality emerged with the discoveries of contemporary science. We see this in the theories of quantum mechanics, emergence, and contemporary biology. Quantum theory (at least in the Copenhagen interpretation) affirms a world of spontaneity founded, at its most basic level, on a fundamental indeterminism.[39] Such indeterminacy reminds us of Aristotle's primary matter—not the actual, measurable "stuff" of Newtonian science, but a principle of sheer possibility. Werner Heisenberg himself made this connection.[40]

The theory of emergence holds that new features arise at various levels in the natural world that cannot be explained by reference to their parts.[41] To study them, one must start with the whole (from the top down) rath-

---

37. Edwin A. Burtt, *The Metaphysical Foundations of Modern Physical Science* (Garden City, N.Y.: Doubleday, 1954), 30, 98–99, 208–9.

38. See David Hume, *An Enquiry Concerning Human Understanding* (Chicago: Open Court, 1930), 75–81.

39. "Those of a realist cast of mind will tend to correlate epistemology closely with ontology, believing that what we know, or what we cannot know, is a reliable guide to what is the case. If this metascientific strategy is followed, unpredictability will be seen as the sign of a degree of causal openness in physical process. In the case of quantum theory, this is indeed the line that has been followed by the majority of physicists, who join with Bohr in interpreting Heisenberg's uncertainty principle as an ontological principle of indeterminism and not merely an epistemological principle of ignorance in the way that Bohm suggests" (John C. Polkinghorne, "Space, Time, and Causality," *Zygon* 41, no. 4 [2006]: 979).

40. Werner Heisenberg, *Physics and Philosophy* (New York: Harper and Brothers, 1958), 160.

41. See Philip Clayton, *Mind and Emergence: From Quantum to Consciousness* (Oxford: Oxford University Press, 2004), 66–69; Mariusz Tabaczek, OP, "The Metaphysics of Downward Causation: Rediscovering the Formal Cause," *Zygon* 48, no. 2 (2013): 380–404.

er than the part (from the bottom up). There are, for instance, "several features of the present-day theory of elementary particles" which suggest that "at certain levels of complexity, matter exhibits 'emergent properties' and 'emergent laws' which can neither be defined nor explained in terms of the properties and laws at a lower level of complexity."[42] As John Polkinghorne points out, "Subatomic particles are not only not 'more real' than a bacterial cell; they also have no greater privileged share in determining the nature of reality."[43] The move away from reductionism to the "top down" causality of the whole invites a reconsideration of Aristotle's notion of substantial form as an intrinsic principle that makes the whole substance to be what it is.

Contemporary biology has embraced the notion of purpose or final causality. As Francisco Ayala explains, "Biologists need to account for the functional features of organisms, their 'design,' in terms of the goals or purposes they serve, which they do by teleological hypotheses or teleological explanations."[44] He argues that "teleological explanations in biology are not only acceptable but indeed indispensable."[45]

Potentiality, form, and finality are modes of causality that cannot be measured. Contemporary science, however, now seems to invite (or require) them as categories of explanation.[46]

Divine Action and Modern Science

The narrow notion of causality that limited our ability to speak of God's action is in many ways still with us.[47] As Keith Ward explains: "The scientific world-view seems to leave no room for God to act, since every-

---

42. Jonathan Powers, *Philosophy and the New Physics* (New York: Methuen, 1982), 155.

43. John Polkinghorne, *Reason and Reality: The Relation between Science and Theology* (Philadelphia: Trinity Press International, 1991), 39.

44. Francisco J. Ayala, "Reduction, Emergence, Naturalism, Dualism, Teleology: A Précis," in *Back to Darwin: A Richer Account of Evolution*, ed. John B. Cobb (Grand Rapids, Mich.: Eerdmans, 2008), 84.

45. Ayala, "Teleological Explanations," 44.

46. On the retrieval of Aristotelian causality in contemporary science, see William A. Wallace, OP, *The Modeling of Nature: Philosophy of Science and Philosophy of Nature in Synthesis* (Washington, D.C.: The Catholic University of America Press, 1996).

47. As Philip Clayton says, "The present-day crisis in the notion of divine action has resulted as much as anything from a shift in the notion of causation" (Philip Clayton, *God and Contemporary Science* [Edinburgh: Edinburgh University Press, 1997], 189).

thing that happens is determined by scientific laws."[48] According to Albert Einstein: "The more a man is imbued with the ordered regularity of all events, the firmer becomes his conviction that there is no room left by the side of this ordered regularity for causes of a different nature. For him, neither the rule of human nor the rule of divine will exists as an independent cause of natural events."[49] Langdon Gilkey argues: "Contemporary theology does not expect, nor does it speak of, wondrous divine events on the surface of natural and historical life. The causal nexus in space and time which Enlightenment science and philosophy introduced into the Western mind . . . is also assumed by modern theologians and scholars."[50]

If causality is reduced to physical force, then God's causality must also be understood as physical force. But when God's action is conceived as one physical force among others in the world, his action inevitably seems to interfere with such forces and to violate the laws of science that describe them. Gordon Kaufman accordingly asks how God can act in the world without "violently ripping into the fabric of history or arbitrarily upsetting the momentum of its powers."[51]

If there is only one kind of causality, it must also characterize God's action, reducing God to just one univocal cause among others. When two univocal causes are involved in the same action, however, the causality of one inevitably interferes with the other. If two people carry a table, for instance, the more weight one lifts, the less there is for the other. Similarly, if we think of God as a cause like any other in the world, the more God does, the less there is for creatures to do. If God is omnipotent, he must rob all creatures of their proper causality. Some theologians have therefore concluded that God's power must be limited if creatures are to retain any causality of their own.

Deists limit God's action to the moment of creation: God made the world, but is no longer needed to explain its continued existence and ac-

---

48. Keith Ward, *Divine Action* (London: Collins, 1990), 1.

49. Albert Einstein, *Out of My Later Years* (New York: Wisdom Library, 1950), 32.

50. Langdon Gilkey, "Cosmology, Ontology and the Travail of Biblical Language," in *God's Activity in the World: The Contemporary Problem*, ed. Owen C. Thomas (Chico, Calif.: Scholars Press, 1983), 31.

51. Gordon D. Kaufman, *God the Problem*, (Cambridge, Mass.: Harvard University Press, 1972), 147.

tivity. Some theologians limit God's action to the confines of the laws of nature. Friedrich Schleiermacher argues, for instance, that "as regards the miraculous, the general interests of science, more particularly of natural science, and the interests of religion seem to meet at the same point, i.e., that we should abandon the idea of the absolutely supernatural."[52] Rudolf Bultmann argues that events in nature are "so linked by cause and effect" as to leave "no room for God's working."[53]

To prevent such divine interference, some theologians limit God's power and knowledge. Maurice Wiles, for instance, thinks that "God's creation of our world necessarily implies a divine self-limitation in relation to traditional understandings of omnipotence and omniscience."[54] Arthur Peacocke argues that "God's omniscience and omnipotence must be regarded, in some respects, as 'self-limited.'"[55] For John Polkinghorne, the presence of chance requires a limitation of divine power: "God chose a world in which chance has a role to play, thereby ... accepting limitation of his power to control."[56] Denis Edwards and Brian Hebblethwaite limit God's knowledge and power in the interest of human freedom.[57]

We must limit God's action if we think that it would otherwise interfere with the causality of creatures. But God's action will seem to entail such interference if it is conceived as a univocal cause. There will be no other way to conceive it, however, if causality itself is viewed as a univocal

---

52. Friedrich Schleiermacher, *The Christian Faith,* ed. H. R. Mackintosh and J. S. Stewart (Edinburgh: T and T Clark, 1976), 183.

53. Rudolf Bultmann, "The Meaning of God as Acting," in *God's Activity in the World: The Contemporary Problem,* ed., Owen C. Thomas (Chico, Calif.: Scholars Press, 1983), 64.

54. Maurice Wiles, *God's Action in the World* (London: SCM Press, 1986), 80.

55. Peacocke, *Theology,* 155.

56. Polkinghorne, *Science and Creation,* 63.

57. "If divine love involves divine respect for and patience with created processes as well as human freedom, this means that God is not absolutely unlimited in freedom and power to achieve the divine purposes.... God's nature, as lovingly respectful of both human freedom and the finite limits and autonomy of natural processes, may involve limitations on divine action in particular circumstances" (Denis Edwards, *How God Acts: Creation, Redemption and Special Divine Action* [Minneapolis: Fortress Press, 2010], 51–52). "Creation is an act of God's omnipotence, but in order to relate himself to the creatures he has made, he must limit himself in a manner appropriate to the nature of what he has made, in the case we are considering, free finite persons.... God's omniscience, like his omnipotence, is self-limited by the nature of what he has made" (Brian L. Hebblethwaite, "Some Reflections on Predestination, Providence, and Divine Foreknowledge," *Religious Studies* 15, no. 4 [1979]: 440–41).

notion. Fortunately, contemporary science has opened a broader notion of causality, allowing for new ways to speak of divine action.

Divine Action and Contemporary Science

Today's science suggests two fundamentally new options for speaking of divine action. The first is to employ the new scientific discoveries themselves theologically. The second is to use not so much the discoveries as the broader notion of causality that they imply. The second invites a retrieval of the classical causality of Aquinas and Aristotle.

Some theologians follow the first option and employ the scientific discoveries themselves in their theology.[58] Robert Russell, for instance, uses the indeterminism of quantum mechanics to show how God might act in the world without interference. He argues that "we can view God as acting in particular quantum events to produce, indirectly, a specific event at the macroscopic level, one which we call an event of special providence.... [Q]uantum mechanics allows us to think of special divine action without God overriding or intervening in the structures of nature."[59] John Polkinghorne suggests that the openness of chaos theory may leave "room for divine maneuver."[60]

The notion of "emergence" has also been used as a model for divine action. Arthur Peacocke, for instance, uses the analogy the "causality of the whole." He argues that God may exert an influence on the whole universe without interfering with its parts in the same way that an emergent

---

58. For an overview of this approach, see Ian G. Barbour, *Religion in an Age of Science* (San Francisco: HarperSanFrancisco, 1990); Robert John Russell, Nancey Murphy, and William R. Stoeger, eds., *Scientific Perspectives on Divine Action: Twenty Years of Challenge and Progress* (Vatican City and Berkeley, Calif.: Vatican Observatory and Center for Theology and the Natural Sciences, 2008).

59. Robert John Russell, "Does the 'God Who Acts' Really Act in Nature?" in *Science and Theology: The New Consonance,* ed. Ted Peters (Boulder, Colo.: Westview Press, 1998), 89, 94. Cf. Robert John Russell, "Does 'The God Who Acts' Really Act? New Approaches to Divine Action in Light of Contemporary Science," in *Cosmology from Alpha to Omega: The Creative Mutual Interaction of Theology and Science* (Minneapolis: Fortress, 2008), 110–50. For Russell's more recent reflections, see Robert John Russell, "What We've Learned from Quantum Mechanics about Non-interventionist Objective Divine Action—and Its Remaining Challenges," in *God's Providence and Randomness in Nature: Scientific and Theological Perspectives,* ed. Robert John Russell and Joshua M. Moritz (West Conshohocken, Penn.: Templeton Press, 2019), 131–72.

60. Polkinghorne, *Science and Providence,* 31.

whole in nature may exert a causal influence on its parts without interference.[61]

All of these approaches implicitly suggest a narrow idea of causality. Their very attempts to describe divine action within the spaces available in quantum, chaos, and emergence theories suggest that they are seeing divine and creaturely causality univocally. Only univocal causes can interfere with one another. Another liability of such approaches is that, as science advances and available spaces for divine action diminish, they run the risk of becoming merely "a sophisticated version of the 'god of the gaps' approach."[62]

Contemporary science itself seems to be reaching towards a multifaceted account of material, formal, efficient, and final causes in nature that theologians can also employ.[63] God can then be seen as the final cause of each creature. Since every action of the creature is for the sake of some real or apparent good, and each thing is good only insofar as it participates in a likeness to the Supreme Good, who is God, "it follows that God himself is the cause of every operation as its end."[64] As final cause, God does not interfere with creaturely action but is rather its source, since the creature would not act at all unless it were moved in some way by some good to be attained through its action. God is also the exemplar formal cause of all things. As the idea or exemplar in the mind of an artist is the source of a work of art, so God is "the first exemplar cause of all things."[65] As the creative idea of the artist does not interfere with her work, so God does not interfere with the activity of creatures.

In addition, God is the first efficient cause of all things. We must not

61. See Arthur Peacocke, "Emergence, Mind, and Divine Action: The Hierarchy of the Sciences in Relation to the Human Mind-Brain-Body," in *The Re-emergence of Emergence: The Emergentist Hypothesis from Science to Religion*, ed. Philip Clayton and Paul Davies (New York: Oxford University Press, 2006), 274–76. For a critique of Peacocke and Polkinghorne, see Taede A. Smedes, *Chaos, Complexity, and God: Divine Action and Scientism* (Leuven: Peeters, 2004).

62. Michael Langford, *Providence* (London: SCM Press, 1981), 79. See also Robert J. Brecha, "Schrödinger's Cat and Divine Action: Some Comments on the Use of Quantum Uncertainty to Allow for God's Action in the World," *Zygon* 37, no. 4 (2002): 921.

63. See Álvaro Balsas, SJ, *Divine Action and the Laws of Nature: An Approach Based on the Concept of Causality Consonant with Contemporary Science* (Braga: Axioma Publicações da Faculdade de Filosofia, 2017).

64. *ST* I, 105, 5, co.

65. *ST* I, 44, 3, co.

understand this causality in the narrow sense of Newtonian physics. God is not merely the force that moves the atoms, but rather the source of the very existence of creatures.[66] Since being is the innermost actuality of each creature, God is most intimately present: "Being is innermost in each thing and most fundamentally inherent.... Hence, it must be that God is in all things and innermostly."[67]

God's efficient causality is also manifest in the action of creatures. Insofar as such action entails being and perfection, it is fully from God and fully from the creature. As Aquinas says: "It is apparent that the same effect is not attributed to a natural cause and to divine power in such a way that it is partly done by God and partly by the natural agent; rather, it is wholly done by both, but in different ways."[68] God does not act in the world as one univocal cause among others, but as the transcendent cause of all.[69] Far from depriving creatures of their proper causality, God is its source: "Because of his goodness, God communicates his perfections to creatures according to their capacity. Consequently, he shares his goodness with them, not only so that they will be good and perfect themselves, but also so that they can, with God's help, give perfection to others. Now, to give perfection to other creatures is the most noble way of imitating

66. *ST* I, 3, 4, co.; *ST* I, 44, 1, co.

67. *ST* I, 8, 1, co.

68. *SCG* III, c.70.8. It is important to note here that evil as such is not a type of being, but rather a *lack* of being. The fact that God is the source of all being in no way implies that God is the source or cause of the evil of sin. See *ST* I, 19, 9.

69. See *In peri herm.* I, lect. 14, no. 22, and the section on "God's Unchanging Will and the Contingency of Creatures" in chapter 5 of this book. "The claim is regularly made that the classical notion of a transcendent God, an immutable and unchanging God, is no longer acceptable to modern scientific notions of the universe. Our existence here is simply the product of a large number of chance events. From this, some atheists conclude that God is no longer needed because chance denies any sense of divine purpose. Others who are believers have concluded that God, too, must change, to accommodate a world of chance and change.... But the claims of those who would place God within the temporal flow are in fact more problematic when viewed against what science is telling us about the nature of space, time, and matter. This conclusion may come as a surprise to those for whom the notion of a changing God has become something of a theological commonplace. However, it does conform with Christian belief in a God who is unchangingly loving, constantly reliable, unswervingly compassionate, a provident God who has counted the hairs on our head and knows when the smallest sparrow falls to the ground. Such a God is a mystery indeed, and divine existence is beyond anything that we can imagine. But such a God sits more than comfortably with everything modern science is telling us about the universe" (Cynthia Crysdale and Neil Ormerod, *Creator God, Evolving World* [Philadelphia: Fortress Press, 2012], 56).

God."[70] God's action cannot be seen as meddling or interfering. Even when God performs miracles, causing events that are beyond the capacity of creatures, his action cannot be said to disturb the worldly order, since the most profound order of the world is its ordering towards God.[71]

Conclusion

As our understanding of causality has been influenced by empirical science, so has our notion of divine action. We might say that when the richly nuanced account of causality in classical philosophy was reduced in the wake of modern Newtonian science to the force that moves the atoms, our theological account of divine action was locked into that narrow understanding. The broadened notion of causality in contemporary science has again unlocked our capacity to speak of divine action in ways that allow us to affirm the transcendent causality of God, his immanence in creation, and the authentic causality of creatures.[72]

70. *De ver.* 9, 2, co. "Again, a thing must first be perfect in itself before it can cause another thing, as we have said already. So, this final perfection comes to a thing in order that it may exist as the cause of others. Therefore, since a created thing tends to the divine likeness in many ways, this one whereby it seeks the divine likeness by being the cause of others takes the ultimate place" (*SCG* III, c.21.8).

71. "If therefore we consider the order of things depending on the first cause, God cannot do anything against this order; for if he did so, he would act against his foreknowledge, or his will or his goodness. But if we consider the order of things depending on any secondary cause, thus God can do something outside such order; for he is not subject to the order of secondary causes, but on the contrary this order is subject to him as proceeding from him not by a natural necessity, but by the choice of his own will; for he could have created another order of things. Wherefore God can do something outside this order when he chooses, for instance by producing the effects of secondary causes without them or by producing certain effects to which secondary causes do not extend" (*ST* I, 105, 6, co.). On miracles, see Anselm Ramelow, OP, "The God of Miracles," in *God: Reason and Reality*, ed. Anselm Ramelow, OP (Munich: Philosophia Verlag, 2013), 303–64; Douglas R. Geivett and Gary R. Habermas, eds., *In Defense of Miracles: A Comprehensive Case for God's Action in History* (Downers Grove, Ill.: Intervarsity Press, 1997).

72. For a fuller account, see Dodds, *Unlocking*.

CONCLUSION

If Aquinas's *Summa Theologica* traces a broad circle from God to the procession of creatures and their return to God in Christ, our discussion has limned a smaller arc. Like Aquinas, we began with both faith in God's revelation and the admission that in this life "we cannot know of God what he is, and thus are united to him as to one unknown."[1] Aware of our limits, we followed Aquinas by considering creation in its most humble aspects: that in this world some things move, some change, some fail, some are better than others, and some act purposefully. These almost trivial aspects of creation, grounding Aquinas's Five Ways, allowed us to ascend to God and affirm his existence even as we discovered the distinctive ways that his influence is evident in the world. Still with our eye on creatures, we used the Five Ways to speak of God's attributes such as simplicity, perfection, goodness, and immutability.

Like Aquinas, we then used those discussions as a sort of laboratory to discover how it is that we know and speak of God, exploring the relationship between God and creatures and the analogous nature of theological language. We then went on to speak of God's knowledge, will, and power.

Having in a sense ascended to God from creatures, we then reversed directions, descending from God to creatures once again in our discussion of God's action in creation, providential care for the world, and government of all things. In this context, we noted the concerns that arose in the wake

---

1. *ST* I, 12, 13, ad 1. "Neither a Catholic nor a pagan knows the very nature of God as it is in itself; but each one knows it according to some idea of causality, or excellence, or remotion" (*ST* I, 13, 10, ad 5).

of modern science when God's influence began to look like something that might interfere with the causality of creatures and the fundamental order of nature. We then saw how the discoveries of contemporary science have opened into a broader notion of causality, inviting a return to the thought of Aquinas in which God is not in competition with the natural world but is the very source of the being and action of creatures.

In all of this, Aquinas has proved a reliable guide, allowing us to address questions that arise in contemporary science, philosophy, and theology, while holding fast to the truth that God has revealed. It is to be hoped that Aquinas's disciples may continue to follow his example, described so well by Josef Pieper:

> In considering the teaching of St. Thomas, we should not understand it merely as the material substance of an explicitly formulated set of doctrines.... A Thomism which limits itself to the consideration of the material substance of the explicitly said necessarily proves itself inadequate in a time which confronts man with wholly new problems and brings him into contact with realities previously barely glimpsed. In times such as these it is imperative to call to mind the qualities which made Thomas what he was: the all-inclusive, fearless strength of his affirmation, his generous acceptance of the whole of reality, the trustful magnanimity of his thought....
>
> On the other hand, what we call here the "Thomist attitude" would have to include, in order to remain true to its master, the resolution not to relinquish a single particle of the heritage of truth; for it is the hallmark of the "modernity" of Albert and Thomas that both refused to disrupt and abandon, for the sake of new ideas, the realm of tradition; they relinquished neither the Bible nor Augustine (nor, consequently, Plato) for the sake of Aristotle.
>
> The new territory which awaits conquest today—or, more exactly, which is conquered already but not yet appropriated and put to use by philosophical speculation—is of virtually immeasurable scope. Some of its provinces may be singled out, however. Firstly, there are the new realms opened up by physics and biology. Secondly, the new dimension of the psyche brought into view by the findings of depth psychology. Thirdly, the wisdom of the East, ready for and apparently in want of absorption into the intellectual structure of Christian philosophical interpretation and the Christian way of life—or it may also be that it is we who need enrichment through this wisdom, in a quite particular manner. In this whole context, Thomas Aquinas might attain to a new timeliness, both affirmative and corrective.[2]

2. Pieper, *The Silence*, 102–4.

KEY PHILOSOPHICAL TERMS
AND CONCEPTS

A Very Short Primer in Scholastic Philosophy

To understand Aquinas's theology, it's necessary to have some understanding of his key philosophical concepts. This appendix offers a quick overview.[1] For easy reference, key terms have been put in **bold type** in places where they are defined or clarified.

Matter and Form

The first thing to catch our eye as we look at the natural world is that things are happening; things are changing. In any change, there is always something that stays the same and something new.[2] When a dog comes at its owner's call,

---

1. For a more detailed presentation of these concepts, see Wallace, *Elements*; Feser, *Scholastic Metaphysics*; Edward Feser, *Aristotle's Revenge: The Metaphysical Foundations of Physical and Biological Science* (Neunkirchen-Seelscheid, Germany: Editiones Scholasticae, 2019); Michael J. Dodds, OP, *Philosophy of Nature* (Oakland, Calif.: Western Dominican Province/Lulu.com, 2010); Michael J. Dodds, OP, *Philosophical Anthropology* (Oakland, Calif.: Western Dominican Province/Lulu.com, 2013).

2. Aristotle explains this using the examples of the "unmusical" person who learns music and the unshaped bronze that becomes a statue: "Whatever comes to be is always complex. There is, on the one hand, (a) something which comes into existence, and again (b) something which becomes that—the latter (b) in two senses, either the subject or the opposite. By 'opposite' I mean

for instance, it remains a dog but attains a new place. This is called **accidental change**. The substance (the dog) stays the same, while its accidents (e.g., place) change. But what if the substance itself changes? If the dog dies, for instance, the original substance (the dog) ceases to be a single substance and becomes a bunch of other substances that make up the carcass. We call this **substantial change**. In this case, what stays the same? A reductionist might say that the dog itself was never anything but a bunch of other substances (atoms, etc.) and that these stay the same when the dog dies. The dog owner knows better. The beloved dog has died, and the pile of chemicals that remains is something else altogether. If the substance itself is changing, it can't be substance that stays the same. It has to be something more basic, more fundamental. For Aristotle, what stays the same is not substance, but the mere possibility of being a substance—what he calls **primary matter** (*prōtē hylē*).[3]

It's true that some things we come across in the world—like log cabins— are just collections of other stuff (building materials that have been put together in a certain way). Before, while, and after the cabin is built, the logs are still logs. But other things, like dogs and cats and people, each exhibit a kind of unity in its being and action that allows us to recognize it as a whole and not just a collection of parts—a bunch of stuff. If that's our intuition, then we need an ontological principle to explain that unity, that oneness. We need a principle to explain why all of the parts of the dog are really dog and why all the parts of you and me (carbon, nitrogen, and so forth) do not exist as other stuff but as you and me. This principle is called **substantial form**.

Every material substance is composed of two principles. One is the mere possibility of being (**primary matter**). It is a principle of possibility or **potency**. It explains why the substance has the possibility or potency to cease to be what it is and become something else. The other is **substantial form**. It is a principle of actuality or **act**. It actualizes the potency to make the substance to be the kind of thing that it is. It's the principle *by which* the substance is the kind of thing that it is.

When the dog dies, its primary matter is no longer disposed to the substantial form of dog, and the substantial forms of the various substances that comprise the dog's carcass are educed from the primary matter of the dog. This is analogous to the way that, when I roll an originally "flat" piece of paper (with the accidental form of "flatness"), the paper ceases to be "disposed" to the acci-

---

the 'unmusical,' by the 'subject' 'man,' and similarly. I call the absence of shape or form or order the 'opposite,' and the bronze or stone or gold the 'subject'" (*Phys.* I, 7 [190b 10–15]).

3. *Phys.* II, 1 (193a 29). See Wallace, *Modeling*, 8.

dental form of flatness, and so a new accidental form of "roundness" is educed from the potentiality of the paper.

This account of substance avoids dualism since neither primary matter nor substantial form is itself a "thing"—a substance. Each is rather a principle of substance. Only together do they constitute a complete substance.

Nature

The **nature** of a substance comprises both substantial form and primary matter, but especially substantial form.[4] In causing the substance to be the kind of thing that it is, the substantial form (or nature) also accounts for the particular structure and characteristic activities of the substance (the barking of the dog or the quacking of the duck). Aristotle therefore sees nature as "the principle of motion and rest."[5] Today, it's often said that things act in certain ways because they obey the **laws of science**. But those laws merely describe the characteristic actions of things. They don't cause such actions. The laws are descriptive, not prescriptive. To explain why things spontaneously act (and react) as they do, we need a principle that explains why they are what they are, and that principle is substantial form or nature.

Potency and Act

Our brief account of change has already introduced the notions of **potency** and **act**. These principles are involved in both substantial and accidental change. In **accidental change**, a certain substance that remains through the change is the principle of potency while some accidental form is the principle of act. In the accidental change of logs being built into a cabin, for instance, the logs are the matter (the principle of potency) that is actualized by the accidental form or structure of the cabin. In **substantial change**, primary matter is the principle of potency while substantial form is the principle of act. Substantial form "actualizes" the potency of primary matter to exist as one sort of substance or another (so the substantial form of the dog is the principle by which the dog exists as a dog).

Aquinas will use the principles of potency and act in many contexts to illustrate and clarify his theology. Yet they are admittedly subtle notions that we

4. "This then is one account of 'nature,' namely that it is the immediate material substratum of things which have in themselves a principle of motion and change. Another account is that 'nature' is the shape or form which is specified in the definition of the thing.... The form indeed is nature rather than the matter" (*Phys.* II, 1 [193a 27–30, 193b 7]).

5. "Nature is the principle of motion and rest in those things to which it belongs properly (*per se*) and not as a concomitant attribute (*per accidens*)" (*Phys.* II, 1 [192b 21–23]).

grasp best through analogies. Even Aristotle sputters a bit when he tries to formulate a few examples to explain them:

> Actuality, then, is the existence of a thing not in the way which we express by "potentially"; we say that potentially, for instance, a statue of Hermes is in the block of wood and the half-line is in the whole, because it might be separated out, and we call even the man who is not studying a man of science, if he is capable of studying; the thing that stands in contrast to each of these exists actually. Our meaning can be seen in the particular cases by induction, and we must not seek a definition of everything but be content to grasp the analogy, that it is as that which is building is to that which is capable of building, and the waking to the sleeping, and that which is seeing to that which has its eyes shut but has sight, and that which has been shaped out of the matter to the matter, and that which has been wrought up to the unwrought. Let actuality be defined by one member of this antithesis, and the potential by the other.[6]

Motion

We're all familiar with motion or change. We all know what it is—until we're asked, "What is it?" Then, we hem and haw and start naming synonyms: motion is a process, or a progression, or a transformation, a going, a moseying, and so forth. Rather than offer synonyms, Aristotle and Aquinas try to define **motion** in terms of **potency** and **act**.

There are two kinds of motion: immanent and transient.[7] The first is called **immanent** since it remains (immanently) in the doer. It includes such operations as knowing and loving. The knowing happens *in* the knower, and the loving happens *in* the lover. It's a simple activity that need not imply potency or imperfection. It's the "act" of a being "in act"—such as the act of a knower who is knowing. The second is called **transient** since it somehow "passes" from

---

6. *Meta.* IX, 6 (1038a 25 – 1048b 36).

7. "Movement is twofold. One is 'the act of something imperfect, i.e. of something existing in potentiality, as such': this movement is successive and is in time. Another movement is 'the act of something perfect, i.e. of something existing in act,' e.g. to understand, to feel, and to will.... This movement is not successive, nor is it of itself in time" (*ST* I-II, 31, 2, ad 1). "It is clear that if we call sensation a change we mean a different sort of change. Movement from one mutually exclusive quality to another is the actuality of a thing in potency; for while the thing is losing one quality, and so long as it still has not the other, its movement is still incomplete and it is in potency. And because the potential as such is imperfect, this kind of movement is an actuality of the imperfect; whereas the kind we are concerned with here is an actuality of what is perfect,—the response of a sense-faculty already actualized by its object. Only the senses in act can have sensations. So their movement is quite different from physical movement. It is this movement also which, together with understanding and willing, is properly called an 'operation': and this also is what Plato referred to when he said that the soul moves itself through knowing and loving itself" (*In de an.* III, lect. 12.2 [§766]).

a doer to a receiver, as the act of heating passes from a flame that is actually hot to the water that is potentially hot. Unlike immanent motion, transient motion always involves potency and imperfection (such as the lack of the actuality of heat). It is defined as "the act of that which exists in potency insofar as it is in potency."[8] The act of heating water to the boiling point, for instance, belongs to the water only insofar as it is being heated but has not yet begun to boil. Before the heating begins, the water is in potency both to the act of boiling (attaining a temperature of 100° Celsius) and to the act of being heated to the boiling point. The latter is transient motion: the act of heating that belongs to the water, which is in potency to boil only insofar as it is not yet boiling but is still in potency to boil.

Transient motion belongs to both the doer and the receiver of the act and may be considered on the part of either. Considered on the part of the doer, it is called **action**." (The flame is actually heating.) In this sense, it does not necessarily imply potency or imperfection. Considered on the part of the receiver, it is called **passion**. (The water is passively being heated and so acquiring a certain perfection of heat.) In this sense it implies potency and imperfection by definition, since it is "the act of a being in potency insofar as it is in potency."

Transient motion also implies complexity since it always entails some subject that endures through the change, but initially lacks and subsequently acquires some actuality. The water, for instance, initially lacks and subsequently attains a certain degree of heat.[9]

Transient motion plays an essential role in Aquinas's First Way of showing the existence of God (*ST* I, 2, 3). Immanent motion will be important in showing how God, though immutable, can "move" (*ST* I, 9, 1), and in Aquinas's theology of the Trinity (*ST* I, 27, 1–4).

Essence and Existence

We've already seen that every material substance involves a fundamental composition of substantial form and primary matter. Substantial form is the principle by which it is the kind of thing that it is (tree, squirrel, or bumble bee),

8. "Motion is the act of that which exists in potency, such that its ordination to its prior potency is designated by what is called 'act,' and its ordination to further act is designated by what is called 'existing in potency.' Hence, the Philosopher has defined motion most adequately by saying that motion is the entelechy, i.e., the act, of that which exists in potency insofar as it is such" (*In phys.* III, lect. 2, no. 285). "The fulfillment [act] of what exists potentially, in so far as it exists potentially is motion" (*Phys.* III, 1 [201a 10–11]).

9. *Phys.* I, 7 (190b 10–15).

while primary matter is its possibility of being something else. Together, they account for "what it is" (its **essence**). But they don't explain the fact "that it is"—that it exists. In addition to essence, therefore, the creature must also have a principle of **existence** by which it actually exists. This is called the **act of existing** or *esse*. By using a verb (*esse* or "to be") to name this principle, Aquinas shows its dynamic character as "the act of all acts and the perfection of all perfections."[10] As primary matter is a principle of potency in relation to substantial form, so essence is a principle of potency in relation to *esse*. Every material thing therefore has a twofold composition of primary matter and substantial form as well as essence and *esse*.[11] Every spiritual creature (angel) has a single composition of act and potency: the potency of the spiritual form or essence and the act of existing (*esse*).[12] In God, there is no composition since God's essence is his existence (*esse*). These notions will be important in Aquinas's discussion of divine simplicity.[13]

Causality

The notion of causality plays an essential role throughout Aquinas's theology. The hallmark of causality is dependency: "Those things upon which others depend for their being or becoming are called causes."[14] There are four kinds of causes: material, formal, efficient, and final.

The **material cause** is the principle of potency, the subject that endures through change. In accidental change, the material cause is some substance (such as an apple that turns red). In substantial change, the material cause is always primary matter. When a dog dies, for instance, only primary matter (the mere possibility of being something or other) endures through the change. The **formal cause** is that by which a thing is what it is. It may be intrinsic or extrinsic. In our discussion of form and matter, we considered the **intrinsic formal cause** that is present in a particular thing (e.g., the accidental form by which a cabin is a cabin or the substantial form by which a dog is a dog). But the formal cause may also be extrinsic. For example, even before the cabin was constructed, its shape or structure existed as an idea in the mind of the builder, and the cabin was built in accordance with that idea. That idea is called the **extrinsic** or

---

10. *De pot.* 7, 2, ad 9. "Existence is the most perfect of all things, for it is compared to all things as that by which they are made actual; for nothing has actuality except so far as it exists" (*ST* I, 4, 1, ad 3).

11. *SCG* II, c.54.9.

12. *SCG* II, c.54.7–8.

13. See *ST* I, 3, 4.

14. *In phys.* I, lect.1 no. 5.

exemplar formal cause. In Aquinas's theology, all things exist eternally as ideas in the divine mind, so God is the ultimate exemplar cause of all things.[15]

The **efficient cause** is the agent or source of change.[16] The sculptor, for instance, is the efficient cause of the statue. Several efficient causes may act together to produce an effect. This can happen in two basic ways. First, when two (or more) efficient causes of the same order act together, the effect is divided between them and is due partly to one and partly to the other. For example, when two people carry a table, the work is divided between them so that the more weight one lifts, the less there is for the other. Second, when two efficient causes of different orders act together, the effect is not divided between them, but belongs wholly to each.[17] Once again, this can happen in two ways: **instrumental causality** and **secondary causality**.

In **instrumental causality**, one agent, called the **principal cause**, acts through another, called the **instrumental cause**, to produce an effect. For example, a person (principal cause) uses a pen (instrumental cause) to write a sentence on a page. The two causes belong to different orders" since the writer is an intelligent agent capable of writing an intelligent sentence, while the pen is not.[18] The effect belongs wholly to each cause: there is no word that the writer did not write, and no mark that the pen did not make. Yet the effect (intelligible marks on the page) exceeds the capacity of the pen. In instrumental causality, the effect always exceeds the capacity of the instrumental cause.

In **secondary causality**, one agent, called the **primary cause**, acts through another, called the **secondary cause**, to produce an effect that belongs wholly to both. In this case, however, the effect does not exceed, but is precisely pro-

---

15. *ST* I, 44, 3.

16. "That from which there is a beginning of motion or rest is in some way called a cause" (*In phys.* II, lect. 5, no. 180).

17. "One action does not proceed from two agents of the same order. But nothing hinders the same action from proceeding from a primary and a secondary agent" (*ST* I, 105, 5, ad 2).

18. "An efficient cause is twofold, principal and instrumental. The principal cause works by the power of its form, to which form the effect is likened; just as fire by its own heat makes something hot.... But the instrumental cause works not by the power of its form, but only by the motion whereby it is moved by the principal agent: so that the effect is not likened to the instrument but to the principal agent: for instance, the couch is not like the axe, but like the art which is in the craftsman's mind.... An instrument has a twofold action; one is instrumental, in respect of which it works not by its own power but by the power of the principal agent: the other is its proper action, which belongs to it in respect of its proper form: thus it belongs to an axe to cut asunder by reason of its sharpness, but to make a couch, in so far as it is the instrument of an art. But it does not accomplish the instrumental action save by exercising its proper action: for it is by cutting that it makes a couch" (*ST* III, 62, 1, co. and ad 2). On these distinctions, see James S. Albertson, "Instrumental Causality in St. Thomas," *New Scholasticism* 28, no. 4 (1954): 409–35.

portionate to, the capacity of the secondary cause—even though the secondary cause could not achieve the effect apart from the influence of the primary cause. Aquinas gives the example of a building project in which "all lower artisans work in accord with the direction of the top craftsman."[19] Each artisan acts only in accordance with his own capacity and skill, yet they could not accomplish the work apart from the influence of the master craftsman. The product can be attributed wholly to the artisans and wholly to the master craftsman.[20] Note that in both secondary and instrumental causality, the activity of the primary or principal cause does not diminish the proper causality of the secondary or instrumental cause, but rather enables it. These concepts will be important in Aquinas's discussion of the relation between divine and creaturely causality in the question of divine action.

The cause of the substantial form as such is another important aspect of efficient causality. This has to do with the role of the efficient cause in substantial change. This notion is a bit technical but is important in explaining the First and Fifth Ways (*ST* I, 2, 3, co.) and in the question of divine action. In substantial change, one substance (the agent) acts on another in such a way that the primary matter of the second substance is no longer disposed to its present substantial form, at which point a new substantial form is educed from the potency of the matter. So when a tiger kills an antelope, we can say (philosophically) that it acts on the antelope in such a way that the primary matter of the antelope is no longer disposed to the substantial form of antelope. At that point, the antelope dies and new substantial forms (those of the various substances that comprise the antelope carcass) are educed from the potency of the matter.

A similar thing happens (in terms of the eduction of substantial form from primary matter) when an animal is generated—as when mama and papa rabbit produce offspring. They first produce gametes (i.e., they dispose primary matter in such a way that the substantial forms of ovum and sperm are educed from

19. *SCG* III, c.67.5. Another example of secondary causality is when a group of musicians (as secondary causes) work under a conductor (as primary cause) to produce a symphony. Though none of the musicians is producing an effect beyond his or her own skill and training, they could not produce the combined sound of the symphony without the influence of the conductor. The performance may be attributed wholly to the conductor and wholly to the musicians.

20. "The terms 'primary' and 'secondary' come into play when we are faced with the situation where one thing is what it is by virtue of the other. So each can be said properly to be a cause, yet what makes one secondary is its intrinsic dependence on the one which is primary. This stipulation clearly distinguishes a secondary cause from an instrument, which is *not* a cause in its own right: it is not the hammer which drives the nails but the carpenter using it" (Burrell, *Freedom*, 97).

it). They then copulate, allowing for the union of ovum and sperm, at which point the substantial form of rabbit is educed from the potency of the primary matter of the ovum and sperm.

Aquinas is careful to note that the parents are the cause of the baby rabbit insofar as they are the cause of the disposition of the matter to the substantial form of rabbit, but they are not the cause of the substantial form as such. (Otherwise, since each of them is a rabbit in virtue of possessing the substantial form of rabbit, each would be a cause of itself.) The parents are the cause of the "becoming" of the baby rabbit, but they are not the cause of its "being" since they are not the cause of the form as such through which it has its being.[21]

The cause of the substantial form as such must still be accounted for. It's an important consideration, since form (nature) is the intrinsic principle of the characteristic activities of the substance, and the agent that causes the form is also the ultimate cause of those activities that follow upon the form.[22] Aquinas

21. "We must observe that an agent may be the cause of the 'becoming' of its effect, but not directly of its 'being.'... For if an agent is not the cause of a form as such [*causa formae inquantum huiusmodi*], neither will it be directly the cause of 'being' which results from that form; but it will be the cause of the effect, in its 'becoming' only. Now it is clear that of two things in the same species one cannot directly cause the other's form as such, since it would then be the cause of its own form, which is essentially the same as the form of the other; but it can be the cause of this form for as much as it is in matter—in other words, it may be the cause that 'this matter' receives 'this form.' And this is to be the cause of 'becoming,' as when man begets man, and fire causes fire. Thus whenever a natural effect is such that it has an aptitude to receive from its active cause an impression specifically the same as in that active cause, then the 'becoming' of the effect, but not its 'being,' depends on the agent" (*ST* I, 104, 1, co.). "The doctrine of the nature of univocal causality (dogs producing dogs and cats cats) should be taken into consideration. A univocal cause presupposes the common nature which it communicates in causing individuals of that nature. The dogs which reproduce are not causes of doghood as doghood, but of doghood-in-this-or-that. To say that they cause doghood would be to make them causes of themselves, and thus prior to themselves, a contradiction in terms. The cause of doghood as doghood must have a nature nobler than doghood" (Dewan, "St. Thomas's Fourth Way," 376).

22. "And so it must be said that a principle of motion is in natural things in the way in which motion belongs to them. Therefore in those things to which it belongs to move, there is an active principle of motion. Whereas in those things to which it belongs to be moved, there is a passive principle, which is matter.... However in heavy and light bodies there is a formal principle of motion.... However the natural form is not the mover. Rather the mover is that which generates and gives such and such a form upon which such motion follows" (*In phys.* II, lect. 1, no. 144). "Nor, again, is this true [that a thing moves itself] of those beings, such as heavy and light bodies, which are moved through nature. For such beings are moved by the generating cause [*a generante*] and the cause removing impediments" (*SCG* I, c.13.8). "Since accidents result from the substantial principles of a thing, the agent who immediately produces the substance of a thing must be able immediately to cause, in relation to this thing, anything whatever that results from the thing's substance. For instance, the generating agent, because it gives the form, gives all the properties and resultant motions [*generans enim, quod dat formam, dat omnes proprietates et motus consequentes*]" (*SCG* III,

calls this agent the "equivocal cause [*agens aequivocum*]" since, unlike the parents (who are the univocal causes of the baby rabbit since they are also rabbits), it does not belong to the same species (rabbit) as the offspring. In Aquinas's cosmology, the role of equivocal cause may be assigned to a heavenly body such as the sun.[23] Ultimately, however, God is discovered as the ultimate cause of the form as such, in whose mind, as first exemplar cause, are the types of all things.[24] God is ultimately therefore the source of the characteristic activities

c.99.4). James Weisheipl summarizes this teaching in the phrase "*qui dat formam dat consequentia formae* [the one who gives the form gives what follows upon the form]," and notes: "This principle is found throughout St. Thomas's writings on the subject" (Weisheipl, "The Principle," 90n39).

23. "Sometimes, however, the effect has not this aptitude to receive the impression of its cause, in the same way as it exists in the agent: as may be seen clearly in all agents which do not produce an effect of the same species as themselves: thus the heavenly bodies cause the generation of inferior bodies which differ from them in species. Such an agent can be the cause of a form as such [*causa formae secundum rationem talis formae*], and not merely as existing in this matter, consequently it is not merely the cause of 'becoming' but also the cause of 'being' [*est causa non solum fiendi, sed essendi*]" (*ST* I, 104, 1, co.). "Whatever perfection exists in an effect must be found in the effective cause: either in the same formality, if it is a univocal agent—as when man reproduces man; or in a more eminent degree, if it is an equivocal agent [*agens aequivocum*]—thus in the sun is the likeness of whatever is generated by the sun's power" (ST I, 4, 2, co.). See also *ST* I, 4, 3, co.; *SCG* III, c.69.24.

24. "[God] also gives created agents their forms and preserves them in being. Therefore he is the cause of action not only by giving the form which is the principle of action, as the generator is said to be the cause of movement in things heavy and light [*non solum est causa actionum inquantum dat formam quae est principium actionis, sicut generans dicitur esse causa motus gravium et levium*], but also as preserving the forms and powers of things; just as the sun is said to be the cause of the manifestation of colors, inasmuch as it gives and preserves the light by which colors are made manifest. And since the form of a thing is within the thing, and all the more, as it approaches nearer to the First and Universal Cause; and because in all things God Himself is properly the cause of universal being which is innermost in all things; it follows that in all things God works intimately" (*ST* I, 105, 5, co.). "God not only gives things their forms [*non solum dat formas rebus*], but he also preserves them in existence, and applies them to act, and is moreover the end of every action" (*ST* I, 105, 5, ad 3). "Now the first mover in the order of corporeal things is the heavenly body. Hence no matter how perfectly fire has heat, it would not bring about alteration, except by the motion of the heavenly body. But it is clear that as all corporeal movements are reduced to the motion of the heavenly body as to the first corporeal mover, so all movements, both corporeal and spiritual, are reduced to the simple First Mover, who is God. And hence no matter how perfect a corporeal or spiritual nature is supposed to be, it cannot proceed to its act unless it be moved by God; but this motion is according to the plan of His providence, and not by necessity of nature, as the motion of the heavenly body. Now not only is every motion from God as from the First Mover, but all formal perfection is from Him as from the First Act. And thus the act of the intellect or of any created being whatsoever depends upon God in two ways: first, inasmuch as it is from Him that it has the form whereby it acts [*inquantum ab ipso habet formam per quam agit*]; secondly, inasmuch as it is moved by Him to act. Now every form bestowed on created things by God has power for a determined act, which it can bring about in proportion to its own proper endowment.... Hence we must say that for the knowledge of any truth whatsoever man needs divine help, that the intellect

of creatures, as they act in accordance with their particular forms, not in such a way as to deprive them of their proper causality but as its source. In our cosmology, we can skip the medieval notion of planets as equivocal causes and move immediately to God as the cause of the substantial form as such.

The **final cause** is defined as "that for the sake of which a thing is done."[25] It is most evident in the activity of intelligent agents who can (usually) say why they are doing something (for instance, studying in order to pass an exam). Aristotle and Aquinas argue, however, that final causality is present everywhere in nature, even among agents without intelligence.[26] The term **teleology** is used for the study of final causality or the use of final causality in philosophical arguments. Final causality will be important in Aquinas's Fifth Way and in describing God as the final end or goal of all creation.

Aristotle and Aquinas also consider **chance** to be a cause. Each substance has a tendency to act in a certain way (according to its nature or substantial form) to produce certain effects regularly, as spiders regularly spin webs. Humans can also intend to produce certain effects freely, as a quarterback may intend to pass a football to a certain receiver. Sometimes, however, either in nature or in human action, the intended effect does not occur and something else happens instead because of the unintended influence of some other cause. For instance, a gust of wind might blow the football off course and allow the opposing team to intercept it. Such effects are attributed to "chance" and may be seen as either "good luck" (for the opposing team) or "bad luck" (for the quarterback). William Wallace offers a handy definition: "Another definition of chance is that it is an interference between, or an intersection of, two lines of natural causality not determined, by the nature of either, to interfere with one another. Such happens, say, when a cosmic ray strikes a gene and results in the production of abnormal offspring."[27]

---

may be moved by God to its act" (*ST* I-II, 109, 1, co.). On tracing the cause of the form back to God, see Reitan, "Aquinas and Weisheipl," 186–90; Dodds, *Unlocking*, 194–98; Twetten, "Why Motion Requires," 247–48.

25. *Phys.* II, 3 (194b 32).

26. *In phys.* II, lect. 5, no. 186. See also *ST* I, 5, 2, ad 1; *In meta.* V, lect. 2, no. 775.

27. Wallace, *Elements*, 47. See also Dodds, *Philosophy of Nature*, 54–56, and Dodds, *Unlocking*, 33–41.

THE EMERGENCE OF MONOTHEISM

How monotheism arose historically in Israel remains a controversial question.[1] As Michael Carella and Ita Sheres observe: "There has never been a satisfactory resolution of what is one of the central issues in all of Biblical scholarship. That issue is the nature and origin of Hebraic monotheism."[2] According to Patrick Miller: "No consensus has been reached on the origins of monotheism in ancient Israel. On the contrary, the distance between perspectives on this question may be farther than it has ever been. There are some who speak with ease of an early polytheism in Israelite religion, while others insist on the priority and generally exclusive worship of the god Yahweh from very early stages in Israelite religion."[3]

Our terminology itself can be a stumbling block in such discussions. For instance, we tend to distinguish between polytheism, monolatry, henotheism, and monotheism, as illustrated in figure A-1. We then apply these terms to various eras and personages of the Old Testament. We might say, for instance, that

1. I am most grateful to Sr. Barbara Green, OP, for her help and advice on this appendix.

2. Michael J. Carella and Ita Sheres, "Hebraic Monotheism: The Evolving Belief, the Enduring Attitude," *Judaism* 37, no. 2 (1988): 229. For a review of current issues, see Mark S. Smith, *The Early History of God: Yahweh and the Other Deities in Ancient Israel*, 2nd ed. (Grand Rapids, Mich.: Eerdmans, 2002), xii–xxx, and Rainer Albertz, *A History of Israelite Religion in the Old Testament Period*, trans. John Bowden, 2 vols. (Louisville, Ky.: Westminster John Knox Press, 1994).

3. Patrick D. Miller, "Foreword to the Second Edition," in Smith, *The Early History of God: Yahweh and the Other Deities in Ancient Israel*, 2nd ed., x.

Term	Greek etymology	Meaning
Polytheism	*poly* (many) + *theos* (god)	belief in many gods
Monolatry	*monos* (alone, only) + *latria* (service)	worship of one god which does not deny the existence of others
Henotheism	*hen* (one) + *theos* (god)	belief in one god which does not deny the existence of others
Monotheism	*monos* (alone, only) + *theos* (god)	belief in one god which denies the existence of others

Figure A-1. Terminology for Monotheism

originally Abraham's family were polytheists. Later, Abraham practiced monolatry, worshipping only the God who had appeared to him while not disputing the existence of other gods. This was a type of henotheism, believing in one god but not denying the reality of others. Only much later did Abraham's descendants begin to practice monotheism, believing in one God and denying the existence of others.

Although such terminology is helpful, we should remember that the Israelites themselves did not think in these categories. As Mark Smith explains:

> The study of Israelite religion often involves studying practices more than creedal beliefs because the Bible more frequently stresses correct practices than correct beliefs or internal attitudes. Christian scholars, however, tend to focus more on beliefs or internal attitudes because Christian theology has often emphasized this aspect of religion. The study of Israelite monotheism is complicated by this factor, as monotheism has usually been defined as a matter of belief in one deity whereas monolatry has been understood as a matter of practice, specifically, the worship of only one deity, sometimes coupled with a tolerance for other peoples' worship of their deities. However, if ancient Israelite religion is to be viewed primarily as a matter of practice, then the modern distinction between monotheism and monolatry is problematic.

Still, he notes that "the distinction between the two phenomena emerged within Israelite religion."[4]

Many historians see ancient Israel as monolatrous but not monotheistic.[5] The Israelites worshipped Yahweh alone but did not deny the existence of oth-

4. Smith, *Early History*, 17.
5. In Smith, *Early History*, 3, Mark Smith mentions several who hold this view, including: William Foxwell Albright, *Yahweh and the Gods of Canaan: A Historical Analysis of Two Contrasting Faiths* (London: Athlone Press, 1968); Yehezkel Kaufmann, *The Religion of Israel from Its Beginnings to the Babylonian Exile*, trans. Moshe Greenberg (New York: Schocken, 1966); and Helmer Ringgren, *Israelite Religion*, trans. David E. Green (Philadelphia: Fortress Press, 1966).

er gods—and there were many available. The Canaanites had a rich pantheon, including the ancient patriarch El, his consort Asherah, their son Baal (a belligerent storm-god), and Baal's sister, Anat (a divine warrior). Accordingly, the Israelites were in constant danger of syncretism. Some historians contend that, although Israel's popular religion at times succumbed to syncretism, its official religion was always monolatrous and gradually became monotheistic. This view finds support in Exodus 34:11–16, which depicts Israel as a distinct people, dedicated to Yahweh, who promises to drive out the native peoples from the land of Canaan and commands the Israelites to tear down their pagan altars and worship Yahweh alone.[6]

Recent historical scholarship, however, questions this narrative and asks whether Israel can be seen as consistently monolatrous.[7] Archeological evidence suggests that Israelites and Canaanites shared a largely common culture in the Iron Age I period (c. 1200–1000 B.C.), from which a distinctive Israelite culture gradually emerged. As Robert Gnuse explains: "The recognition that Israelites were not made of a people who entered the land of Palestine from the outside and thus were radically discontinuous with the native Canaanites in cultural matters is of foundational significance in reflection upon Israelite identity.... Archaeology has led us to perceive that Israel emerged in the highlands of Palestine in Iron Age I in a peaceful and internal process that took centuries to accomplish."[8] Johannes De Moor notes:

There is a growing consensus nowadays that the early Israelites must have been Canaanites themselves. To a very large extent they shared their names, their language, their culture, and even their religion with their neighbors. This is not to say that the tradition describing them as settlers who came in from the desert is unreliable. This tradition is so persistently present that it must reflect a fundamental experience of at least some of the early Israelites.[9]

If Israel initially shared a common culture with Canaan, then "the emergence of Israelite monolatry was an issue of Israel's breaking with its own 'Canaanite' past, and not simply one of avoiding 'Canaanite' neighbors.... In early Israel, the cult of Yahweh generally held sway. However, this statement does not fully characterize pre-exilic Israelite religion as a whole. Rather, Israelite religion apparently included worship of Yahweh, El, Asherah and Baal."[10]

6. Smith, *Early History*, 3.
7. See ibid., 5–14.
8. Robert Karl Gnuse, *No Other Gods: Emergent Monotheism in Israel* (Sheffield, U.K.: Sheffield Academic Press, 1997), 346.
9. Johannes C. de Moor, *The Rise of Yahwism: The Roots of Israelite Monotheism* (Leuven: Leuven University Press, 1997), 108.
10. Smith, *Early History*, 7.

As Israel distinguished itself from Canaan (or from its own earlier practices), there was a gradual "convergence" in which the features of various deities were included in the notion of Yahweh. The storm imagery associated with Baal in Ugaritic writings, for instance, is applied to Yahweh in biblical texts such as Psalm 29, and imagery describing the Canaanite goddess Asherah can be recognized in the feminine personification of Wisdom in Proverbs 1–9.[11] Psalm 18 seems to identify Yahweh and El: "The Lord [Yahweh] thundered from heaven; the Most High ['elyôn] made his voice resound."[12] Elsewhere the identification is more explicit: "The Priestly theological treatment of Israel's early religious history in Exodus 6:2–3 identifies the old god El Shadday with Yahweh. In this passage Yahweh appears to Moses: 'And God said to Moses, "I am Yahweh. I appeared to Abraham, to Isaac, and to Jacob, as El Shadday, but by my name Yahweh I did not make myself known to them.""'[13] The identification of Yahweh and El may be quite ancient: "One indication that Yahweh and El were identified at an early stage is that there are no biblical polemics against El. At an early point, Israelite tradition identified El with Yahweh or presupposed this equation."[14]

In the midst of such "convergence" there was also a gradual "differentiation" of Israel's cult from that of Canaan, as certain defining features of Canaanite religion (such as homage to Baal) were rejected and worship came to be centered on Yahweh alone.[15]

The Patriarchal Period (c. 1850–1250 B.C.)

The actual historical practice of the patriarchs is difficult to reconstruct, since the period itself is in some ways a construct of later generations who wrote down the patriarchal stories after monotheism was already established. It seems likely, however, that the patriarchs worshipped God under the name of the Canaanite god, El. The very name "Israel" seems to be a compound with the name "El," suggesting "that El was the original chief god of the group named Israel."[16]

---

11. Ibid., 54, 80–91, 133–37. On the wisdom tradition in the Old Testament, see John Jarick, ed., *Perspectives on Israelite Wisdom: Proceedings of the Oxford Old Testament Seminar* (New York: Bloomsbury, 2016).

12. Ps 18:14. See Smith, *Early History*, 55.

13. Ibid., 34.

14. Ibid., 33. See also Ringgren, *Israelite Religion*, 44–45; Mark S. Smith, *God in Translation: Deities in Cross-Cultural Discourse in the Biblical World* (Tübingen: Mohr Siebeck, 2008), 96–99.

15. On the ideas of "convergence" and "differentiation," see Smith, *Early History*, 7–9, 54–59.

16. Ibid., 32.

Abraham is pictured as coming from a people who worshiped many gods: "Thus says the Lord, the God of Israel: In times past your ancestors, down to Terah, father of Abraham and Nahor, lived beyond the River and served other gods. But I brought your father Abraham from the region beyond the River and led him through the entire land of Canaan."[17] God does not identify himself as the *only* God, but simply promises to be *Abraham's* God: "I will maintain my covenant with you and your descendants after you throughout the ages as an everlasting pact, to be your God and the God of your descendants after you."[18] The patriarchal narratives represent God as having precedence over all other gods and as being able to act effectively for his people, wherever they are. Unlike pagan deities, God has no relatives—no father, mother, consort, or children. He is known not through the cycles of nature but through his actions in the history of his people.

The Mosaic Period (c. 1250–1200 B.C.)

To what extent monotheism was established by the time of Moses is debated. God makes known his name as Yahweh, "I am who am."[19] He sovereignly controls the events of the Exodus and liberates his people from Egypt. In the Covenant of Sinai, he forbids the worship of other gods: "You shall not have other gods beside me."[20] Yet the people immediately fall into idolatry, worshiping the golden calf.[21] Yehezkel Kaufmann argues that the instantiation of the sin of idolatry marks the beginning of Israelite monotheism:

With Moses the sin of idolatry—particularly as a national sin—comes into existence. Before, idolatry was nowhere interdicted and punished. The stories depicting idolatry as a national sin presuppose the existence of a monotheistic people. Since such stories begin only with Moses, we infer that it was in his time that the great transformation took place. By making Israel enter a covenant with the one God, he made it a monotheistic people that . . . was punishable for the sin of idolatry.[22]

Some texts, however, suggest that Yahweh was still seen as one god among others. In delivering his people from Egypt, God describes himself as "executing judgment on all the gods of Egypt—I, the Lord!"[23] When Moses's father-

17. Jos 24:2–3
18. Gn 17:7.
19. Ex 3:14.
20. Ex 20:3.
21. Ex 32:1–35.
22. Kaufmann, *Religion*, 230.
23. Ex 12:12.

in-law, Jethro, a Midianite priest, hears of God's mighty works, he exclaims: "Blessed be the Lord who has rescued you from the power of the Egyptians and of Pharaoh. Now I know that the Lord is greater than all the gods."[24] The existence of other gods is not denied; Yahweh is simply greater than they are. The first commandment of the Decalogue also refers to other gods, but as John L. McKenzie points out:

> The first commandment can scarcely be interpreted as a selection of one god out of many. Other gods are totally rejected as simply irrelevant for Israel; they are not recognized as possessing any power or as active in any way, and Yahweh is not engaged in combat with them.... It seems that to some degree to ask whether Moses and early Israel were monotheists is to answer it; for other ancient Semitic religions the question cannot even be asked.[25]

The Judges (c. 1200–1025 B.C.)

After Sinai, the biblical account presents Israel as a distinctive cultural group (with a unique Yahwistic religion) that conquers and takes possession of the land of Canaan yet slips continually back into practices now proscribed. The actual history is difficult to determine. It may have involved a gradual amalgamation of various groups: "Israel developed its self-consciousness or ethnic identity in large measure through its religious foundation—a breakthrough that led a subset of Canaanite culture, coming from a variety of places, backgrounds, prior affiliations, and livelihoods, to join a supertribe united under the authority of a devotion to a supreme deity, revealed to Moses as Yahweh."[26]

The Israelites had many grounds for their distinctiveness: "Separate religious traditions of Yahweh, separate traditions of origins in Egypt for at least some component of Israel, and separate geographical holdings in the hill country contributed to the Israelites' sense of difference from their Canaanite neighbors."[27] Yet they shared much in common, prompting some scholars to see Israelite culture "as a subset of Canaanite culture."[28] If Israelite monotheism emerged from Canaanite polytheism, at least to some extent, then the purification of Israel from pagan practices may have entailed not just distinguishing

---

24. Ex 18:10–11.

25. John L. McKenzie, SJ, *Dictionary of the Bible* (New York: Macmillan, 1977), 585.

26. Lawrence E. Stager, "Forging an Identity: The Emergence of Ancient Israel," in *The Oxford History of the Biblical World*, ed. Michael D. Coogan (New York: Oxford University Press, 1998), 141–42. See also William Dever, *Who Were the Early Israelites, and Where Did They Come From?* (Grand Rapids, Mich.: Eerdmans, 2003).

27. Smith, *Early History*, 31.

28. Ibid., 25.

themselves from their Canaanite neighbors, but also purifying their religion from its own polytheistic past, often by assimilating to Yahweh certain aspects of the gods they had previously worshiped.[29]

The Monarchy (c. 1030–587 B.C.)

The unique worship of Yahweh continued to emerge during the time of the monarchy. A "Yahweh-alone movement" gradually led from monolatry to the explicit monotheism achieved at the time of the Exile.[30] Aspects of Baal, the warrior God, were assimilated to Yahweh, who helped the kings in their battles or withdrew his help when they were unfaithful. In 931 B.C., when David's son Solomon died, the state was divided into northern and southern kingdoms, Israel and Judah. The unfaithfulness of Solomon is named as the reason for this.[31] In Judah, the covenant relationship between Yahweh and David's house was emphasized and reinforced as worship was centralized at the temple in Jerusalem. Although many political and economic factors were involved in the eventual fall of the kingdom of Israel, the biblical narrative names the unfaithfulness of the people themselves as the fundamental reason for their defeat and deportation by the Assyrians in 721 B.C.[32]

In Judah during the reign of Josiah, the Book of the Law was discovered in the temple in 622 B.C. Josiah had the book read in the presence of all the people and so renewed the covenant: "The king … made a covenant in the presence of the Lord to follow the Lord and to observe his commandments, statutes, and decrees with his whole heart and soul, and to re-establish the words of the covenant written in this book. And all the people stood by the covenant."[33]

Historians generally consider the Book of the Law as an early form of the Book of Deuteronomy.[34] The development of writing during this time helped to normalize the law and religious customs.[35] In the second half of the monarchy, "the written form may have become the more common mode of communi-

---

29. Ibid., 7–8.

30. See Bernhard Lang, "No God but Yahweh! The Origin and Character of Biblical Monotheism," in *Monotheism*, ed. Claude Geffré, Jean-Pierre Jossua, and Marcus Lefébure (Edinburgh: T and T Clark, 1985), 41–49. See also Smith, *Early History*, 195–96.

31. 1 Kgs 11:29–39.

32. 2 Kgs 17:6–12.

33. 2 Kgs 23:3.

34. McKenzie, *Dictionary*, 459.

35. Smith, *Early History*, 187–88. For an intriguing, historically and scripturally based, fictional account of the influence of writing on the Israelite tradition at the time of the Exile, see Barbara Green, OP, *Mindful* (Charleston, S.C.: Book Surge Publishing, 2008), esp. 178–200.

cating the prophetic word."[36] Deuteronomy itself presents the Ten Commandments "precisely as a written product penned by Yahweh, the divine scribe."[37]

Despite the reform attempts of Josiah, the southern kingdom also fell away from the practice of the law. Again, although there were many historical factors involved, the biblical narrative sees unfaithfulness as the reason for the exile of the people of Judah to Babylon in 587 B.C.[38]

The Exile and Afterward

The experience of the Exile (587–538 B.C.) fostered the development of monotheism. The exiles had their own communities where they studied the writings and traditions of Israel. The historical books of the Old Testament were collected, and the Deuteronomic editors began the work of codifying Hebrew law.[39] The moral lesson was that unfaithfulness to the covenant regularly led to divine retribution as manifested in suffering and military defeats.[40]

The political situation of the Exile may also have served as a catalyst for the transition from monolatry to monotheism. Monolatry is inevitably "localized." Those of this family, or village, or state will worship this god who will help and protect them, even if there are other gods who favor other people. Worship becomes "temporalized." In time of drought one prays to the rain god, and in time of war to the warrior god. Bernhard Lang calls this "temporary monolatry."[41]

When a god of monolatry ceases to be worshipped, it also ceases to exist for practical purposes. So the gods of different civilizations seem to die when their respective peoples perish. The new political situation of the Exile made it clear that Yahweh transcended all political and temporal boundaries. God used the Babylonian empire to exile his people as punishment for their sins, just as he would use Persia to restore them when the time of chastisement was over.[42]

Yahweh came to be seen not just as the God the exiles happened to worship, but as the *one and only* God whose dominion was universal.

Judah's reduced status on the world scene also required new thinking about divinity.... Yahweh became an "empire-god," the god of all the nations but in a way that no longer

---

36. Smith, *Early History*, 191.
37. Ibid., 191.
38. 2 Kgs 24–25.
39. McKenzie, *Dictionary*, 197, 255.
40. "The language, style, and theological ideas of Deuteronomy, in particular the rather strict ideas of temporal reward and punishment for keeping the law, are reflected in the subsequent historical books down to the end of 2 Kings" (McKenzie, *Dictionary*, 197).
41. Lang, "No God," 47–48.
42. See Jer 29: 4, 10–11.

closely tied the political fortunes of Judah to the status of this god. With the old order of divine king and his human, royal representation on earth reversed, Yahweh stands alone in the divine realm, with all the other gods as nothing. In short, the old head-god of monarchic Israel became the Godhead of the universe.[43]

As Rainer Albertz notes, "It is certainly no coincidence that the monotheistic tendency of Yahweh religion could only be realized fully in the exile, after the collapse of society and beyond the level of a political national religion."[44]

André Lemaire describes the transformation from monolatry to monotheism.

First, Yahwism, a local cult in the southern desert around the 13th century B.C.E., developed into an Israelite monolatry. Over time YHWH became the exclusive God of the Israelites, to the exclusion of all foreign gods.... Second, the national religion of Yahwism was thrown into a crisis with the Babylonian Exile—that is, with the collapse of Judah and the resettlement of Judahites in Babylonia. This event could well have marked the end of Yahwism as a monolatry (with YHWH, the God of Israel, defeated by the gods of Babylonia). Thanks to the prophets, however, monolatrous Yahwism was transformed into a universal monotheism; this is attested in Deutero-Isaiah's prophecies from the mid-sixth century B.C.E.... Yahwism was kept alive—in a transcendental, monotheistic form—by the strong sense of religious feeling among the Israelites prior to and then during the Exile. Also, the fact that their worship was aniconic—meaning that YHWH was not localized by images of him placed in his temples— allowed Yahwism to be transportable. YHWH's presence, the presence of the God Most High, could even be felt by the waters of Babylon.[45]

Gösta Ahlström also notes the fundamentally new understanding of Yahweh occasioned by the Exile.

The Babylonian exile led to the reordering of religious thought about the presence of Yahweh among his people and the membership of his cultic community. Babylonia was not Yahweh's territory; both politically and religiously, Yahwistic worship had no place in Babylonia. The adoption of the worship of Babylonian gods would have been the natural response to the new situation, since it was normal practice to worship the gods of the land where one was living. The polemics in Deutero-Isaiah against Babylonian gods [Is 40:19 ff] reflect an attempt to stem this growing tide in the exilic community, in fear that the abandonment of the worship of Yahweh would result in the extinction of Yahweh's people. Faced with the possible loss of identity, the religious leaders of the exiles made the bold and radical assertion that Yahweh was not bound to a state or a particular

43. Smith, *Early History*, 194.
44. Albertz, *History*, 1:64.
45. André Lemaire, *The Birth of Monotheism: The Rise and Disappearance of Yahwism* (Washington, D.C.: Biblical Archaeological Society, 2007), 133–34.

territory like other deities. Ezekiel, for instance, asserted that Yahweh had followed his people into exile and thus, could still be worshiped, even if the nation and its temple no longer existed [Ezek 11:14 ff].[46]

Jeremiah emphasizes the universal reign of the one God and the unreality of others: "The cult idols of the nations are nothing.... Like a scarecrow in a cucumber field are they, they cannot speak.... Nothingness are they, a ridiculous work.... Not like these is the portion of Jacob: he is the creator of all things; Israel is his very own tribe, Lord of hosts is his name."[47] Deutero-Isaiah (c. 550 B.C.) also testifies: "Thus says the Lord, Israel's King and redeemer, the Lord of hosts: 'I am the first and I am the last; there is no God but me.... I am the Lord and there is no other, there is no God besides me.'"[48] The Book of Deuteronomy (also a product of the Exile in its redaction) attributes such explicit monotheism to Moses, who, reviewing God's wonders in Egypt, says: "All this you were allowed to see that you might know the Lord is God and there is no other.... This is why you must now know, and fix in your heart, that the Lord is God in the heavens above and on earth below, and there is no other."[49] The Exile ended with the decree of Cyrus (538 B.C.), and the exiles returned to Jerusalem to rebuild the temple, completing it in 515 B.C.[50]

Conclusion

It has been argued that the development of Israel's monolatry and the transition to monotheism involved "both an 'evolution' and a 'revolution' in religious conceptualization."[51] As evolution, Israel's religion grew out of its roots in Canaanite culture and its assimilation of features of Canaanite deities to

46. Gösta W. Ahlström, *Who Were the Israelites?* (Winona Lake, Ind.: Eisenbrauns, 1986), 109–110.

47. Jer 10:3, 5, 15–16. See also Jer 27:5–7.

48. Is 44:6–7; Is 45:5.

49. Dt 4:35, 39.

50. See Is 45:1–3.

51. Smith, *Early History*, 198. "Israelites moved toward monotheism over a six century process until its culmination or breakthrough in the Babylonian exile. In consideration of a number of significant scholars we observed a general consensus emerging. Significant crises or socio-historical developments in the pre-exilic period fueled this advance, so that monotheism appears to emerge as a culmination of several 'jumps' with a final major breakthrough in the exile. Authors, therefore, see this movement as both evolutionary and revolutionary in its advance. It is evolutionary in that it takes centuries to emerge. However, it is revolutionary in that the process really occurs in a relatively short period of time compared to the greater scope of human history, and the final breakthrough in the exile to radical monotheism was not the inevitable result of the gradual process, but rather it was a quantum leap prepared for by many previous smaller revolutions" (Gnuse, *No Other Gods*, 347).

Yahweh. As revolution, the Israelites understood their religion as founded on God's action in their history, liberating them from slavery in Egypt and establishing a covenantal relationship with them, embodied in the Law that was given at Mount Sinai. The experience of God in that covenant relationship allowed them gradually to understand Yahweh not only as the God who alone should be worshiped but as God who alone exists.

The change does not involve simply Yahweh as the only deity, nor does it concern only a change in the understanding of divinity as one "stable" reality or order of reality. The change involved the combination or identification of these two features of reality in tandem, *both* Yahweh as the only deity *and* deity (in terms of name, personality and images, roles and functions, and realms of operation) stabilized and made one (or at least ontologically participating singly) in the figure of Yahweh.[52]

The gradual emergence of monotheism in the history of Israel is in some ways like the dawning realization of Trinitarianism in the early church. In each case, a unique divine revelation was given—at Sinai for the Israelites and in the person and actions of Christ for the Christian community. As the truth of monotheism was implicitly present among the Israelites, not as an abstract idea but in their actual worship of God alone, so the truth of the Trinity was implicitly present in the faith of the early Christians, not as a defined dogma, but in their faithfulness to "the teaching of the apostles and to the communal life, to the breaking of the bread and to the prayers," as well as to baptism "in the name of the Father and of the Son and of the Holy Spirit."[53] As the prayerful life of the Israelites opened them to the truth of monotheism, so the prayerful practice of Christians led them to the truth of the Trinity.[54] As the Holy Spirit brought the church gradually, through all the controversies of the early Christian communities, to the explicit doctrine of the Trinity, so the Spirit of God brought the Israelites, through all the complexities of their history, to the explicit confession of the One God: "Hear, O Israel! The Lord our God is one Lord!"[55]

52. Smith, *God in Translation*, 146.

53. Acts 2:42; Mt 28:19.

54. "In the Bible, monotheism is not a philosophical question but the fruit of religious experience and an expression of practice based on faith. At issue is a practical monotheism" (Kasper, *The God*, 239). "It is a revelation to study what, amid all the highly philosophical subtleties of these Greek minds, which were also Christian, in the end governed their conciliar conclusion. Not indeed their philosophy, but the Church's tradition of 'devotion to Christ.' ... The fathers of the Council gave more weight to this devotional practice among Christians than to philosophical thinking; and because of that the Church was able to break with the middle Platonism which for two centuries had governed the thinking of the theologians" (Edward Schillebeeckx, OP, *Jesus: An Experiment in Christology*, trans. Hubert Hoskins [New York: Seabury Press, 1979], 565–66).

55. Dt 6:4.

BIBLIOGRAPHY

Works of Thomas Aquinas

Catena aurea in Joannem. Vol. 5 of *Opera omnia ut sunt in Indice Thomistico*, 128–246. Stuttgart: Frommann-Holzboog, 1980.

Collationes credo in Deum. [English translation with Latin text of the Leonine Edition on facing pages: *The Sermon-Conferences of St. Thomas Aquinas on the Apostles' Creed.* Translated and edited by Nicholas Ayo, CSC. Notre Dame, Ind.: University of Notre Dame Press, 1988.]

Commentarium in Aristotelis libros Peri hermeneias. Turin and Rome: Marietti, 1955. [English translation: *Commentary on Aristotle's On Interpretation.* In *Aristotle: On Interpretation. Commentary by St. Thomas and Cajetan.* Translated by Jean T. Oesterle. Milwaukee: Marquette University Press, 1962.]

Commentarium in libros Aristotelis De caelo et mundo. Vol. 3 of *Opera omnia.* Rome: Typographia polyglotta, 1886. [English translation: *Exposition of Aristotle's Treatise on the Heavens.* Translated by Fabian R. Larcher and Pierre H. Conway. College of St. Mary of the Springs, Ohio, 1963–64.]

Contra errores Graecorum. Vol. 1 of *Opuscula theologica*, 315–46. Turin and Rome: Marietti, 1954.

Contra impugnantes Dei cultum et religionem. Vol 41 of *Opera omnia.* Rome: Typographia polyglotta, 1970. [English Translation: *Against Those Who Attack the Religious Profession.* In *An Apology for the Religious Orders.* Translated by John Proctor, OP. St. Louis, Mo.: B. Herder, 1902.]

De aeternitate mundi. Vol. 43 of *Opera omnia*, 85–89. Rome: Typographia polyglotta, 1976. [English translation: *On the Eternity of the World.* In *St. Thomas Aquinas, Siger of Brabant, St. Bonaventure, On the Eternity of the World*, 19–25. Edited by Cyril Vollert et al. Milwaukee, Wisc.: Marquette University Press, 1964.]

De articulis fidei et ecclesiae sacramentis. In *Corpus Thomisticum*, accessed December 22, 2018, http://www.corpusthomisticum.org/oss.html.

De ente et essentia. Vol. 43 of *Opera omnia*, 369–81. Rome: Typographia polyglotta, 1976. [English translation: *On Being and Essence.* In *Selected Writings of St. Thomas*

Aquinas, 29–67. Translated by Robert P. Goodwin. New York: Bobbs-Merrill Company, Inc., 1965.]

Epistola ad Bernardum abbatem casinensem. Vol. 42 of *Opera omnia.* Rome: Typographia polyglotta, 1979.

Epistola exhortatoria de modo studendi ad fratrem Joannem. [English translation: The Letter of Thomas Aquinas to Brother John on How to Study], *Opuscula Theologica* 1:451 (Rome: Marietti, 1954).]

Expositio super Iob ad litteram. Vol. 26 of *Opera omnia.* Rome: Typographia polyglotta, 1965.

Expositio super librum Boethii De Trinitate. Edited by B. Oecker. Leiden: Brill, 1959. [English translation of Questions 5–6: *The Division and Method of the Sciences.* Translated by Armand Maurer. Toronto: Pontifical Institute of Mediaeval Studies, 1963. English translation of Questions 1–4: *Faith, Reason, and Theology: Questions I-IV of His Commentary on the De Trinitate of Boethius.* Translated by Armand Maurer. Toronto: Pontifical Institute of Mediaeval Studies, 1987.]

In Aristotelis librum De anima commentarium. Vol. 45/1 of Opera ommnia. Rome: Typographia polyglotta, 1984. [English translation: *Aristotle's De Anima in the Version of William of Moerbeke and the Commentary of St. Thomas Aquinas.* Translated by Kenelm Foster, OP, and Silvester Humphries, OP. London: Routledge and Kegan Paul, 1951.]

In librum beati Dionysii De divinis nominibus expositio. Turin and Rome: Marietti, 1950.

In Metaphysicam Aristotelis commentaria. Turin and Rome: Marietti, 1926. [English translation: *Commentary on the Metaphysics of Aristotle.* 2 vols. Translated by J. Rowan. Chicago: Regnery, 1961.]

In octo libros Physicorum Aristotelis expositio. Turin and Rome: Marietti, 1965. [English translation: *Commentary on Aristotle's Physics.* Translated by R. Blackwell et al. New Haven, Conn.: Yale, 1963.]

Quaestiones disputatae de malo. Vol. 23 of *Opera omnia.* Rome: Typographia polyglotta, 1982. [English translation: *On Evil.* Translated by Jean Oesterle. Notre Dame, Ind.: University of Notre Dame Press, 1995.]

Quaestiones disputatae de potentia. Turin and Rome: Marietti, 1965. [English translation: *On the Power of God.* Translated by the English Dominican Fathers. Westminster, Md.: Newman Press, 1952.]

Quaestiones disputatae de veritate. Vol. 22/1–3 of *Opera omnia.* Rome: Typographia polyglotta, 1972–76. [English translation: *Truth.* 3 vols. Translated by R. Mulligan et al. Chicago: Regnery, 1952–54.]

Quaestiones quodlibetales. Turin and Rome: Marietti, 1949.

Scriptum super libros Sententiarum. Vols. 7–11 of *Opera omnia.* Paris: Vivès, 1882–89.

Summa contra Gentiles. 3 vols. Turin and Rome: Marietti, 1961. [English translation: *On the Truth of the Catholic Faith:* Summa contra Gentiles. 4 vols. Translated by Anton C. Pegis et al. Garden City, N.Y.: Image Books, 1955–57.]

Summa theologiae. Rome: Editiones Paulinae, 1962. [English translations: *Summa Theologica.* 3 vols. Translated by the Fathers of the English Dominican Province. New York: Benziger Bros., 1946; *Summa Theologiae.* 61 vols. Translated by Thomas Gilby, OP, et al. London: Eyre and Spottiswoode, 1964–81.]

Super epistolam ad Colossenses lectura, in *Expositio et lectura super epistolas Pauli apostoli.* 2 vols. Turin and Rome: Marietti, 1953.

Super epistolam ad Ephesios lectura, in *Expositio et lectura super epistolas Pauli apostoli.* 2 vols. Turin and Rome: Marietti, 1953.

Super evangelium S. Ioannis lectura. Turin and Rome: Marietti, 1952. [English translation: *Commentary on the Gospel of John.* 3 vols. Translated by Fabian Larcher and James A. Weisheipl, OP. Washington, D.C.: The Catholic University of America Press, 2010.]

Super evangelium S. Matthaei lectura. Turin and Rome: Marietti, 1951.

Super librum De causis expositio. Edited by H. D. Saffrey. Fribourg-Louvain: Société Philosophique, 1954. [English translation: *Commentary on the Book of Causes.* Translated by Vincent A. Guagliardo, OP, Charles R. Hess, OP, and Richard C. Taylor. Washington, D.C.: The Catholic University of America Press, 1996.]

Other Works

Aersten, Jan A. "Aquinas's Philosophy in Its Historical Setting." In *The Cambridge Companion to Aquinas,* edited by Norman Kretzmann and Eleonore Stump, 12–37. Cambridge: Cambridge University Press, 1993.

Ahlström, Gösta W. *Who Were the Israelites?* Winona Lake, Ind.: Eisenbrauns, 1986.

Albertson, James S. "Instrumental Causality in St. Thomas." *New Scholasticism* 28, no. 4 (1954): 409–35.

Albertz, Rainer. *A History of Israelite Religion in the Old Testament Period.* Translated by John Bowden. 2 vols. Louisville, Ky.: Westminster John Knox Press, 1994.

Albright, William Foxwell. *Yahweh and the Gods of Canaan: A Historical Analysis of Two Contrasting Faiths.* London: Athlone Press, 1968.

Anderson, James F. *Reflections on the Analogy of Being.* The Hague: Martinus Nijhoff, 1967.

Anselm, St. *Proslogion.* In *The Existence of God.* Edited by John Hick, 25–30. New York: Macmillan, 1964.

Aristotle. *The Basic Works of Aristotle.* Edited by Richard McKeon. New York: Random House, 1941. (Includes *Categories*; *Metaphysics*; *Nicomachean Ethics*; *On the Soul*; *Physics*.)

Arp, Robert, ed. *Revisiting Aquinas' Proofs for the Existence of God.* Leiden: Brill, 2016.

Ashley, Benedict M., OP. "Research into the Intrinsic Final Causes of Physical Things." *Proceedings of the American Catholic Philosophical Association* 26 (April 1952): 185–94.

———. *The Way toward Wisdom: An Interdisciplinary and Intercultural Introduction to Metaphysics.* Notre Dame, Ind.: University of Notre Dame Press, 2006.

Asimov, Isaac. *Understanding Physics.* London: Bracken Books, 1966.

Ayala, Francisco J. "Teleological Explanations in Evolutionary Biology." In *Nature's Purposes: Analyses of Function and Design in Biology,* edited by Colin Allen, Marc Bekoff, and George Lauder, 29–49. Cambridge, Mass.: MIT Press, 1998.

———. "Intelligent Design: The Original Version." *Theology and Science* 1, no. 1 (2003): 9–32.

———. "Reduction, Emergence, Naturalism, Dualism, Teleology: A Précis." In *Back to Darwin: A Richer Account of Evolution,* edited by John B. Cobb, 76–87. Grand Rapids, Mich.: Eerdmans, 2008.

Baggini, Julian. *Atheism: A Very Short Introduction.* New York: Oxford University Press, 2003.

Balsas, Álvaro, SJ. *Divine Action and the Laws of Nature: An Approach Based on the Concept of Causality Consonant with Contemporary Science.* Braga: Axioma Publicações da Faculdade de Filosofia, 2017.

Barbour, Ian G. *Religion in an Age of Science.* San Francisco: HarperSanFrancisco, 1990.

———. "God's Power: A Process View." In *The Work of Love: Creation as Kenosis,* edited by John Polkinghorne, 1–20. Grand Rapids, Mich.: Eerdmans, 2001.

Barnes, Corey L. "Natural Final Causality and Providence in Aquinas." *New Blackfriars* 95, no. 1057 (2014): 349–61.

Bauerschmidt, Frederick Christian. *Thomas Aquinas: Faith, Reason, and Following Christ.* Oxford: Oxford University Press, 2013.

Beck, David. "A Fourth Way to Prove God's Existence." In *Revisiting Aquinas' Proofs for the Existence of God,* edited by Robert Arp, 147–71. Leiden: Brill, 2016.

Beebee, Helen, Christopher Hitchcock, and Peter Menzies. "Introduction." In *The Oxford Handbook of Causation,* edited by Helen Beebee, Christopher Hitchcock, and Peter Menzies, 1–18. Oxford: Oxford University Press, 2012.

Behe, Michael J. *Darwin's Black Box: The Biochemical Challenge to Evolution.* New York: Free Press, 1996.

———. "The Modern Intelligent Design Hypothesis: Breaking Rules." In *God and Design: The Teleological Argument and Modern Science,* edited by Neil A. Manson, 277–91. London: Routledge, 2003.

Blocher, Henri. "Divine Immutability." In *The Power and Weakness of God: Impassibility and Orthodoxy,* edited by Nigel M. de S. Cameron, 1–22. Edinburgh: Rutherford House Books, 1990.

Bobik, Joseph. "Aquinas's Fourth Way and the Approximating Relation." *Thomist* 51, no. 1 (1987): 17–36.

Boland, Vivian, OP. *Ideas in God according to Saint Thomas Aquinas: Sources and Synthesis.* Leiden: Brill, 1996.

Bonansea, Bernardino M., OFM. *God and Atheism: A Philosophical Approach to the Problem of God.* Washington D.C.: The Catholic University of America Press, 1979.

Bonino, Serge-Thomas, OP. "Contemporary Thomism through the Prism of the Theology of Predestination." In *Thomism and Predestination: Principles and Disputa-*

tions, edited by Steven A. Long, Roger W. Nutt, and Thomas Joseph White, OP, 29–50. Ave Maria, Fla.: Sapientia Press, 2017.

Bonnette, Dennis. *Aquinas' Proofs for God's Existence. St. Thomas Aquinas on: "The Per Accidens Necessarily Implies the Per Se."* The Hague: Martinus Nijhoff, 1972.

Boyle, Leonard E., OP. "The Setting of the *Summa Theologiae*." In *Aquinas's "Summa Theologiae": Critical Essays*, edited by Brian Davies, OP, 1–24. Lanham, Md.: Rowman and Littlefield, 2006.

Braaten, Carl E., and Robert W. Jenson, eds. *Either/Or: The Gospel or Neopaganism.* Grand Rapids, Mich.: Eerdmans, 1995.

Braine, David. *The Reality of Time and the Existence of God: The Project of Proving God's Existence.* New York: Oxford University Press, 1988.

Brecha, Robert J. "Schrödinger's Cat and Divine Action: Some Comments on the Use of Quantum Uncertainty to Allow for God's Action in the World." *Zygon* 37, no. 4 (2002): 909–24.

Brierley, Michael W. "The Potential of Panentheism for Dialogue Between Science and Religion." In *The Oxford Handbook of Religion and Science*, edited by Philip Clayton and Zachary Simpson, 635–51. Oxford: Oxford University Press, 2006.

Buckley, Michael J., SJ. *At the Origins of Modern Atheism.* New Haven, Conn.: Yale University Press, 1987.

———. *Denying and Disclosing God: The Ambiguous Progress of Modern Atheism.* New Haven, Conn.: Yale University Press, 2004.

Bultmann, Rudolf. "The Meaning of God as Acting." In *God's Activity in the World: The Contemporary Problem*, edited by Owen C. Thomas, 61–76. Chico, Calif.: Scholar's Press, 1983.

Bunge, Mario. *Causality and Modern Science.* New York: Dover Publications, 1979.

Burrell, David B., CSC. *Analogy and Philosophical Language.* New Haven, Conn.: Yale University Press, 1973.

———. "Divine Practical Knowing: How an Eternal God Acts in Time." In *Divine Action: Studies Inspired by the Philosophical Theology of Austin Farrer,* edited by Brian Hebblethwaite and Edward Henderson, 93–102. Edinburgh: T and T Clark, 1990.

———. *Freedom and Creation in Three Traditions.* Notre Dame, Ind.: University of Notre Dame Press, 1993.

———. *Deconstructing Theodicy: Why Job Has Nothing to Say to the Puzzle of Suffering.* Grand Rapids, Mich.: Baker Academic, 2008.

Burtt, Edwin A. *The Metaphysical Foundations of Modern Physical Science.* Garden City, N.Y.: Doubleday, 1954.

Cahn, Stephen M. "Does God Know the Future?" In *Questions about God: Today's Philosophers Ponder the Divine*, edited by Steven M. Cahn and David Shatz, 147–52. Oxford: Oxford University Press, 2002.

Carella, Michael J., and Ita Sheres. "Hebraic Monotheism: The Evolving Belief, the Enduring Attitude." *Judaism* 37, no. 2 (1988): 229–39.

Carroll, Lewis. *Alice's Adventures in Wonderland*. Chicago: Volume One Publishing, 1998.

Carroll, William E. "Creation and Science in the Middle Ages." *New Blackfriars* 88, no. 1018 (2007): 678–89.

———. *Creation and Science: Has Science Eliminated God?* London: Catholic Truth Society, 2011.

Catechism of the Catholic Church. Mahwah, N.J.: Paulist Press, 1994.

Cates, Diana Fritz. *Aquinas on the Emotions: A Religious-Ethical Inquiry*. Washington, D.C.: Georgetown University Press, 2009.

Cessario, Romanus, OP. *A Short History of Thomism*. Washington, D.C.: The Catholic University of America Press, 2005.

Cessario, Romanus, OP, and Cajetan Cuddy, OP, *Thomas and the Thomists: The Achievement of Thomas Aquinas and His Interpreters*. Minneapolis: Fortress Press, 2017.

Chenu, Marie-Dominique, OP. *Toward Understanding Saint Thomas*. Translated by A.-M. Landry, OP, and D. Hughes, OP. Chicago: H. Regnery, 1964.

———. *Aquinas and His Role in Theology*. Translated by Paul Philibert, OP. Collegeville, Minn.: Liturgical Press, 2002.

Chesterton, G. K. *Saint Thomas Aquinas: The Dumb Ox*. Garden City, N.Y.: Doubleday, 1960.

Chisholm, Robert B. "Does God 'Change his Mind?'" *Bibliotheca Sacra* 152 (October–December 1995): 387–99.

Clarke, William Norris, SJ. "Is a Natural Theology Still Possible Today?" In *Physics, Philosophy, and Theology: A Common Quest for Understanding*, edited by Robert J. Russell, William R. Stoeger, and George V. Coyne, 103–23. Vatican City and Berkeley, Calif.: Vatican Observatory and Center for Theology and the Natural Sciences, 1988.

———. "The Limitation of Act by Potency: Aristotelianism or Neoplatonism?" In *Explorations in Metaphysics: Being—God—Person*, 65–88. Notre Dame, Ind.: University of Notre Dame Press, 1994.

———. "What Is Most and Least Relevant in the Metaphysics of St. Thomas Today?" In *Explorations in Metaphysics: Being—God—Person*, 1–30. Notre Dame, Ind.: University of Notre Dame Press, 1994.

Clayton, Philip. *God and Contemporary Science*. Edinburgh: Edinburgh University Press, 1997.

———. *Mind and Emergence: From Quantum to Consciousness*. Oxford: Oxford University Press, 2004.

———. "Panentheism in Metaphysical and Scientific Perspective." In *In Whom We Live and Move and Have Our Being: Panentheistic Reflections on God's Presence in a Scientific World*, edited by Philip Clayton and Arthur R. Peacocke, 73–91. Grand Rapids, Mich.: Eerdmans, 2004.

Cohoe, Caleb. "There Must Be a First: Why Thomas Aquinas Rejects Infinite, Essentially Ordered, Causal Series." *British Journal for the History of Philosophy* 21, no. 5 (2013): 838–56.

Connolly, Thomas Kevin, OP. "The Basis of the Third Proof for the Existence of God." *Thomist* 17, no. 3 (1954): 281–349.

Cooper, John W. *Panentheism: The Other God of the Philosophers: From Plato to the Present*. Grand Rapids, Mich.: Baker Books, 2006.

Copleston, Frederick C., SJ. *Aquinas*. Baltimore, Md.: Penguin Books, 1975.

Cotter, Christopher R., Philip Andrew Quadrio, and Jonathan Tuckett, eds. *New Atheism: Critical Perspectives and Contemporary Debates*. Cham, Switzerland: Springer, 2017.

Craig, William Lane. *God, Time, and Eternity*. Dordrecht: Kluwer, 2001.

———. *Time and Eternity: Exploring God's Relationship to Time*. Wheaton, Ill.: Crossway Books, 2001.

Crean, Thomas, OP. *God Is No Delusion: A Refutation of Richard Dawkins*. San Francisco: Ignatius Press, 2007.

Creel, Richard E. *Divine Impassibility: An Essay in Philosophical Theology*. Cambridge: Cambridge University Press, 1986.

Cross, Frank Leslie, and Elizabeth A. Livingstone, eds. *The Oxford Dictionary of the Christian Church*. 3rd rev. ed. Oxford: Oxford University Press, 2005.

Crysdale, Cynthia, and Neil Ormerod. *Creator God, Evolving World*. Philadelphia: Fortress Press, 2012.

Cullen, Christopher M. "Transcendental Thomism: Realism Rejected." In *The Failure of Modernism: The Cartesian Legacy and Contemporary Pluralism*, edited by Brendan Sweetman, 72–86. Mishawaka, Ind.: American Maritain Association, 1999.

Davies, Brian, OP. *Thinking about God*. London: Geoffrey Chapman, 1985.

———. "Aquinas on What God Is Not." In *Thomas Aquinas: Contemporary Philosophical Perspectives*, edited by Brian Davies, OP, 227–42. Oxford: Oxford University Press, 2002.

———. "Introduction." In *Aquinas's "Summa Theologiae": Critical Essays*, edited by Brian Davies, OP, vii–xix. Lanham, Md.: Rowman and Littlefield, 2006.

———. *The Reality of God and the Problem of Evil*. New York: Continuum, 2006.

———. *Thomas Aquinas's "Summa Theologiae": A Guide and Commentary*. Oxford: Oxford University Press, 2014.

———. *Thomas Aquinas's "Summa contra Gentiles": A Guide and Commentary*. Oxford: Oxford University Press, 2016.

———. "The *Summa Theologiae* on What God Is Not." In *Aquinas's "Summa Theologiae": A Critical Guide*, edited by Jeffrey Hause, 47–67. Cambridge: Cambridge University Press, 2018.

Dawkins, Richard. *The God Delusion*. London: Bantam Press, 2006.

De La Torre, Monty. "In Defense of the Fourth Way and Its Metaphysics." PhD dissertation, Australian Catholic University, 2016.

De Moor, Johannes C. *The Rise of Yahwism: The Roots of Israelite Monotheism*. Leuven: Leuven University Press, 1997.

De Nys, Martin J. "If Everything Can Not-Be There Would Be Nothing: Another Look at the Third Way." *Review of Metaphysics* 56, no. 1 (2002): 99–122.

Deferrari, Roy J. *A Latin-English Dictionary of St. Thomas Aquinas.* Boston: St. Paul Editions, 1960.

Dennett, Daniel Clement. *Breaking the Spell: Religion as a Natural Phenomenon.* New York: Viking, 2006.

Dever, William. *Who Were the Early Israelites, and Where Did They Come From?* Grand Rapids, Mich.: Eerdmans, 2003.

Dewan, Lawrence, OP. "St. Thomas's Fourth Way and Creation." *Thomist* 59, no. 3 (1995): 371–78.

———. "Saint Thomas and the Principle of Causality." In *Form and Being: Studies in Thomistic Metaphysics,* 61–80. Washington, D.C.: The Catholic University of America Press, 2006.

———. "The Existence of God: Can It Be Demonstrated?" *Nova et Vetera* (English ed.) 10, no. 3 (2012): 731–56.

Dionysius the Areopagite. "The Divine Names." In *The Divine Names and The Mystical Theology.* Translated by C. E. Rolt, 50–190. London: SPCK, 1979.

Dodds, Michael J., OP. "Thomas Aquinas, Human Suffering, and the Unchanging God of Love." *Theological Studies* 52, no. 2 (1991): 330–44.

———. "Ultimacy and Intimacy: Aquinas on the Relation between God and the World." In *Ordo Sapientiae et Amoris: Hommage au Professeur Jean-Pierre Torrell, OP,* edited by Carlos-Josaphat Pinto de Oliveira, 211–27. Fribourg: Editions Universitaires, 1993.

———. *The Unchanging God of Love: Thomas Aquinas and Contemporary Theology on Divine Immutability.* Washington, D.C.: The Catholic University of America Press, 2008.

———. *The Philosophy of Nature.* Oakland, Calif.: Western Dominican Province/ Lulu.com, 2010.

———. *Unlocking Divine Action: Contemporary Science and Thomas Aquinas.* Washington, D.C.: The Catholic University of America Press, 2012.

———. "The God of Life, the Science of Life, and the Problem of Language." In *God: Reason and Reality,* edited by Anselm Ramelow, OP, 197–233. Munich: Philosophia Verlag, 2013.

———. *Philosophical Anthropology.* Oakland, Calif.: Western Dominican Province/ Lulu.com, 2013.

Dolezal, James E. *God without Parts: Divine Simplicity and the Metaphysics of God's Absoluteness.* Eugene, Ore.: Pickwick Publications, 2011.

———. *All That Is in God: Evangelical Theology and the Challenge of Classical Christian Theism.* Grand Rapids, Mich.: Reformation Heritage Books, 2017.

Donceel, Joseph, SJ. "Can We Still Make a Case in Reason for the Existence of God?" In *God Knowable and Unknowable,* edited by Robert J. Roth, 159–86. New York: Fordham University Press, 1973.

————. *The Searching Mind: An Introduction to a Philosophy of God.* Notre Dame, Ind.: University of Notre Dame Press, 1979.

Doolan, Gregory T. "The Causality of the Divine Ideas in Relation to Natural Agents in Thomas Aquinas." *International Philosophical Quarterly* 44, no. 3 (2004): 393–409.

————. *Aquinas on the Divine Ideas as Exemplar Causes.* Washington, D.C.: The Catholic University of America Press, 2008.

Doran, Chris. "Intelligent Design: It's Just Too Good to Be True." *Theology and Science* 8, no. 2 (2010): 223–37.

Edwards, Denis. *How God Acts: Creation, Redemption and Special Divine Action.* Minneapolis: Fortress Press, 2010.

Einstein, Albert. *Out of My Later Years.* New York: Wisdom Library, 1950.

Elders, Leo. *The Philosophical Theology of St. Thomas Aquinas.* Leiden: Brill, 1990.

————. "Faith and Reason: The Synthesis of St. Thomas Aquinas." *Nova et Vetera* (English ed.) 8, no. 3 (2010): 527–52.

Emery, Gilles, OP. *The Trinitarian Theology of Saint Thomas Aquinas.* New York: Oxford University Press, 2007.

Emery, Gilles, OP, and Matthew Levering, eds. *Aristotle in Aquinas's Theology.* Oxford: Oxford University Press, 2015.

Emonet, Pierre-Marie. *God Seen in the Mirror of the World: An Introduction to the Philosophy of God.* New York: Crossroad, 2016.

Eslick, Leonard. "From the World to God: The Cosmological Argument." *Modern Schoolman* 60, no. 3 (1983): 145–69.

Fabro, Cornelio. *God in Exile: Modern Atheism.* Translated by Arthur Gibson. New York: Paulist Press, 1968.

————. *God: An Introduction to Problems in Theology.* Translated by Joseph T. Papa. Edited by Nathaniel Dreyer. Cullum, Md.: IVE Press, 2017.

Faricy, Robert L., SJ. "The Establishment of the Basic Principle of the Fifth Way." *New Scholasticism* 31, no. 2 (1957): 189–208.

Feser, Edward. *The Last Superstition: A Refutation of the New Atheism.* South Bend, Ind.: St. Augustine's Press, 2008.

————. *Aquinas: A Beginner's Guide.* London: Oneworld Publications, 2009.

————. *Scholastic Metaphysics: A Contemporary Introduction.* Heusenstamm, Germany: Editiones Scholasticae, 2014.

————. "Natural Theology Must Be Grounded in the Philosophy of Nature, Not in Natural Science." In *Neo-Scholastic Essays,* 61–83. South Bend, Ind.: Saint Augustine's Press, 2015.

————. *Five Proofs of the Existence of God.* San Francisco: Ignatius Press, 2017.

————. *Aristotle's Revenge: The Metaphysical Foundations of Physical and Biological Science* Neunkirchen-Seelscheid, Germany: Editiones Scholasticae, 2019.

Fiddes, Paul S. *The Creative Suffering of God.* Oxford: Clarendon Press, 1988.

Fretheim, Terrance E. *The Suffering God: An Old Testament Perspective.* Philadelphia: Fortress Press, 1984.

Gavrilyuk, Paul L. *The Suffering of the Impassible God: The Dialectics of Patristic Thought*. New York: Oxford University Press, 2004.

Geisler, Norman L. *Thomas Aquinas: An Evangelical Appraisal*. Grand Rapids, Mich.: Baker Book House, 1991.

Geivett, R. Douglas. "The Evidential Value of Miracles." In *In Defense of Miracles: A Comprehensive Case for God's Action in History*, edited by R. Douglas Geivett and Gary R. Habermas, 178–95. Downers Grove, Ill.: Intervarsity Press, 1997.

———. "The Evidential Value of Religious Experience." In *The Rationality of Theism*, edited by Paul Copan and Paul K. Moser, 175–203. New York: Routledge, 2003.

Geivett, R. Douglas, and Gary R. Habermas, eds. *In Defense of Miracles: A Comprehensive Case for God's Action in History*. Downers Grove, Ill.: Intervarsity Press, 1997.

Gilkey, Langdon. "Cosmology, Ontology and the Travail of Biblical Language." In *God's Activity in the World: The Contemporary Problem*, edited by Owen C. Thomas, 29–44. Chico, Calif.: Scholars Press, 1983.

Gilson, Etienne. *God and Philosophy*. New Haven, Conn.: Yale University Press, 1941.

———. *The Unity of Philosophical Experience*. Westminster, Md.: Christian Classics, 1982.

———. *The Christian Philosophy of St. Thomas Aquinas*. Translated by L. K. Shook. Notre Dame, Ind.: University of Notre Dame Press, 2006.

Gnuse, Robert Karl. *No Other Gods: Emergent Monotheism in Israel*. Sheffield, U.K.: Sheffield Academic Press, 1997.

Goetz, Ronald. "The Suffering God: The Rise of a New Orthodoxy." *Christian Century* 103, no. 13 (April 16, 1986): 385–89.

Gonzalez, Angel Luis. *Ser y participación: Estudio sobre la cuarta vía de Tomás de Aquino*. Pamplona: Ediciones Universidad de Navarra, 1995.

Goris, Harm J. M. J. *Free Creatures of an Eternal God: Thomas Aquinas on God's Infallible Foreknowlege and Irresistible Will*. Leuven: Peeters, 1996.

Grant, W. Matthews. "Aquinas, Divine Simplicity, and Divine Freedom." *Proceedings of the American Catholic Philosophical Association* 77 (2003): 129–44.

Green, Barbara, OP. *Mindful*. Charleston, S.C.: Book Surge Publishing, 2008.

Gutenson, Charles E. "Does God Change?" In *God under Fire: Modern Scholarship Reinvents God*, edited by Douglas S. Huffman and Eric L. Johnson, 231–52. Grand Rapids, Mich.: Zondervan, 2002.

Haack, Susan. *Defending Science within Reason: Between Scientism and Cynicism*. Amherst, N.Y.: Prometheus Books, 2003.

Haldane, John. "Analytical Thomism: How We Got Here, Why It Is Worth Remaining and Where We May Go to Next." In *Analytical Thomism: Traditions in Dialogue*, edited by Craig Paterson and Matthew S. Pugh, 303–10. Burlington, Vt.: Ashgate, 2006.

Hankey, Wayne. "The Place of the Proof for God's Existence in the *Summa Theologiae* of Thomas Aquinas." *Thomist* 46, no. 3 (1982): 370–93.

———. *God in Himself: Aquinas' Doctrine of God as Expounded in the "Summa Theologiae."* New York: Oxford University Press, 1987.

Harris, Sam. *The End of Faith: Religion, Terror, and the Future of Reason*. New York: W. W. Norton, 2005.

Hart, David Bentley. *Atheist Delusions: The Christian Revolution and Its Fashionable Enemies*. New Haven, Conn.: Yale University Press, 2009.

———. *The Experience of God: Being, Consciousness, Bliss*. New Haven, Conn.: Yale University Press, 2013.

Hartshorne, Charles. *The Divine Relativity: A Social Conception of God*. New Haven, Conn.: Yale University Press, 1948.

Hasker, William. "Does God Change?" In *Questions about God: Today's Philosophers Ponder the Divine*, edited by Steven M. Cahn and David Shatz, 137–45. Oxford: Oxford University Press, 2002.

Haught, John F. *God and the New Atheism: A Critical Response to Dawkins, Harris, and Hitchens*. Louisville, Ky.: Westminster John Knox, 2008.

Hebblethwaite, Brian L. "Some Reflections on Predestination, Providence, and Divine Foreknowledge." *Religious Studies* 15, no. 4 (1979): 433–48.

Heisenberg, Werner. *Physics and Philosophy*. New York: Harper and Brothers, 1958.

Helm, Paul. *Eternal God: A Study of God without Time*. New York: Oxford University Press, 1988.

Henle, Robert J., SJ. "Transcendental Thomism: A Critical Assessment." In *One Hundred Years of Thomism: "Aeterni Patris" and Afterwards, A Symposium*, edited by Victor B. Brezik, 90–116. Houston: Center for Thomistic Studies, 1981.

Henry, Martin. "Does Hell Still Have a Future?" *The Heythrop Journal* 56, no. 1 (2015): 120–35.

Hick, John. *An Interpretation of Religion: Human Responses to the Transcendent*. 2nd ed. New Haven, Conn.: Yale University Press, 2004.

Highfield, Ron. *The Faithful Creator: Affirming Creation and Providence in an Age of Anxiety*. Downers Grove, Ill.: IVP Academic, 2015.

Hill, William J., OP. *Knowing the Unknown God*. New York: Philosophical Library, 1971.

———. "Does God Know the Future? Aquinas and Some Moderns." *Theological Studies* 36, no. 1 (1975): 3–18.

———. "Two Gods of Love: Aquinas and Whitehead." *Listening* 14, no. 3 (1979): 249–65.

———. "Does Divine Love Entail Suffering in God?" In *God and Temporality*, edited by Bowman L. Clarke and Eugene T. Long, 55–71. New York: Paragon, 1984.

———. "The Implicate World: God's Oneness with Mankind as a Mediated Immediacy." In *Beyond Mechanism: The Universe in Recent Physics and Catholic Thought*, edited by David L. Schindler, 78–98. Lanham, Md.: University Press of America, 1986.

Hitchens, Christopher. *God Is Not Great: How Religion Poisons Everything*. New York: Warner Twelve, 2007.

The Holy Bible: Revised Standard Version. New York: Collins, 1973.

Hughes, Christopher. *On a Complex Theory of a Simple God: An Investigation in Aquinas' Philosophical Theology.* Ithaca, N.Y.: Cornell University Press, 1989.

Hume, David. *An Enquiry Concerning Human Understanding.* Chicago: Open Court, 1930.

Hütter, Reinhard. "Attending to the Wisdom of God—from Effect to Cause, from Creation to God: A *Relecture* of the Analogy of Being according to Thomas Aquinas." In *The Analogy of Being: Invention of the Antichrist or the Wisdom of God?* edited by Thomas Joseph White, OP, 209–45. Grand Rapids, Mich.: Eerdmans, 2011.

Huxley, Thomas Henry. "Biogenesis and Abiogenesis." Presidential Address for the British Association for the Advancement of Science, 1870, https://mathcs.clarku.edu/huxley/CE8/B-Ab.html.

Jaeger, Lydia. "The Contingency of Creation and Modern Science." *Theology and Science* 16, no. 1 (2018): 54–78.

Jansen, Henry. "Moltmann's View of God's (Im)mutability: The God of the Philosophers and the God of the Bible." *Neue Zeitschrift für systematische Theologie und Religionsphilosophie* 36, no. 3 (1994): 284–301.

Jantzen, Grace. *God's World, God's Body.* Philadelphia: Westminster, 1984.

Jarick, John, ed. *Perspectives on Israelite Wisdom: Proceedings of the Oxford Old Testament Seminar.* New York: Bloomsbury, 2016.

Jenkins, John. *Knowledge and Faith in Thomas Aquinas.* Cambridge: Cambridge University Press, 1997.

John Paul II, Pope. *Crossing the Threshold of Hope.* Edited by Vittorio Messori. Toronto: Alfred A. Knopf, Inc., 1994.

———. *Fides et ratio: On the Relationship between Faith and Reason.* Encyclical Letter. September 14, 1998. Washington, D.C.: United States Catholic Conference, 1998.

Johnson, Elizabeth A. *She Who Is: The Mystery of God in a Feminist Theological Discourse.* New York: Crossroad, 1992.

Johnson, Mark F. "Aquinas's *Summa theologiae* as Pedagogy." In *Medieval Education,* edited by Ronald B. Begley and Joseph W. Koterski, SJ, 133–42. New York: Fordham University Press, 2005.

Jordan, Mark D. "Theology and Philosophy." In *The Cambridge Companion to Aquinas,* edited by Norman Kretzmann and Eleonore Stump, 232–51. Cambridge: Cambridge University Press, 1993.

———. *Rewritten Theology: Aquinas after His Readers.* Oxford: Blackwell, 2006.

Journet, Charles. *The Meaning of Grace.* Translated by A. V. Littledale. New York: P. J. Kenedy and Sons, 1960.

———. *The Meaning of Evil.* Translated by Michael Barry. New York: P. J. Kenedy and Sons, 1963.

Kaiser, Walter C., Jr. *Malachi: God's Unchanging Love.* Grand Rapids, Mich.: Baker Book House, 1984.

Kasper, Walter. *The God of Jesus Christ.* Translated by Matthew J. O'Connell. New York: Crossroad, 1984.

Kaufman, Gordon D. *God the Problem*. Cambridge, Mass.: Harvard University Press, 1972.

Kaufmann, Yehezkel. *The Religion of Israel from Its Beginnings to the Babylonian Exile*. Translated by Moshe Greenberg. New York: Schocken, 1966.

Keating, James F., and Thomas Joseph White, OP, eds. *Divine Impassibility and the Mystery of Human Suffering*. Grand Rapids, Mich.: Eerdmans, 2009.

Kenny, Anthony. "Introduction." In *Aquinas: A Collection of Critical Essays*, edited by Anthony Kenny, 1–12. Notre Dame, Ind.: University of Notre Dame Press, 1976.

———. *The Five Ways: Saint Thomas Aquinas' Proofs of God's Existence*. Notre Dame, Ind.: University of Notre Dame Press, 1980.

Kerr, Fergus, OP. "Theology in Philosophy: Revisiting the Five Ways." *International Journal for Philosophy of Religion* 50, no. 1 (2001): 115–30.

———. *After Aquinas: Versions of Thomism*. Oxford: Blackwell, 2002.

Kerr, Fergus, OP, ed. *Contemplating Aquinas: On the Varieties of Interpretation*. London: SCM, 2003.

Kerr, Gaven, OP. *Aquinas's Way to God: The Proof in "De Ente et Essentia."* New York: Oxford University Press, 2015.

———. "The Relevance of Aquinas' Uncaused Cause Argument." In *Revisiting Aquinas' Proofs for the Existence of God*, edited by Robert Arp, 71–86. Leiden: Brill, 2016.

———. "Essentially Ordered Series Reconsidered Once Again." *American Catholic Philosophical Quarterly* 91, no. 2 (2017): 155–74.

Krempel, A. *La doctrine de la relation chez saint Thomas*. Paris: Librairie Philosophique J. Vrin, 1952.

Kretzmann, Norman. *The Metaphysics of Theism: Aquinas's Natural Theology in "Summa contra Gentiles" I*. Oxford: Clarendon Press, 1997.

Kuhn, Thomas S. *The Structure of Scientific Revolutions*. Chicago: University of Chicago Press, 1970.

Lactantius. *A Treatise on the Anger of God*. In *The Ante-Nicene Fathers: Translations of the Writings of the Fathers down to A.D. 325,* vol. 7, edited by Alexander Roberts and James Donaldson, 259–80. Grand Rapids, Mich.: Eerdmans, 1994.

LaCugna, Catherine Mowry. *God for Us: The Trinity and Christian Life*. San Francisco: Harper, 1992.

Lang, Bernhard. "No God but Yahweh! The Origin and Character of Biblical Monotheism." In *Monotheism*, edited by Claude Geffré, Jean-Pierre Jossua, and Marcus Lefébure, 41–49. Edinburgh: T and T Clark, 1985.

Langford, Michael. *Providence*. London: SCM Press, 1981.

Lash, Nicholas. "Where Does the God Delusion Come From?" *New Blackfriars* 88 (2007): 507–21.

Lauer, Rosemary. "The Notion of Efficient Cause in the *Secunda Via*." *Thomist* 38, no. 4 (1974): 754–67.

Laughlin, Peter. "Divine Necessity and Created Contingency in Aquinas." *The Heythrop Journal* 50, no. 4 (2009): 649–57

Leibniz, Gottfried Wilhelm. *Theodicy: Essays on the Goodness of God, the Freedom of Man, and the Origin of Evil.* New Haven, Conn.: Yale University Press, 1952.

Leinsle, Ulrich G. *Introduction to Scholastic Theology.* Translated by Michael J. Miller. Washington, D.C.: The Catholic University of America Press, 2010.

Lemaire, André. *The Birth of Monotheism: The Rise and Disappearance of Yahwism.* Washington, D.C.: Biblical Archaeological Society, 2007.

Levering, Matthew. "Aquinas on Romans 8: Predestination in Context." In *Reading Romans with St. Thomas Aquinas,* edited by Matthew Levering and Michael Dauphinais, 196–215. Washington, D.C.: The Catholic University of America Press, 2012.

———. *Engaging the Doctrine of Creation: Cosmos, Creatures, and the Wise and Good Creator.* Grand Rapids, Mich.: Baker Academic, 2017.

Levering, Matthew, Marcus Plested, and Charles Raith II, eds. *Oxford Handbook of Reception of Aquinas.* Oxford: Oxford University Press, forthcoming.

Lewis, C. S. *The Great Divorce.* New York: Macmillan, 1976.

Lister, Rob. *God Is Impassible and Impassioned: Toward a Theology of Divine Emotion.* Wheaton, Ill.: Crossway, 2012.

Lombardo, Nicholas E., OP. *The Logic of Desire: Aquinas on Emotion.* Washington, D.C.: The Catholic University of America Press, 2011.

Long, Steven A. *Analogia Entis: On the Analogy of Being, Metaphysics, and the Act of Faith.* Notre Dame, Ind.: University of Notre Dame Press, 2011.

———. "St. Thomas Aquinas, Divine Causality, and the Mystery of Predestination." In *Thomism and Predestination: Principles and Disputations,* edited by Steven A. Long, Roger W. Nutt, and Thomas Joseph White, OP, 51–76. Ave Maria, Fla.: Sapientia Press, 2017.

Long, Steven A., Roger W. Nutt, and Thomas Joseph White, OP, eds. *Thomism and Predestination: Principles and Disputations.* Ave Maria, Fla.: Sapientia Press, 2017.

Luisi, Pier Luigi. *The Emergence of Life: From Chemical Origins to Synthetic Biology.* New York: Cambridge University Press, 2010.

Macquarrie, John. *The Humility of God.* Philadelphia: Westminster, 1978.

Mansini, Guy, OSB. *Fundamental Theology.* Washington, D.C: The Catholic University of America Press, 2018.

Maritain, Jacques. *Saint Thomas and the Problem of Evil.* Milwaukee, Wisc.: Marquette University Press, 1942.

———. *The Range of Reason.* New York: Charles Scribner's Sons, 1952.

———. *Approaches to God.* New York: Macmillan, 1954.

Markham, Ian S. *Against Atheism: Why Dawkins, Hitchens, and Harris are Fundamentally Wrong.* Malden, Mass.: Wiley-Blackwell, 2010.

Marmion, Declan, and Rik Van Nieuwenhove. *An Introduction to the Trinity.* New York: Cambridge University Press, 2010.

Marshall, Bruce D. "*Quod sit una uetula*: Aquinas on the Nature of Theology." In *The Theology of Thomas Aquinas,* edited by Rik Van Nieuwenhove and Joseph Wawrykov, 1–35. Notre Dame, Ind.: University of Notre Dame Press, 1995.

Martin, Michael, ed. *The Cambridge Companion to Atheism*. New York: Cambridge University Press, 2007.

Matava, Robert Joseph. *Divine Causality and Human Free Choice: Domingo Bañez, Physical Premotion and the Controversy de Auxiliis Revisited*. Leiden: Brill, 2016.

McCabe, Herbert, OP. "The Involvement of God." *New Blackfriars* 66, no. 785 (1985): 464–76.

———. *On Aquinas*. Edited by Brian Davies, OP. New York: Continuum, 2008.

———. *God and Evil in the Theology of St. Thomas Aquinas*. Edited by Brian Davies, OP. New York: Continuum, 2010.

McCool, Gerald A., SJ. *From Unity to Pluralism: The Internal Evolution of Thomism*. New York: Fordham University Press, 1989.

———. *Nineteenth-Century Scholasticism: The Search for a Unitary Method*. New York: Fordham University Press, 1989.

———. *The Neo-Thomists*. Milwaukee, Wisc.: Marquette University Press, 1994.

McFague, Sallie. *Models of God: Theology for an Ecological, Nuclear Age*. Philadelphia: Fortress Press, 1987.

———. *The Body of God: An Ecological Theology*. Minneapolis: Fortress Press, 1993.

McGinn, Bernard. "The Development of the Thought of Thomas Aquinas on the Reconciliation of Divine Providence and Contingent Action." *Thomist* 39, no. 4 (1975): 741–52.

———. *Thomas Aquinas's "Summa theologiae": A Biography*. Princeton, N.J.: Princeton University Press, 2014.

McGrath, Alister. *The Twilight of Atheism: The Rise and Fall of Disbelief in the Modern World*. New York: Doubleday, 2004.

McGrath, Alister, and Joanna Collicutt McGrath. *The Dawkins Delusion? Atheist Fundamentalism and the Denial of the Divine*. Downers Grove, Ill.: IVP Books, 2007.

McInerny, Ralph. *Aquinas and Analogy*. Washington, D.C.: The Catholic University of America Press, 1996.

———. *Praeambula fidei: Thomism and the God of the Philosophers*. Washington, D.C.: The Catholic University of America Press, 2006.

McKenzie, John L., SJ. *Dictionary of the Bible*. New York: Macmillan, 1977.

McWhorter, Matthew R. "Aquinas on God's Relation to the World." *New Blackfriars* 94, no. 1049 (2013): 3–19.

Merton, Thomas. *New Seeds of Contemplation*. New York: New Directions Publishing, 2007.

Miller, Patrick D. "Forward to the Second Edition." In *The Early History of God: Yahweh and the Other Deities in Ancient Israel*. 2nd ed. By Mark S. Smith, x–xi. Grand Rapids, Mich.: Eerdmans, 2002.

Miyakawa, Toshiyuki. "The Value and the Meaning of the Tertia Via of St. Thomas Aquinas." *Aquinas* 6, no. 2 (1963): 239–95.

Moltmann, Jürgen. *The Crucified God*. New York: Harper and Row, 1974.

———. *The Trinity and the Kingdom*. Translated by M. Kehl. New York: Harper and Row, 1981.

————. *History and the Triune God: Contributions to Trinitarian Theology.* New York: Crossroad, 1992.

Monod, Jacques. *Chance and Necessity: An Essay on the Natural Philosophy of Modern Biology.* New York: Alfred A. Knopf, 1972.

Montagnes, Bernard. *The Doctrine of the Analogy of Being according to Thomas Aquinas.* Translated by E. M. Macierowski. Milwaukee, Wisc.: Marquette University Press, 2004.

Moreland, Anna Bonta. *Known by Nature: Thomas Aquinas on Natural Knowledge of God.* New York: Crossroad, 2010.

Moreno, Antonio, OP. "The Law of Inertia and the Principle *'Quidquid movetur ab alio movetur.'" Thomist* 38, no. 2 (1974): 306–31.

Mulchahey, Michèle M. *"First the Bow is Bent in Study. . .": Dominican Education before 1350.* Toronto: Pontifical Institute of Mediaeval Studies, 1998.

Muñiz, Francisco P., OP. "La 'quarta via' de Santo Tomás para demonstrar la existencia de Dios." *Revista de Filosofía* 3, no. 10 (1944): 385–433; 4, no. 12 (1945): 49–101.

————. "*Introducción a la cuestion 2.*" Vol. 1 of *Suma Teológica.* By Tomás de Aquino. Translated by Raimundo Suarez, OP, 282–313. Madrid: Biblioteca de Autores Cristianos, 1964.

Murphy, Nancey. "Science and the Problem of Evil: Suffering as a By-product of a Finely Tuned Cosmos." In *Physics and Cosmology: Scientific Perspectives on the Problem of Natural Evil,* edited by Nancey Murphy, Robert John Russell, and William Stoeger, 131–51. Vatican City and Berkeley, Calif.: Vatican Observatory and Center for Theology and the Natural Sciences, 2007.

Nahm, Milton C. *Selections from Early Greek Philosophy.* New York: Appleton-Century-Crofts, 1964.

New American Bible. Revised Edition. Charlotte, N.C.: Saint Benedict Press, 2011.

Newton, Isaac. *Mathematical Principles of Natural Philosophy.* In *Sir Isaac Newton's Mathematical Principles of Natural Philosophy and His System of the World,* edited and translated by Andrew Motte and Florian Cajori, 1–547. Berkeley, Calif.: University of California Press, 1946.

Newton, William. "A Case of Mistaken Identity: Aquinas's Fifth Way and Arguments of Intelligent Design." *New Blackfriars* 95, no. 1059 (2014): 569–78.

Nichols, Aidan, OP. *Discovering Aquinas: An Introduction to His Life, Work, and Influence.* Grand Rapids, Mich.: Eerdmans, 2002.

Nutt, Roger W. "Providence, Wisdom, and the Justice of Job's Afflictions: Considerations from Aquinas' *Literal Exposition on Job.*" *The Heythrop Journal* 56, no. 1 (2015): 44–66.

Oliver, Simon. *Philosophy, God and Motion.* New York: Routledge, 2005.

————. "Aquinas and Aristotle's Teleology." *Nova et Vetera* (English ed.) 11, no. 3 (2013): 849–70.

O'Meara, Thomas F., OP. *Thomas Aquinas: Theologian.* Notre Dame, Ind.: University of Notre Dame Press, 1997.

O'Rourke, Fran. *Pseudo-Dionysius and the Metaphysics of Aquinas.* Leiden: Brill, 1992.

Paley, William. *Natural Theology: Or, Evidences of the Existence and Attributes of the Deity, Collected from the Appearances of Nature.* Boston: Gould, Kendall and Lincoln, 1842.

Paluch, Michał, OP. *La profondeur de l'amour divin: Evolution de la doctrine de la prédestination dans l'oeuvre de Thomas d'Aquin.* Paris: J. Vrin, 2004.

———. "Recovering a Doctrine of Providence." *Nova et Vetera* (English ed.) 12, no. 4 (2014): 1159–72.

Pasnau, Robert, and Christopher John Shields. *The Philosophy of Aquinas.* Boulder, Colo.: Westview Press, 2004.

Pawl, Timothy. "The Five Ways." In *The Oxford Handbook of Aquinas,* edited by Brian Davies, OP, and Eleonore Stump, 115–31. New York: Oxford University Press, 2011.

Peacocke, Arthur. *Theology for a Scientific Age: Being and Becoming—Natural, Divine, and Human.* Minneapolis: Fortress Press, 1993.

———. "Emergence, Mind, and Divine Action: The Hierarchy of the Sciences in Relation to the Human Mind-Brain-Body." In *The Re-emergence of Emergence: The Emergentist Hypothesis from Science to Religion,* edited by Philip Clayton and Paul Davies, 257–78. New York: Oxford University Press, 2006.

Pegis, Anton C. *St. Thomas and Philosophy.* Milwaukee, Wisc.: Marquette University Press, 1964.

Pelikan, Jaroslav. *The Emergence of the Catholic Tradition.* Chicago: University of Chicago Press, 1971.

Pesch, Otto Hermann. *The God Question in Thomas Aquinas and Martin Luther.* Philadelphia: Fortress Press, 1972.

———. "Thomas Aquinas and Contemporary Theology." In *Contemplating Aquinas: On the Varieties of Interpretation,* edited by Fergus Kerr, 185–216. London: SCM, 2003.

Pieper, Josef. *Happiness and Contemplation.* Translated by Richard and Clara Winston. London: Faber and Faber, 1958.

———. *Scholasticism: Personalities and Problems of Medieval Philosophy.* New York: McGraw Hill, 1960.

———. *Guide to Thomas Aquinas.* Translated by Richard and Clara Winston. New York: New American Library, 1964.

———. *The Silence of Saint Thomas.* Translated by John Murray and Daniel O'Connor. Chicago: Henry Regnery, 1966.

Pimentel, Stephen. "Thomas's Elusive Proof: A Reconstruction of the 'Existential Argument' for the Existence of God." *Proceedings of the American Catholic Philosophical Association* 78 (2004): 93–105.

Pinnock, Clark H. *Most Moved Mover: A Theology of God's Openness.* Grand Rapids, Mich.: Baker Books, 2001.

Piper, John. *The Pleasures of God: Meditations on God's Delight in Being God.* Sisters, Ore.: Multnomah Publishers, 2000.

Placher, William C. *Narratives of a Vulnerable God: Christ, Theology, and Scripture.* Louisville, Ky.: Westminster John Knox Press, 1994.

———. *The Domestication of Transcendence: How Modern Thinking about God Went Wrong.* Louisville, Ky.: Westminster John Knox Press, 1996.

Polkinghorne, John C. *One World: The Interaction of Science and Theology.* Princeton, N.J.: Princeton University Press, 1986.

———. *Science and Creation: The Search for Understanding.* Boston: Shambhala, 1989.

———. *Science and Providence: God's Interaction with the World.* Boston: New Science Library, 1989.

———. *Reason and Reality: The Relation between Science and Theology.* Philadelphia: Trinity Press International, 1991.

———. *Belief in God in an Age of Science.* New Haven, Conn.: Yale University Press, 1998.

———. "Space, Time, and Causality." *Zygon* 41, no. 4 (2006): 975–83.

Powers, Jonathan. *Philosophy and the New Physics.* New York: Methuen, 1982.

Quinn, John M., OSA. "The Third Way to God: A New Approach." *Thomist* 42, no. 1 (1978): 50–68.

Rahner, Karl. "Remarks on the Dogmatic Treatise 'De Trinitate.'" Vol. 4 of *Theological Investigations.* Translated by K. Smyth, 77–102. Baltimore, Md.: Helicon Press, 1966.

Ramelow, Anselm, OP. "The God of Miracles." In *God: Reason and Reality*, edited by Anselm Ramelow, OP, 303–64. Munich: Philosophia Verlag, 2013.

Regis, Edward. *What Is Life? Investigating the Nature of Life in the Age of Synthetic Biology.* New York: Farrar, Straus and Giroux, 2008.

Reitan, Eric A., OP. "Aquinas and Weisheipl: Aristotle's Physics and the Existence of God." In *Philosophy and the God of Abraham: Essays in Memory of James A. Weisheipl, O.P.*, edited by R. James Long, 179–90. Toronto: Pontifical Institute of Mediaeval Studies, 1991.

Ringgren, Helmer. *Israelite Religion.* Translated by David E. Green. Philadelphia: Fortress Press, 1966.

Rocca, Gregory P. *Speaking the Incomprehensible God: Thomas Aquinas on the Interplay of Positive and Negative Theology.* Washington, D.C.: The Catholic University of America Press, 2004.

Rota, Michael. "Infinite Causal Chains and Explanation." *Proceedings of the American Catholic Philosophical Association* 81 (2007): 109–22.

Rowe, William V. "Adolf von Harnack and the Concept of Hellenization." In *Hellenization Revisited: Shaping a Christian Response within the Greco-Roman World*, edited by Wendy E. Helleman, 69–98. Lanham, Md.: University Press of America, 1994.

Russell, Robert John. "Does the 'God Who Acts' Really Act in Nature?" In *Science and Theology: The New Consonance*, edited by Ted Peters, 77–102. Boulder, Colo.: Westview Press, 1998.

———. "Does 'The God Who Acts' Really Act? New Approaches to Divine Action in Light of Contemporary Science." In *Cosmology from Alpha to Omega: The Creative Mutual Interaction of Theology and Science*, 110–50. Minneapolis: Fortress, 2008.

———. "What We've Learned from Quantum Mechanics about Non-interventionist Objective Divine Action—and Its Remaining Challenges," in *God's Providence and Randomness in Nature: Scientific and Theological Perspectives*, edited by Robert John Russell and Joshua M. Moritz, 131–72. West Conshohocken, Penn.: Templeton Press, 2019.

Russell, Robert John, Nancey Murphy, and William R. Stoeger, eds. *Scientific Perspectives on Divine Action: Twenty Years of Challenge and Progress*. Vatican City and Berkeley, Calif.: Vatican Observatory and Center for Theology and the Natural Sciences, 2008.

Ryan, Fáinche. *Formation in Holiness: Thomas Aquinas on Sacra doctrina*. Dudley, Mass.: Peeters, 2007.

Schaab, Gloria L. "A Procreative Paradigm of the Creative Suffering of the Triune God: Implications of Arthur Peacocke's Evolutionary Theology." *Theological Studies* 67, no. 3 (2006): 542–66.

———. "The Creative Suffering of the Triune God: An Evolutionary Panentheistic Paradigm." *Theology and Science* 5, no. 3 (2007): 289–304.

Schenk, Richard, OP. "The Epoché of Factical Damnation? On the Costs of Bracketing Out the Likelihood of Final Loss." In *Soundings in the History of a Hope: New Studies on Thomas Aquinas*, 131–61. Ave Maria, Fla.: Sapientia Press, 2016.

Schillebeeckx, Edward, OP. *Jesus: An Experiment in Christology*. Translated by Hubert Hoskins. New York: Seabury Press, 1979.

———. *Christ: The Experience of Jesus as Lord*. Translated by John Bowden. New York: Crossroad, 1983.

———. *Church: The Human Story of God*. Translated by John Bowden. New York: Crossroad, 1993.

Schilling, S. Paul. *God and Human Anguish*. Nashville, Tenn.: Abingdon, 1977.

Schleiermacher, Friedrich. *The Christian Faith*. Edited by H. R. Mackintosh and J. S. Stewart. Edinburgh: T and T Clark, 1976.

Schudt, Karl. "Edith Stein's Proof for the Existence of God from Consciousness." *American Catholic Philosophical Quarterly* 82, no. 1 (2008): 105–25.

Schulte, Raphael. "Wie ist Gottes Wirken in Welt und Geschichte theologisch zu verstehen?" [How is God's action in the world and in history to be understood theologically?] In *Vorsehung und Handeln Gottes*, edited by Theodor Schneider and Lothar Ullrich, 116–67. Leipzig: St. Benno Verlag, 1988.

Shackleford, John M. *Faith Seeking Understanding: Approaching God through Science*. New York: Paulist Press, 2007.

Shanley, Brian J., OP. "Eternity and Duration in Aquinas." *Thomist* 61, no. 4 (1997): 525–48.

———. "Eternal Knowledge of the Temporal in Aquinas." *American Catholic Philosophical Quarterly* 71, no. 2 (1997): 197–224.

———. "Divine Causation and Human Freedom in Aquinas." *American Catholic Philosophical Quarterly* 72, no. 1 (1998): 99–122.

———. "Analytical Thomism." *Thomist* 63, no. 1 (1999): 125–37.

———. *The Thomist Tradition.* Dordrecht: Kluwer Academic Publishers, 2002.

Sheehan, Thomas. "Rahner's Transcendental Project." In *The Cambridge Companion to Karl Rahner,* edited by Declan Marmion and Mary E. Hines, 29–42. New York: Cambridge University Press, 2005.

Siniscalchi, Glenn. "Fine-Tuning, Atheist Criticism, and the Fifth Way." *Theology and Science* 12, no. 1 (2014): 64–77.

Smedes, Taede A. *Chaos, Complexity, and God: Divine Action and Scientism.* Leuven: Peeters, 2004.

Smith, Mark S. *The Early History of God: Yahweh and the Other Deities in Ancient Israel.* 2nd ed. Grand Rapids, Mich.; Eerdmans, 2002.

———. *God in Translation: Deities in Cross-Cultural Discourse in the Biblical World.* Tübingen: Mohr Siebeck, 2008.

Smith, Vincent E. "The Prime Mover: Physical and Metaphysical Considerations." *Proceedings of the American Catholic Philosophical Association* 28 (1954): 78–94.

Spaemann, Robert, and Reinhard Löw. *Die Frage Wozu? Geschichte und Wiederentdeckung des teleologischen Denkens* [The question, "to what purpose?" History and rediscovery of teleological thinking]. München: Piper, 1985.

Spitzer, Robert J., SJ. *New Proofs for the Existence of God: Contributions of Contemporary Physics and Philosophy.* Grand Rapids, Mich.; Eerdmans, 2010.

Stager, Lawrence E. "Forging an Identity: The Emergence of Ancient Israel." In *The Oxford History of the Biblical World,* edited by Michael D. Coogan, 123–75. New York: Oxford University Press, 1998.

Stannard, Russell. *The God Experiment: Can Science Prove the Existence of God?* London: Faber and Faber, 1999.

Stoeger, William R., SJ. "The Origin of the Universe in Science and Religion." In *Cosmos, Bios, Theos: Scientists Reflect on Science, God and the Origins of the Universe, Life, and Homo Sapiens,* edited by Henry Margenau and Roy Abraham Varghese, 254–69. LaSalle, Ill.: Open Court, 1992.

———. "The Big Bang, Quantum Cosmology, and *creatio ex nihilo.*" In *Creation and the God of Abraham,* edited by David B. Burrell, Carlo Coglioti, Janet Soskice, and William R. Stoeger, 152–75. New York: Cambridge University Press, 2010.

Stump, Eleonore. *Aquinas.* New York: Routledge, 2003.

———. *Wandering in Darkness: Narrative and the Problem of Suffering.* Oxford: Oxford University Press, 2013.

Stump, Eleonore, and Norman Kretzmann. "Eternity." *Journal of Philosophy* 78, no. 8 (1981): 429–58.

———. "God's Knowledge and Its Causal Efficacy." In *The Rationality of Belief and the Plurality of Faith: Essays in Honor of William P. Alston.* Edited by Thomas D. Senor, 94–124. Ithaca, N.Y.: Cornell University Press, 1995.

Sullivan, Thomas D. "Omniscience, Immutability and the Divine Mode of Knowing." *Faith and Philosophy* 8, no. 1 (1991): 21–35.

Svensson, Manfred, and David VanDrunen. *Aquinas among the Protestants*. Oxford: Wiley Blackwell, 2018.

Swinburne, Richard. *The Existence of God*. 2nd ed. Oxford: Oxford University Press, 2004.

Synan, Edward A. "Aquinas and the Children of Abraham." In *Philosophy and the God of Abraham: Essays in Memory of James A. Weisheipl, O.P.*, edited by R. James Long, 203–16. Toronto: Pontifical Institute of Mediaeval Studies, 1991.

Tabaczek, Mariusz, OP. "Hegel and Whitehead: In Search for Sources of Contemporary Versions of Panentheism in the Science-Theology Dialogue." *Theology and Science* 11, no. 2 (2013): 143–61.

———. "The Metaphysics of Downward Causality: Rediscovering the Formal Cause." *Zygon* 48, no. 2 (2013): 380–404.

Tanner, Kathryn. *God and Creation in Christian Theology: Tyranny or Empowerment?* New York: Basil Blackwell, 1988.

Tapp, Christian, and Edmund Runggaldier, eds. *God, Eternity, and Time*. Burlington, Vt: Ashgate, 2011.

Taylor, Charles. *A Secular Age*. Cambridge, Mass.: Harvard University Press, 2007.

Taylor, Richard. "Introduction." In *The Ontological Argument from St. Anselm to Contemporary Philosophers*, edited by Alvin Plantinga, vii–xvii. Garden City, N.Y.: Doubleday, 1965.

Te Velde, Rudi A. "Natural Reason in the *Summa contra Gentiles*." In *Thomas Aquinas: Contemporary Philosophical Perspectives*, edited by Brian Davies, OP, 117–40. Oxford: Oxford University Press, 2002.

———. *Aquinas on God: The "Divine Science" of the "Summa Theologiae"*. Aldershot: Ashgate, 2006.

Thomas, Owen C. "Problems in Panentheism." In *The Oxford Handbook of Religion and Science*, edited by Philip Clayton and Zachary Simpson, 652–64. Oxford: Oxford University Press, 2006.

Torrell, Jean-Pierre, OP. *Saint Thomas Aquinas*. Vol. 1, *The Person and His Work*. Vol. 2, *Spiritual Master*. Translated by Robert Royal. Washington, D.C.: The Catholic University of America Press, 1996, 2003.

———. *Aquinas's "Summa": Background, Structure, and Reception*. Translated by Benedict M. Guevin, OSB. Washington, D.C.: The Catholic University of America Press, 2005.

Tracy, David. *Blessed Rage for Order: The New Pluralism in Theology*. New York: Seabury, 1975.

Tracy, Thomas F. "Particular Providence and the God of the Gaps." *CTNS Bulletin* 15, no. 1 (1995): 1–18.

———. "The Lawfulness of Nature and the Problem of Evil." In *Physics and Cosmology: Scientific Perspectives on the Problem of Natural Evil*, edited by Nancey Murphy,

Robert John Russell, and William Stoeger, 153–78. Vatican City and Berkeley, Calif.: Vatican Observatory and Center for Theology and the Natural Sciences, 2007.

Tugwell, Simon, OP, ed. *Albert and Thomas: Selected Writings*. New York: Paulist Press, 1988.

Turner, Denys. *Faith, Reason and the Existence of God*. Cambridge: Cambridge University Press, 2004.

———. "On Denying the Right God: Aquinas on Atheism and Idolatry." *Modern Theology* 20, no. 1 (2004): 141–61.

———. *Thomas Aquinas: A Portrait*. New Haven, Conn.: Yale University Press, 2013.

Turner, Geoffrey. "St. Thomas Aquinas on the 'Scientific' Nature of Theology." *New Blackfriars* 78, no. 921 (1997): 464–76.

Twetten, David B. "Why Motion Requires a Cause: The Foundation for a Prime Mover in Aristotle and Aquinas." In *Philosophy and the God of Abraham: Essays in Memory of James A. Weisheipl, O.P.*, edited by R. James Long, 235–54. Toronto: Pontifical Institute of Mediaeval Studies, 1991.

———. "Clearing a 'Way' for Aquinas: How the Proof from Motion Concludes to God." *Proceedings of the American Catholic Philosophical Association* 70 (1996): 259–78.

Umphrey, Stewart. *The Aristotelian Tradition of Natural Kinds and Its Demise*. Washington, D.C.: The Catholic University of America Press, 2018.

Urban, Hugh B. *New Age, Neopagan, and New Religious Movements: Alternative Spirituality in Contemporary America*. Oakland, Calif.: University of California Press, 2015.

Valkenberg, Wilhelmus G. B. M. *Words of the Living God: Place and Function of Holy Scripture in the Theology of St. Thomas Aquinas*. Leuven: Peeters, 2000.

Van de Beek, A. *Why? On Suffering, Guilt and God*. Grand Rapids, Mich.: Eerdmans, 1990.

Van Steenberghen, Fernand. *Hidden God: How Do We Know that God Exists?* St. Louis, Mo.: Herder, 1966.

Vann, Gerald, OP. *Saint Thomas Aquinas*. New York: Benziger Brothers, 1947.

———. *The Pain of Christ and the Sorrow of God*. New York: Alba House, 2000.

Vatican Council I. *Dei Filius*. April 24, 1870. In *The Christian Faith in the Doctrinal Documents of the Catholic Church*, 5th ed., edited by J. Neuner, SJ, and J. Dupuis, SJ. New York: Alba House, 1990.

Vatican Council II. *Dei verbum*. November 18, 1965. In *The Documents of Vatican II*, edited by Austin P. Flannery, OP. New York: Pillar Books, 1975.

———. *Gaudium et Spes*. December 7, 1965. In *The Documents of Vatican II*, edited by Austin P. Flannery, OP. New York: Pillar Books, 1975.

Velecky, Lubor. *Aquinas' Five Arguments in the Summa Theologiae 1a 2, 3*. Kampen, The Netherlands: Kok Pharos, 1994.

Von Harnack, Adolf. *History of Dogma*. Translated by Neil Buchanan. New York: Russell and Russell, 1958.

Vos, Arvin. *Aquinas, Calvin, and Contemporary Protestant Thought: A Critique of Protestant Views on the Thought of Thomas Aquinas.* Washington, D.C.: Christian University Press, 1985.

Wallace, William A., OP. "Newtonian Antinomies against the Prima Via." *Thomist* 19, no. 2 (1956): 151–92.

———. *Causality and Scientific Explanation.* 2 vols. Ann Arbor: University of Michigan Press, 1972.

———. *The Elements of Philosophy: A Compendium for Philosophers and Theologians.* New York: Alba House, 1977.

———. "Aquinas and Newton on the Causality of Nature and of God: The Medieval and Modern Problematic." In *Philosophy and the God of Abraham: Essays in Memory of James A. Weisheipl, O.P.,* edited by R. James Long, 255–79. Toronto: Pontifical Institute of Mediaeval Studies, 1991.

———. *The Modeling of Nature: Philosophy of Science and Philosophy of Nature in Synthesis.* Washington, D.C.: The Catholic University of America Press, 1996.

Ward, Keith. *Divine Action.* London: Collins, 1990.

———. *The God Conclusion: God and the Western Philosophical Tradition.* London: Darton, Longman and Todd, 2009.

Weinandy, Thomas G., OFM Cap. *Does God Change? The Word's Becoming in the Incarnation.* Still River, Mass.: St. Bede's Publications, 1985.

———. *Does God Suffer?* Notre Dame, Ind.: University of Notre Dame Press, 2000.

Weingartner, Paul. *God's Existence: Can It Be Proven? A Logical Commentary on the Five Ways of Thomas Aquinas.* Frankfurt: Ontos Verlag, 2010.

Weisheipl, James A., OP. "The Meaning of *Sacra Doctrina* in *Summa Theologiae* I, q. 1." *Thomist* 38, no. 1 (1974): 49–80.

———. *Friar Thomas D'Aquino: His Life, Thought and Works.* Washington, D.C.: The Catholic University of America Press, 1983.

———. "The Principle '*Omne quod movetur ab alio movetur*' in Medieval Physics." In *Nature and Motion in the Middle Ages,* edited by William E. Carroll, 75–97. Washington, D.C.: The Catholic University of America Press, 1985.

White, Thomas Joseph, OP. *Wisdom in the Face of Modernity: A Study in Thomistic Natural Theology.* Naples, Fla.: Sapientia Press of Ave Maria, 2009.

———. "Catholic Predestination: The Omnipotence and Innocence of Divine Love." In *Thomism and Predestination: Principles and Disputations,* edited by Steven A. Long, Roger W. Nutt, and Thomas Joseph White, OP, 94–126. Ave Maria, Fla.: Sapientia Press, 2017.

White, Victor, OP. "Prelude to The Five Ways." In *Aquinas's "Summa Theologiae": Critical Essays,* edited by Brian Davies, OP, 25–44. Lanham, Md.: Rowman and Littlefield, 2006.

Whitehead, Alfred North. *Process and Reality.* New York: Free Press, 1978.

Wilcox, John R. "Our Knowledge of God in *Summa Theologiae, Prima Pars, Quaestiones 3–6*: Positive or Negative?" *Proceedings of the American Catholic Philosophical Association* 72 (1998): 201–11.

Wildman, Wesley J. "Incongruous Goodness, Perilous Beauty, Disconcerting Truth: Ultimate Reality and Suffering in Nature." In *Physics and Cosmology: Scientific Perspectives on the Problem of Natural Evil*, edited by Nancey Murphy, Robert John Russell, and William Stoeger, 267–94. Vatican City and Berkeley, Calif.: Vatican Observatory and Center for Theology and the Natural Sciences, 2007.

Wiles, Maurice. *God's Action in the World*. London: SCM Press, 1986.

Wilken, Robert Louis. *The Spirit of Early Christian Thought: Seeking the Face of God*. New Haven, Conn.: Yale University Press, 2003.

Wippel, John F. *Thomas Aquinas on the Divine Ideas*. Toronto: Pontifical Institute of Mediaeval Studies, 1993.

———. "The Five Ways." In *The Metaphysical Thought of Thomas Aquinas: From Finite Being to Uncreated Being*, 442–500. Washington, D.C.: The Catholic University of America Press, 2000.

———. "Thomas Aquinas on Creatures as Causes of Esse." *International Philosophical Quarterly* 40, no. 2 (2000): 197–213.

Wright, John H., SJ. "Divine Knowledge and Human Freedom: The God who Dialogues." *Theological Studies* 38, no. 3 (1977): 450–77.

Young, William W. "From Describing to Naming God: Correlating the Five Ways with Aquinas's Doctrine of the Trinity." *New Blackfriars* 85, no. 999 (2004): 527–41.

INDEX

Aersten, Jan A., 22n82

Ahlström, Gösta W., 196

Albert the Great, St., 5, 81, 175

Albertson, James S., 183n18

Albertz, Rainer, 188n2, 196

Albright, William Foxwell, 189n5

analogy, 13: 74, 93, 102, 110, 111, 118–19, 147, 154, 159–61, 170, 180; and language for God, 87–92

Anderson, James F., 89n43

Anselm, St., 12, 25–27, 45n70

Aristotle, 4–5, 9, 17n63, 18–19, 33n33, 33n36, 34n38; 37n47, 46n71, 51, 52n86, 72n49, 77, 85, 108n39, 116, 153, 160,, 163n27, 165–67, 170, 175, 177n2, 178–80, 187

Arp, Robert, 29n21, 30n24, 30n25, 36n46

Ashley, Benedict M., OP, 23n86, 28n16, 50n82

Asimov, Isaac, 39

atheism, 30, 56–60

Averroes, 17

Avicenna, 17, 18n69

Ayala, Francisco J., 51n83, 138, 167

Baggini, Julian, 56n104

Balsas, Álvaro, SJ., 171n63

Barbour, Ian G., 138n57, 170n58

Barnes, Corey L., 127n9

Bauerschmidt, Frederick Christian, 12n43, 12n44, 20n75, 23n86, 24n1

Beck, David, 30n24, 46n71

Beebee, Helen, 41n60

Behe, Michael J., 53n91, 53n92, 53n93

Big Bang, 33n34; and the doctrine of creation, 161–62

biology, 53n93, 108, 163n26, 166, 175; and final causality, 51, 167. *See also* evolution

Blocher, Henri, 122n23

Bobik, Joseph, 49n79

Boland, Vivian, OP, 65n17

Bonansea, Bernardino M., OFM., 56n104, 57n107, 57n108

Bonino, Serge-Thomas, OP, 133n37, 135n43

Bonnette, Dennis, 34n41, 40

Boyle, Leonard E., OP, 2n5, 5n17

Braaten, Carl E, 78n82

Braine, David, 55

Brecha, Robert J., 171n62

Brierley, Michael W., 70n41

Buckley, Michael J., SJ, 56n104

Bultmann, Rudolf, 169

Bunge, Mario, 41n60, 165

Burrell, David B., CSC, 88n39, 106n18, 137n51, 141n74, 162n20, 184n20

Burtt, Edwin A., 166n37

Cahn, Stephen M., 104n12, 107n24

Carella, Michael J., 188

Carroll, Lewis, 95

Carroll, William E., 40n56, 161n15, 162n20

Catechism of the Catholic Church, 27, 131n27

Cates, Diana Fritz, 119n3

cause, 24, 28–31, 33, 34n41, 35, 39, 45;
47n74, 48n75, 49–50; as constant conjunction, 41; and contemporary science,
165–67; efficient, 35n43, 41–42, 183;
exemplar (extrinsic formal cause) 18–83;
final (purpose, teleology), 50–54, 126–27,
167, 182–83, 187; of the form as such,
38, 44n67, 52, 184–87; formal (intrinsic
formal cause, substantial form), 178,
182; material (primary matter), 178, 182;
primary and secondary, 45, 183–84; principal and instrumental, 183; and series of
causes, 35–37, 42. *See also* biology; divine
action; God; univocal cause
Cessario, Romanus, OP, 20n75
chance, 42, 52, 105, 115–17, 127–28, 187. *See
also* God
chaos theory, 170–71
Chesterton, G. K., 4n11
Chisholm, Robert B., 115n25
Clarke, William Norris, SJ, 27n11, 54n95,
68n31, 97
Clayton, Philip, 70n41, 166n41, 167n47,
171n61
Cohoe, Caleb, 36n46
Connolly, Thomas Kevin, OP, 43n65
Cooper, John W, 70n41
Copleston, Frederick C., SJ, 22n82
Cotter, Christopher R., 56n106
Craig, William Lane, 78n81, 97, 106
Crean, Thomas, OP, 56n106
creation, 4, 13, 48, 69, 72, 104–5, 112,
119–20, 127, 137–40, 143, 150–51, 155,
157–59, 168–69, 178; act of, 159–62, 174,
187. *See also* Big Bang; God
Creel, Richard E., 106
Cross, Frank Leslie, 70n42, 71n44
Crysdale, Cynthia, 172n69
Cuddy, Cajetan, OP, 20n75
Cullen, Christopher M., 22n84

Davies, Brian, OP, 2n5, 3n8, 6n21, 18n69,
20n78, 22n82, 29n21, 55n101, 71n46,
84n23, 88n39, 137n51
Davies, Paul, 171n61

Dawkins, Richard, 46n73, 56n106, 57,
58n110
De La Torre, Monty, 49n79
De Moor, Johannes C., 190
De Nys, Martin J., 43n65
Deferrari, Roy J., 46n71
deism, 53, 69–70
Dei Filius (Vatican I), 27n13
Dei verbum, 27n13
Dupuis, J., SJ, 27n13
design, 97, 139, 167; and the Fifth Way, 53;
intelligent design (ID), 53
Dever, William, 193n26
Dewan, Lawrence, OP, 28n14, 32n31, 38n51,
41n60, 185n21
Dionysius the Areopagite (Pseudo-
Dionysius), 8n31, 66n27, 75–76, 82–83,
84n19, 98n70, 119
divine action: and contemporary science,
170–73; and modern science, 167–70. *See
also* God
Dodds, Michael J., OP, 15n57, 37n49, 42n63,
50n81, 63, 72n50, 72n53, 73n55, 84n19,
87n36, 93n56, 100n80, 105n15, 108n36,
113n13, 114n23, 117n30, 120n11, 121n14,
124n35, 162n20, 165n35, 173n72, 177n1,
186n24, 187n27
Dolezal, James E., 21n81, 62n3
Donceel, Joseph, SJ, 55n98
Doolan, Gregory T., 65n17, 164n31
Doran, Chris, 53n93
dualism, 179

Edwards, Denis, 169
Einstein, Albert, 168
Elders, Leo, 13n48, 22n82, 29n19
emergence: and divine action, 170–71;
theory of, 166–67
Emery, Gilles, OP, 16n59, 18n69, 161n16
Emonet, Pierre-Marie, 70n37
Eslick, Leonard, 40n57
essence, 181–82. *See also* God
evil: natural (*malum naturae*), 140–41; moral (*malum culpae*), 141–42. *See also* God;
sin; suffering

evolution, 42, 163n26. *See also* biology

existence (*esse*), 181–82. *See also* God

Leinsle, Ulrich G., 3n9
Lemaire, André, 196
Levering, Matthew, 18n69, 21n79, 62n3, 65n17, 128n11, 161n17
Lewis, C.S., 131n28
Lister, Rob, 121n14
Livingstone, Elizabeth A., 70n42
Lombardo, Nicholas E., OP, 119n3
Long, Steven A., 88n39, 133n37, 133n39, 134n41, 135n43
Löw. Reinhard, 51n85
Luisi, Pier Luigi, 108n37

Macquarrie, John, 122
Mansini, Guy, OSB, 29n18
Maritain, Jacques, 46n72, 46n73, 55, 57n107, 57n108, 58n111, 60n117, 143n80
Maréchal, Joseph, SJ, 55
Markham, Ian S., 56n106
Marmion, Declan, 16n59, 22n84
Marshall, Bruce D., 11n40
Martin, Michael, 56n104
Matava, Robert Joseph, 134n41
McCabe, Herbert, OP, 20n78, 71, 121n14, 137n53
McCool, Gerald A., SJ, 20n75, 22n84
McDermott, Timothy, OP, 52n88, 53n90
McFague, Sallie, 62n4, 87n36
McGinn, Bernard, 2n5, 7n26, 7n28, 20n75, 20n77, 21n81, 80n2, 128n10
McGrath, Alister, 56n104, 56n106
McGrath, Joanna Collicutt, 56n106
McInerny, Ralph, 29n18, 88n39
McKenzie, John L., SJ, 193, 194n34, 195n39, 195n40
McWhorter, Matthew R., 99n72
mechanism, philosophy of, 32, 159, 163
Menzies, Peter, 41n60
Merton, Thomas, 74
method: of Aquinas's philosophy, 3, 9–10; of Aquinas's theology, 3, 10–15, 18, 30, 56, 129; of empirical science, 165–66
Miller, Patrick D., 188
miracles, 7, 55, 71n44, 84n20, 173
Miyakawa, Toshiyoki, 44n67

Moltmann, Jürgen, 72n49, 122, 123n31
Monod, Jacques, 163n26
monolatry, 188–90, 194–97
monotheism, 1n1, 78–79; emergence of, 188–98
Montagnes, Bernard, 49n77
Moreland, Anna Bonta, 17n63, 28n14
Moreno, Antonio, OP, 40n56
Moses Maimonides, 18
motion, 9n34, 10n36, 28n16, 31–40, 52, 72, 76–77, 81, 160–61, 179–80; immanent, 74, 102, 108–9, 111, 147, 180–81; transient, 74–75, 102, 108; 111, 147, 180–81
Mulchahey, Michèle M., 5n17
Muñiz, Francisco, OP, 43n64, 47n74
Murphy, Nancey, 138, 170n58

Nahm, Milton C., 35n44
Neuner, J., SJ, 27n13
Newton, Isaac, 39–40, 52
Newton, William, 53n91
Nichols, Aidan, OP, 20n75
Nutt, Roger W., 133n37, 133n39, 134n41, 135n43, 144n84

occasionalism, 164n30
Oliver, Simon, 30n23, 33n34, 52n86
O'Meara, Thomas F., OP, 22n83, 30n23
O'Rourke, Fran, 84n19
Ormerod, Neil, 172n69
ontological argument, 25–27, 45n70

Paley, William, 53
Paluch, Michał, OP, 128n10, 128n11, 135
panentheism, 70–71
pantheism, 69–71
Pasnau, Robert, 22n82
Pawl, Timothy, 29n21
Peacocke, Arthur, 105, 169–70, 171n61
Pegis, Anton C., 8n29
Pelikan, Jaroslav, 14
Pesch, Otto Hermann, 20n75, 21n81
Pieper, Josef, 3n9, 8n30, 9n35, 16n62, 17n66, 19n72, 20n73, 20n78, 15–56, 175
Pimentel, Stephen, 55n96

Pinnock, Clark H., 105n15
Piper, John, 156
Placher, William C., 20n76, 69n33, 122, 134n42
Plato, 18n69, 53n92, 175, 180n7
Plested, Marcus, 21n79
Polkinghorne, John C., 14n51, 127n5, 137, 138n57, 166n39, 167, 169–70, 171n61
polytheism, 78, 188, 189fA1, 191
Powers, Jonathan, 167n42
predestination, 126, 128–36
providence. *See* God

Quadrio, Philip Andrew, 56n106
quantum physics, 42, 138, 166, 170–71
Quinn, John M., OSA, 44n67

Rahner, Karl, 16n59, 22n84, 55
Raith, Charles II, 21n79
Ramelow, Anselm, OP, 108n36, 173n71
Regis, Edward, 108n38
Reitan, Eric A., OP, 33n33, 34n38, 37n47, 186n24
relationship: mixed, 94–96; real, 94–95; of reason only, 94. *See also* God
Ringgren, Helmer, 189n5, 191n14
Rocca, Gregory P, 88n39
Rota, Michael, 36n46
Rowe, William V., 15n54
Runggaldier, Edmund, 78n81
Russell, Robert John, 27n11, 138n55, 138n56, 138n58, 170
Ryan, Fáinche, 11n42

Schaab, Gloria L., 105n15, 155
Schenk, Richard, OP, 131n28
Schillebeeckx, Edward, OP, 131n28, 137n53, 141n74, 142n76, 148, 198n54
Schilling, S. Paul, 122
Schleiermacher, Friedrich, 169
Schudt, Karl, 55n99
Schulte, Raphael, 99n72
science, 3, 9–10; contemporary, 161, 166–67, 170–73, 175; empirical, 13, 28, 31, 33, 38–39, 50n81, 56, 59, 164, 173; modern

(Newtonian), 50, 165–70, 173, 175; laws of, 179; philosophy as, 11, 13n48, 37n47; theology as, 10–13, 17n63. *See also* chaos theory; emergence; evolution; method; quantum physics
scientism, 50, 58, 165
Shackleford, John M., 56n103
Shanley, Brian J., OP, 20n75, 23n85, 78n79, 103n7, 134n40, 134n41, 134n42
Sheehan, Thomas, 22n84
Sheres, Ita, 188
Shields, Christopher John, 22n82
sin, 114, 130, 132, 133n37, 136, 141–42, 144, 145n88, 149, 172n68, 192. *See also* evil
Siniscalchi, Glenn, 53n91
Smedes, Taede A., 171n61
Smith, Mark S., 188n2, 188n3, 189, 190n6, 190n10, 191n12, 191n14, 191n15, 193n27, 194n30, 194n35, 195n36, 196n43, 197n51, 198n52
Smith, Vincent E., 33n37
Spaemann, Robert, 51n85
Spitzer, Robert J., SJ., 56n103, 162n20
Stager, Lawrence E., 193n26
Stannard, Russell, 56n103
Stein, Edith, 55
Stoeger, William R., SJ, 27n11, 138n55, 138n56, 138n58, 162n20, 170n58
Stump, Eleonore, 22n82, 22n83, 29n21, 78n81, 106n18, 137n51, 143n80
suffering, 59, 126, 137n53, 142n76, 143n80, 144, 145n88, 146. *See also* evil; God
Sullivan, Thomas D., 108n35
Svensson, Manfred, 21n81
Synan, Edward A., 45n69

Tabaczek, Mariusz, OP, 70n41, 166n41
Tanner, Kathryn, 69n34
Tapp, Christian, 78n81
Taylor, Charles, 59
Taylor, Richard, 25n3, 25n5, 26n7
Te Velde, Rudi A., 6n21, 10n37, 17
teleology, 51n83, 51n85, 187. *See also* cause
theodicy, 126, 136, 137n51, 138–39. *See also* evil; God

The One Creator God in Thomas Aquinas and Contemporary Theology was designed in Garamond, with Scala Sans and Garda Titling display type, and composed by Kachergis Book Design of Pittsboro, North Carolina. It was printed on 60-pound House Natural Smooth and bound by Sheridan Books of Chelsea, Michigan.